LIVING WITH *Speed*

LIVING WITH *Speed*

Speed hillclimbing through the eyes of Britain's
most consistently successful team —
Roy Lane, with Steel King

By Norman Burr

Photography by Matthew Gartside
Technical Editor Jerry Sturman

Text © 1997 by Norman Burr.
Except where otherwise credited, all photos © 1997 Matthew Gartside

Other photographs and illustrations from:
Brockbank, Norman Burr, Julie Chalmers, Arnie Corbet, Guy Griffiths Motofoto, Frank E Hall, Mark Harvey, John Hayward, Ian Henderson, W K Henderson, Derek Hibbert, Bob Light, Jerry Sturman, Symonds & Ware, Len Thorpe, Steve Wilkinson, Mark Writtle Productions.
Wherever possible the author has obtained the copyright holder's permission to publish, but with some of older photos particularly, it has not been possible to locate the photographers concerned. The author would be obliged if those individuals, or their agents or heirs, would contact him on 01524 782437.

ISBN 0 9530772 0 9

Designed and typeset by Norman Burr

Printed in England by Pagefast Ltd, Lancaster (01524 841010)

Published 1997 by the author

All rights reserved. No part of this publication may be reproduced, stored in a retrieval system, or transmitted in any form, or by any means, electrical, mechanical, photocopying, recording, or otherwise, without the prior permission of the copyright owner.
Every effort has been made to ensure accuracy and all information is believed correct at the time of going to press, but no responsibility can be accepted for errors.

Page 1 photo
Roy Lane at Gurston Down, May meeting.
Page 3 photo
Roy Lane at Curborough test day.

CONTENTS

Living with Speed

	About Steel King		6
	Foreword	*By Patrick Wood*	7
	Acknowledgements		8
	Preface		9
	Introduction		10
Chapter 1	'I'm going to enjoy this sport'	Curborough Test Day	11
Chapter 2	'All I need now is no job'	Loton Park	16
Chapter 3	'In the clearing stands a Cobra'	Wiscombe Park	24
Chapter 4	'He had no need to do that, but he still went for it'	Prescott	34
Chapter 5	'It's God's law that you'll have a couple of bad results'	Barbon Manor	44
Chapter 6	'A tremendously challenging place'	Lerghy Frissell	51
Chapter 7	'The banana yellow machine looks strangely naked'	Gurston Down	54
Chapter 8	'A brave man at the end of the day'	Shelsley Walsh	62
Chapter 9	'Takes no prisoners, this place'	Doune	72
Chapter 10	'A big rain cloud is clearly visible from the paddock'	Harewood	81
Chapter 11	'I think I'll leave it to the experts'	Bouley Bay	90
Chapter 12	'Local knowledge can be a distinct advantage'	Le Val des Terres	95
Chapter 13	'I tried there, I really did'	Return to Shelsley Walsh	99
Chapter 14	'You bastard, you're going to fly now'	Return to Gurston Down	106
Chapter 15	'Fighting back the tears'	Return to Prescott	113
Chapter 16	'One or two pheasants may be eaten later on today'	Return to Wiscombe Park	120
Chapter 17	'Eighteen till I die'	Return to Doune	129
Tailpiece 1	'If you're going to do something, do it properly'	At home with the Guv'nor	136
Tailpiece 2	'Pay attention to detail'	At work with the Guv'nor	159
Appendix A	The Hillclimb & Sprint Association		166
Appendix B	Championship Winners		167
Appendix C	Speed Championships in the UK		168

LIVING WITH SPEED

About Steel King

Steel King was founded in 1957 as a division of the original Colton Brothers wholesale footwear business to supply industrial footwear on contract, trading from its original premises in Irchester. Expansion of the business caused the need to acquire two further warehouses in Wellingborough. This arrangement became increasingly inconvenient and in September 1996 the current premises were acquired on a one acre site in a prime position on Wellingborough Road, Rushden.

Today, the Steel King warehouse can hold a stock of over 50,000 pairs of Steel King and Doctor Martin quality safety and industrial boots conforming with the European EN345/200 Joules specification, safety wellingtons, training shoes, men's classic shoes, rugged boots and general footwear.

Steel King's byword has always been quality and everything stocked is full grade with leather uppers.

Also at the Wellingborough Road premises is a 1000ft² trade and retail shop which offers the finest quality goods to industry and the public.

For the past 40 years Steel King has been a major supplier of boots to local authorities, hospitals, ambulance service, police, fire brigade, industrial companies and schools throughout Great Britain, and also supplies retail traders locally and nationally on a cash and carry basis.

As a national promotion, for 18 years Steel King has sponsored the car of Roy Lane in the RAC British Speed Hillclimb Championships. This is a specially developed racing car with a 3.5 litre 650bhp ex-Formula One Judd engine which runs in the Steel King livery of silver and green. Roy Lane has never finished outside the top five, and was successful in winning the championship outright in 1992 and again in 1996.

A team of representatives and a Mercedes Benz mobile shop are available to visit industrial premises and issue boots on site to customer's own requirements. Visitors to Crown House on Wellingborough Road are always welcome, and a new 1997-8 full colour safety and industrial poster is now available on request.

For further information, telephone either Malcolm Tobin (Contract & Industrial enquiries) or Robert Mawby (Retail Trade, Cash & Carry and Export) on 01933 314141.

Foreword

By Patrick Wood, Chairman
Hillclimb & Speed Association

Norman has managed to combine many fine qualities in this excellent book about speed hillclimbing. He portrays the friendly but fiercely competitive atmosphere perfectly, drawing the reader into the emotions of the drivers and their 'teams'. You feel the elation, the frustration, the joy and despair, as though you were there. For sure, all the necessary technical detail is here too, but presented in easily understood layman's language.

The result is a book that will have wide appeal: rather like a good novel, once started it is difficult to put down.

Patrick Wood

LIVING WITH SPEED

Acknowledgements

It almost goes without saying that the person who deserves the greatest thanks for his help with this book is Roy Lane himself. Without the enthusiasm and forbearance of Roy and his family, their hospitality and helpfulness, and their willingness to answer dumb questions without the slightest hint of condescension, this book would not exist.

However, there are two other men whose contributions have been absolutely fundamental. One is Richard Colton of Steel King, without whose financial support the book could never have been produced to the standard you now see. His commitment turned what could so easily have been a highly esoteric publication with a tiny circulation into something which the broader public could enjoy.

The other is Jerry Sturman, whose encyclopaedic knowledge of the sport has rescued me from many potential editorial gaffes. His work as Technical Editor has been invaluable. Moreover, he has filled gaps in other ways, covering the Channel Island rounds which family holiday commitments made it impossible to attend, preparing the appendices and answering 101 oddball queries.

I also wish to record my appreciation to Patrick Wood, not only for writing the foreword but also for being so infallibly approachable. His attitude was not atypical — I have lost count of the number of competitors and officials who gave freely of their time and I am grateful to them all — but Patrick in particular could always manage an encouraging word or an intelligent suggestion, even when he was in the thick of preparation in the paddock and really had better things to do.

An unseen but absolutely indispensable contribution has been made by my family, who for several months have put up with seeing far less of me than is healthy for normal family life. My 13 year-old son Tom at least had the compensation of five great days out, at Barbon, Gurston Down, Doune, Prescott and Shelsley respectively, but for my daughter Jocelyn and my wife Wendy the scoresheet was rather more negative, and I am extremely grateful for their understanding and support.

Last but not least I must acknowledge the part played by photographer Matthew Gartside, whose classy pictures make my own efforts look amateurish in the extreme. Before I started this project I scarcely knew him; now I count him as a valued colleague and friend.

Thank you all, for your contribution to a memorable year.

Norman Burr
Priest Hutton, April 1997

Preface

Books which try to be all things to all men run a serious risk of being of no value to anybody.

This uncomfortable reality has never been far from the front of my mind during the planning and writing of *Living with Speed*.

The book grew out of my conviction that hillclimbing is a fascinating sport which genuinely deserves a wider audience.

I've watched hillclimbs for many years, have marshalled at them, have even competed in a very modest way, and have enjoyed every role immensely.

I reasoned that anything which introduced the sport to more people, or at least helped to dispel the depressingly popular notion that it has something to do with persuading cars to go further up impossibly steep and muddy slopes than the law of gravity ever intended, must be a good thing.

Speed hillclimbing is very much a participation sport. Although the longer established venues like Shelsley Walsh and Prescott attract substantial numbers of casual spectators, it remains true that a surprisingly high proportion of those who watch are themselves either competitors or ex-competitors, and many of the spectators who don't fall into either category are probably the family or friends of people who do. Any book too shallow to interest them would simply not be worth publishing.

My formula for squaring this circle involves giving up any pretence of being a dispassionate observer and instead hitching myself to one team for a whole season, concentrating on the RAC British Hillclimb Championship rounds. That way, I hope to offer newcomers a first-hand insight into the sport while rewarding hardened hillracers with technical detail, paddock gossip and the odd touch of nostalgia.

It is Roy Lane whom I must thank for making this approach possible. Experienced hillclimbers will not need telling that there is no better organised, better liked or more experienced crew that I could hope to team up with than Steel King, but for the casual reader I'd better explain that Roy Lane's competition record is unparalleled in the 50 year history of the sport.

He has now won the RAC British Hillclimb Championship four times, including once on a maximum 100-point score. Finished in the top ten every year since 1968. Won more championship rounds than anyone else, ever. Regularly beats men little more than a third of his age. Teaches at a hillclimbing school. Builds hillclimbing cars. Sells competition parts. If you want to understand the sport, travel with the guv'nor.

There were also personal reasons why he was my first choice as a partner for this exercise, for even though I didn't know him before the project started, I felt sure I'd enjoy working with him. I'd been a Lane fan ever since he, alone of all the competitors at Wiscombe Park in 1970, had taken the trouble to thank each group of marshals as he trundled down the hill after his last run of the day. The gesture stayed with me as I wandered back from my post at the top hairpin and has stuck in my mind ever since.

So while the team is Roy's and the season is 1996, this book does not pretend to be an authoritative record of either. Photographer Matthew Gartside and I have attempted to paint a picture of a sport. If we have done our job well, the portrait will still come alive ten years from now, even though some of the names will have changed.

LIVING WITH SPEED

Introduction

In many branches of motorsport no journalist would be able to gain a first-hand insight into the workings of a top team. The rivalry is too intense, the desire for secrecy too strong, the financial pressure too great.

But hillclimbing isn't like that. Even at the highest level, where driver skills and engineering standards stand comparison with the most glamorous branches of motorsport, you'll find the keenest of rivals inspecting each other's cars, lending each other parts and sharing a joke in the paddock.

There are plenty of other branches of motorsport where such camaraderie can be found, but there are surely none which combine such an atmosphere with such high standards of driving and machinery.

It's the nature of the competition itself which makes this possible. As a test against the clock on narrow but immaculately surfaced private roads, it is far gentler on man and machine than most competitive motoring disciplines. Typically, a hill will be tackled half a dozen times over a weekend, with even the longer ones taking only a minute or so to complete. For practical purposes you're alone on the track for the whole of that minute — bend the car and you have only yourself to blame. No one is going to push you into the armco, there's no Senna wannabe behind to worry about, only the road in front.

It follows that expensive accidents and serious injuries are both relatively rare. And because the car is only used in anger over short distances, it wears comparatively slowly. The top single-seaters may be paying £750 for a set of slicks and may be built to a standard that would not disgrace a F1 team, but they'll only get through three sets of tyres in a whole season and one engine could last several years. Circuit racers can consume those rations in one meeting.

It's just as well that costs are generally lower than on the circuits, for sponsorship levels are too. Even the top competitors have trouble attracting four-figure deals and most are happy just to get their entry fee paid. Maybe if hillclimbing were regularly televised things would be different. But it isn't, and in truth it's probably the better for it.

Speed hillclimbing is very much a British phenomenon. There are hillclimbs on the Continent, but the topography is so much more dramatic that the nature of the sport is quite different. Storming up a 15 mile alpine pass bears no relation to a 20-odd second dash up Barbon fell in Cumbria.

Not surprisingly, there has never been a significant international element to hillclimbing in Britain — foreign competitors are extremely rare and no international hillclimb championships have regular rounds on British soil.

With its Britishness and its amateur status, it is tempting to describe hillclimbing as the last gentlemanly branch of motorsport — tempting but wrong. For although the friendliness and sportsmanship would certainly have found an echo amongst the Brooklands crowd, the classlessness of it would not. On the hills, the man — or woman — who arrives from a suburban semi in a Westfield, competes on road tyres and drives home pleased at beating their personal best is every bit as welcome as the Championship contender in a Judd-engined Pilbeam. And just as vital to the sport.

Kids, Wiscombe Park and Mark & Ann Goodyear's Vision.

10

CHAPTER 1

'I'm going to enjoy this sport'   Curborough Test Day

First time out: The Ralt at Curborough, March 1996.

A gaggle of half a dozen cars is parked around the loop of tarmac which constitutes the start paddock at Curborough. Matthew and I edge the BX gingerly on to the circuit and down to the loop, aware that we are rather late and that there is already activity. There are no marshals to tell us what is safe: this is strictly a test day. There won't be much in the way of action today, but it should at least give us a feel for the season ahead.

The place is owned the by Shenstone & District Car Club and club member Roy Lane has hired it for the day. In spring and summer it's used as a sprint venue, but now it is March and we are greeted by a heavily overcast sky and a cold wind. At this time of year, it's not a place where you would volunteer to stand outside all day.

Unless you have a car to test that is, or in Roy's case, two. Under one cover is the Pilbeam MP58 which took him to third in last year's British Hillclimb Championship. Under another is a brand new Ralt-Judd CV RT37 which has yet to turn a wheel. With its honeycomb/carbonfibre monocoque and its suspension tucked horizontally into the centre of the car, F1 style, it's very different from the Pilbeam MP58s which have dominated hillclimbing in recent years. Today will provide the first clue as to whether it will usher in a new era.

In a more modest way, today is already proving to be something of a new era for Russ Mason. To defray the hire costs, Roy has invited other hillclimbers along for the day and Russ has taken him up on the offer. Russ's transport is altogether more modest: a Westfield with a Ford 1700 crossflow engine. It's a track car, but a low budget one, and the big development this winter has been a reworked front suspension. After a few laps to explore the handling, Russ is reduced to staying out simply to enjoy himself: the car is 'transformed' and he is well pleased. A season awaits.

Roy is pleased too. His company, Tech-Craft, carried out the mods to the Westfield and he likes a satisfied customer as much as the next man.

Next out is Simon Durling. His car too is pretty familiar to Roy. It should be: not

LIVING WITH SPEED

only did he win the 1992 Championship in it, he also spent the winter rebuilding the Cosworth-engined Pilbeam around a new monocoque after Simon crashed it badly at Doune in 1995. Simon doesn't say a lot, but he seems happy enough, commenting that apart now being painted red instead of blue, the car looks and feels exactly the same as it did before the accident — which after all was the object of the exercise.

He shares the MP58 with Tim Barrington and, as with all dual-driver cars, there is great rivalry between them. In circuit racing or rallying, team mates can always argue that one car was a tad better than another on the day, but when both drive the same machine on the same course within 10 minutes of each other, there is little room for excuses.

The willingness of organisers to accept dual entries, and the fact that the nature of the competition permits them, is one of the great strengths of hillclimbing. Not only does it bring in people who could never afford to compete on their own, it also adds interest for drivers and spectators alike. Even if your car is no match for the class leaders, knock three seconds off your mate's time and you've proved a point.

Some pairings take the word 'mate' literally. Husband and wife teams are not uncommon in hillclimbing and there's one here today: Pete and Sue Griffiths. They're here strictly for the fun: their immaculate Chevron B47 is the same car they put in the garage at the end of last season and today is simply a cobweb-blowing exercise, a chance to work some aggression into the wrists and ankles.

The Chevron will not be a contender for outright honours in the Championship. For one thing, its 4 cylinder Millington 2 litre (loosely derived from the Sierra Cosworth unit) lacks the sheer grunt of a V8 Cosworth or Judd engined machine. For another, the car is 17 years old. For a third, Pete says 'it's better at sprints than hills', probably because it was built as a F3 car. Many owners of ex-track cars have experienced the same phenomenon and generally attribute it to suspension design. The hills are so tight and twisting, and involve so many camber changes, that the very limited suspension movement typical of track car design is something of a handicap.

In the 1995 season Graham Hickman found this out the hard way when he campaigned an ex-F1 Jordan on the hills. It was not a conspicuous success, not least because its sheer size made it unwieldy. The wheelbase was simply too long. It drew crowds in the paddock, but not at the winners' rostrum.

None of this matters overmuch to Pete and Sue. Their Chevron is part of the family and they accept its strengths and weaknesses as part of the character of the car. As long as they continue to enjoy driving and owning it, their names will continue to appear on entry lists. The only competition car they have ever owned, it is now entering its fourth season in their hands.

Sue's main concern is to keep whittling down the 8-9 second margin that tends to exist between Pete's times and hers. Pete's not saying what his main concern is, but it's probably to improve fast enough to keep it there!

One class down, in the up to 1600cc category, is Barry Goodyear and his Reynard. Barry is about to start his first season of hillclimbing and like many competitors will take in a few sprints as well.

Although no stranger to competition driving — he has rallied in the past — he's under no illusions about where he will end in the league table. 'Probably right down at the bottom' is his assessment. 'But I chose hillclimbing because I regard it as the last gentlemanly form of motorsport'.

The Reynard is a technically interesting design, neatly executed. The whole transmission and final drive is housed in a unique-to-Reynard magnesium casing which houses the ubiquitous Hewland internals and provides pick-up points for the suspension. Engine is a 1598cc Cosworth BDD.

Off the start line, Barry's car squats down noticeably more than anyone else's and there is clearly room for improvement there. For Barry though, the task today is as much to develop the driver as to develop the car. It's all so new that every lap is a learning experience.

My observations are broken by the unmistakable sound of a V8. Not the howl of a flat-crank racing unit but the double-beat of a production-derived design with 90% crank throws. Maybe it isn't the purest of engine notes, but it's surely the one which reaches deepest into the soul. If you aren't stirred by the sound of John Fellows warming up the Rover V8 in his Argo JM9 Rover, then there's something wrong with you.

John is the archetypal down-to-earth Midlander and his car reflects this. The maroon car known as the 'Wraith Rover' is tidy but most certainly not immaculate. 'Roy's probably spent more on his engine than I've spent on this car in five years', he grins, and he may well be right. Last year he concentrated on sprints, coming home 14th in the RAC British Sprint Championship, this year the hills are the target. He remains deeply committed to sprinting, however, and is closely involved with a recent British Motor Sprint Association initiative aimed at raising its profile.

There's no doubt that sprinting is currently the poor relation of hillclimbing. If hillclimbing is small beer in terms of the overall motorsport scene, sprinting is a half of shandy. One idea for changing this is to organise demo sprints as a lunchtime entertainment at GPs and other major circuit events. Indeed the BARC took up this initiative in 1996, running a successful 'Supersprint' event as part of September's Thruxton Festival of Motorsport.

The relationship between sprinting and hillclimbing is an interesting one. The ethos of the two is very similar, as is the mix of machinery and the list of drivers. But sprints impose different demands in that the courses are generally flat and offer more room for error by way of run-off areas and the like. Sprint courses and formats vary considerably, some involving a lap, or sometimes more, of a racing circuit, others using distinct start and finish positions on courses such as airfields. Some are very twisty, others quite fast. All set the cars off individually, though a few may have three or four racing simultaneously, released at intervals. Curborough is a twisting loop ending with a half-mile straight which takes you back to the start but travelling in the opposite direction. On test days like today a link is used which cuts off the start/finish and turns it into a short circuit.

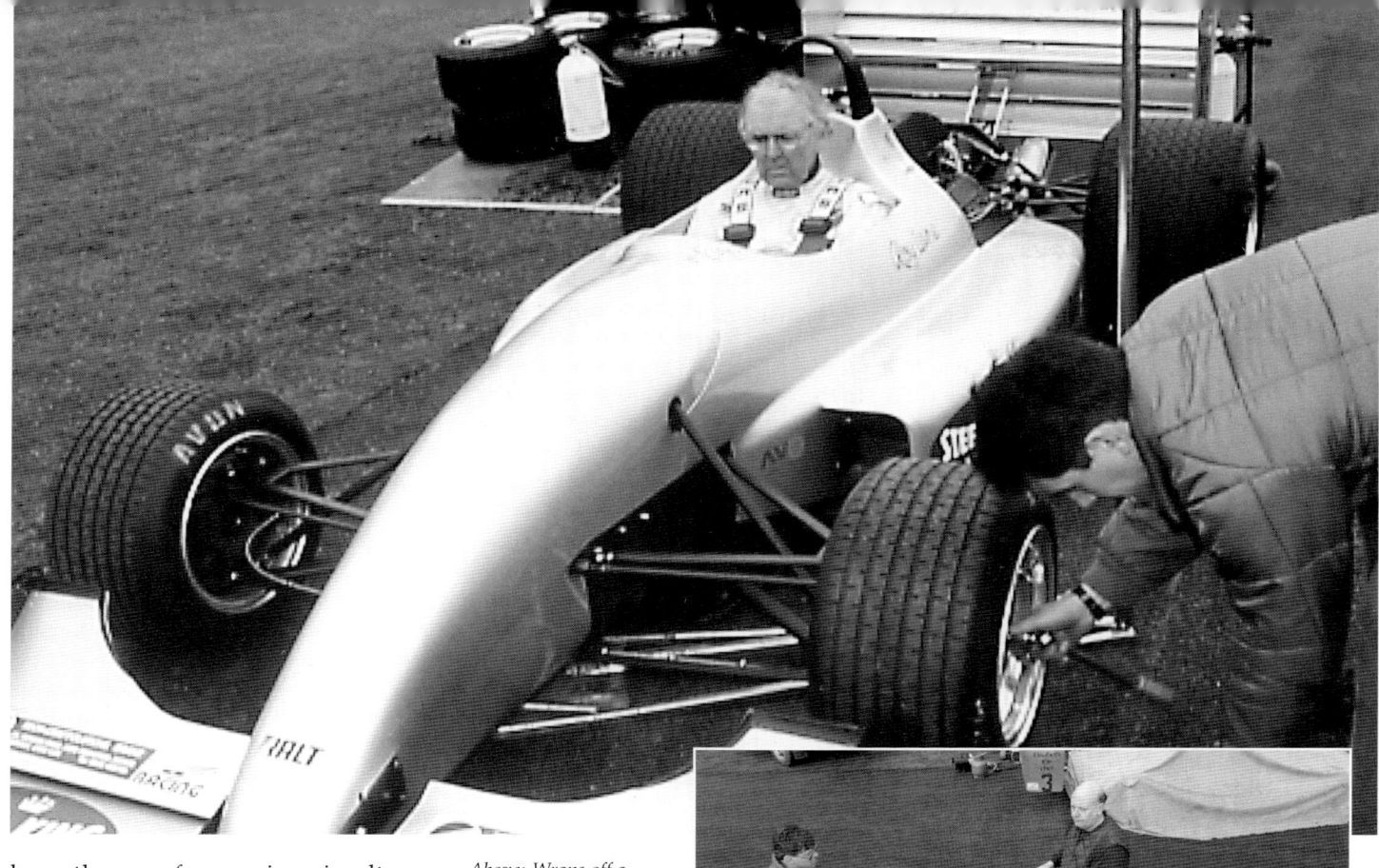

John rumbles off to play. The engine note rises, the car squats down on the start line, lays a neat line of rubber and then disappears. Sure as hell beats working for a living.

Back in the Lane camp, the wraps are being brought off the Ralt for the first time. Painted silver like all his cars in recognition of main sponsor Steel King, it looks stunning: neat, compact, purposeful. If looks won championships, Roy would be home and dry.

Son Antony and son-in-law John Chalmers warm it up. When they pronounce themselves satisfied, Roy settles into the carbonfibre cockpit. 'It's very tight' he observes, before trickling carefully down to the line. Foot down and away.

Why did they decide to build a new car when the old one was clearly still competitive? Antony's answer is almost philosophical: 'The Pilbeam MP58 was designed around 1987 and is hard to improve on. But sometimes you've got

Above: Wraps off a new car as Roy Lane, deep in thought, familiarises himself with the Ralt's cockpit while John Chalmers checks tyre pressures.

Right and below: programming the Ralt's engine management.

13

Gurston Down, July meeting.

Man on the Hill

Simon Durling

Simon's first motorsport experience was as a passenger with his father in sporting trials at the tender age of 5, in 1948.

'I actually had my picture in *Autosport* in 1950, so when they have their 50th anniversary celebration, I shall expect to be asked to attend! I started sporting trials on my own in 1960, as soon as I had a licence.'

He's been involved in the trials scene on and off ever since, including some long-distance trials in Dellows and the like. With trialing in the winter and hillclimbing in the summer, he finds the two sports complementary.

As a boy he watched hillclimbing with his father, both here and at Shelsley. Dad never competed but they knew Bob Dayson well from the trials scene and in 1958 Bob had a Turner laying around. 'He said "do you want to drive it? If you do, there it is, take it away, make it into a raceworthy proposition", which we did'.

The car was quite successful although it was up against tough opposition. 'The classes were slightly different in those days, it was up to 1600 for the Modsports, and I was against the Caterhams. We had a pushrod Ford with a special downdraught ex-1 litre Formula 3 head'.

Amazingly, the car is still competing.

'From the Turner I went on to the 1100 Delta which Scott Moran now uses, then I had an MP52 Pilbeam, which is a spaceframe ex-Formula Ford 2000 car with a 1600 BDA — I had that for a couple of seasons.'

By now he was firmly in the Pilbeam orbit and his next car was another Bourne machine, an MP62 'in which Tony Tewson now runs a BDA, although I had it with a Vauxhall engine. Then I went to this big Pilbeam.'

He is cautious about his championship chances, acknowledging that his accident last year at Doune has slowed him down. Later in the year he is to observe 'There are places where I can be quick and there are places where I find myself backing off a bit because apart from the fact that I don't want to hurt myself again, I don't particularly want to rebuild the car all over again.

'I think I'm probably going to push my luck to win it. But I'd like to do as well as possible. After the accident I didn't know how I was going to do at all, so any wins are a bit of a bonus.'

This year he is sharing the car with Tim Barrington, which brings its own constraints: no one wants to let their partner down by demolishing the car. 'It's very difficult', he acknowledges.

And the future? 'I've packed the businesses up' — he was a housebuilder and garage owner — 'and I shall be living off the money'.

And hillclimbing off the money. 'My middle son's quite interested, and I'd like to do something with him. That will involve going back into sports cars or little racing cars, or whatever.'

---

to take the bull by the horns and try to progress.'

After a few laps Roy comes in. John and Antony are concerned: there's oil spattered over the engine. It turns out to be nothing more than blow-off from a catch tank so the car is cleaned and refuelled ready for others to have a go. 'As men get older their toys get bigger', Roy observes as John prepares for this first run.

Letting John and then Antony drive is far from being just a sop to the mechanics who have helped him build the car. At 60, Roy admits that 'the lads do a tremendous amount of work and without them I wouldn't be doing it. These days it's them who drive me on'.

He's still hungry to win, but he's hungry for them too. You get the impression that he genuinely wants them to be as successful as him.

However it will not be easy, for Roy has been in the top ten of the hillclimb championship every year since 1968, has won the championship three times (1975, 1976 and 1992) and has achieved Fastest Time of the Day (FTD) at practically every hill in the country at some stage.

This year they will probably drive the Ralt more than he will. The plan is for the three of them shake the new car down with some sprints and non-championship rounds early in the season and only introduce it into the championship hillclimb schedule when and if it is ready: maybe part way through the season, maybe not at all. In the meantime last year's car will be Roy's main mount.

Both cars use Judd V8s, though at present it's the Pilbeam which has the state-of-the-art 4 litre EV unit. The Ralt is currently fitted with an older 3.5 litre CV unit, developing 580hp at 11,500rpm, plus another 100rpm to allow for the ignition cutout's progression.

In GP trim it would develop fully 620hp and would sport a much higher rev limit, but in that tune it would be useless for hillclimbing. The engine mapping wouldn't even start until 5000rpm and torque out of slow corners would be practically non-existent. This engine is mapped from 2000: 'It's all about sheer torque and tremendous grunt' Roy explains.

The Pilbeam is readied. As required by the rules, number 3 has been stuck on the nose: its driver's finishing position in last year's British championship. (Numbers 1 to 10 are always reserved for last season's high flyers, other numbers vary from meeting to meeting at the whim of the organisers). Nothing else has been changed since last year, except the engine mapping — this one too has had the grunt treatment.

Roy tries it out and comes back looking pleased. The required thrust in the kidneys is more in evidence, everything else is just as he remembered it.

But most of the driving, and the interest, centres on the Ralt. John, Antony and Roy all take turns. Sean Gould, himself a hillclimber of no mean ability, is there and cadges a ride. His father David, a retired hillclimber (surprise!) still very much involved with the sport on an engineering and consultancy basis, is enthused. John hooks up a laptop PC and reprograms the engine management: in addition to the default pro-

Derek Hibbert

gramme, they have a set-up worked out for each venue. Then another series of runs. It reminds me of kids trying out each other's bikes.

By 2:30 Roy has learned all he wants to for today and is content to let the younger men amuse themselves with his 580hp mountain bike.

Two things need attention, he concludes. Firstly, the front dampers are too stiff: even backed off to maximum rebound they are not letting the springs do their job and as a result the front of the car has a tendency to patter on bumpy corners. The valving needs to be changed to make the present maximum adjustment the centre point.

Secondly, the ergonomics are not working well. The confined cockpit is making cross-gate gearchanges awkward, and Roy is wondering whether the seat which they have lovingly designed may have to be ditched because it pushes the driver too far forward. As it is, he finds his foot fouling the steering joint when he brakes — most disconcerting — and the steering wheel is wrongly positioned.

For a brand new car though, it's an encouragingly short list.

Most people here are either customers or friends of Roy, or both, and as we pack up to go home various arrangements are made to build on the lessons of the day. 'We'll lift the steering wheel up one slot', Simon suggests, as he briefs Roy about what needs doing to the Pilbeam after the first run in what is effectively a new car. In F1 terms this is analogous to Frank Williams helping Ron Dennis build a better McLaren, but here it seems perfectly natural.

Barry walks up. 'You're going to have to do something about that back end', advises Roy. 'The change of camber when you go off the line is absolutely drastic. You want to have a good look at your dampers but you might need to stiffen up the rear springs as well. You've got to slow that back end down. I was sitting in the Discovery and I could see it even looking in the mirror'.

But no amount of rear squat is going to remove the smile on Barry's face. 'I'm going to enjoy this sport', he announces.

Curborough, March 1996.

Car on the Hill

Pilbeam-Judd MP58

Roy Lane, Racing Cars Over 2000cc

The MP58 is one of Mike Pilbeam's most successful designs and has dominated top class hillclimbing for the best part of a decade. No example has done more to further the model's reputation than Roy Lane's, for although visually it looks very similar to several other MP58s on the hills, in practice it is faster than any of them, thanks largely to the development work done on the engine by J&F Engines and the Steel King team.

The key to its performance is torque, huge quantities of it. There are a number of 4 litre V8s now competing, but none has the colossal bottom-end thrust of Roy's example. The twist action doesn't come at the expense of power either: Roy quotes 580bhp, but some of his rivals think that's distinctly conservative.

The car even sounds different, its engine note noticeably deeper than any of its competitors'. Not surprisingly, the precise details of the engine set-up are something of a team secret, but the results are public enough, as the chart shows. The Judd EV produces serious torque from as low as 3500 rpm, an invaluable advantage on tight tracks where maximum acceleration is needed out of a hairpin.

Opinion is divided as to whether the Judd V8 is inherently more torquey than the Cosworth, but there's no doubt about the ability of this one.

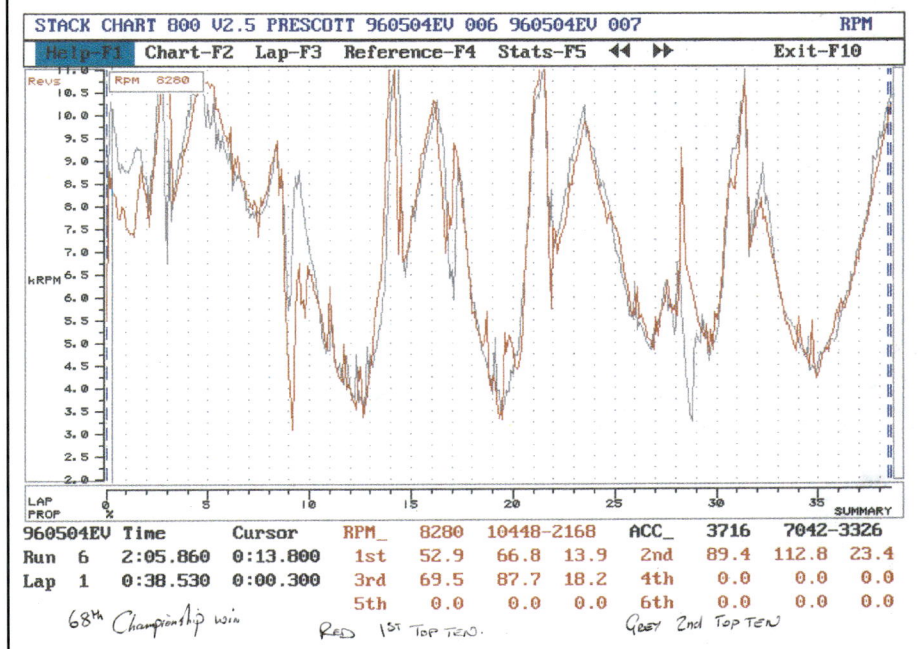

Typical engine management print out, this one recording Roy's winning run at Prescott (see Chap 4).

LIVING WITH SPEED

'All I need now is no job'

Loton Park

Loton Park

Location
near the village of Alberbury on the B4393 west of Shrewsbury.

Organising club
Hagley & District Light Car Club,
c/o Mrs P Fisher,
3 Cofton Church Lane,
Barnt Green,
Birmingham B45 8PS.

Length 1475 yards.

Outright hill records at start of 8.4.96 meeting
Overall: Roy Lane, 47.94sec.
Ladies: Maggie Blankstone, 52.23sec.

Roy's Run

'A highly technical hill with exceptionally good grip, that's why everybody enjoys it so much.

'Two ways to tackle it. One is to change up into second only 20-30 yards off the line, then back to first for the first left-hander, then up to second for Loggerheads. Hold that until the entrance to Triangle which you take in first. Go into second just before the start of the next bend, take third on the straight, put it back into second at end of the straight and hold that to the finish.

'My other (preferred and illustrated) method is to hold first all the way up to and round the first corner, change up into 'second' before Loggerheads, hold that to Triangle which you take in 'third', a slightly lower ratio good for 85mph. Stay in 'third' along the short straight and round the bends until you are emerging on to the straight. Then change up into fourth, a 115mph gear, back off obviously for the kink, at the end of the straight change back into 'third' gear and take fourth again before the finishing line.

'There's very little between the two methods.'

KEY

Track shading indicates gear ratio...
- White striped is first gear
- Tints are intermediates (darker tone equals higher gear)
- Black is top gear

Because ratios and patterns in racing gearboxes can be altered at will, a particular shading on one map does not indicate the same ratio as on another: shading is relative only to that particular venue.

V indicates good viewing area

0 — 100yd

Map labels: FINISH, Fallow, Museum Corner, Cedar Straight, Keepers Corner, Triangle, Loggerheads, PADDOCK, Pond, START, Hall Corner

---

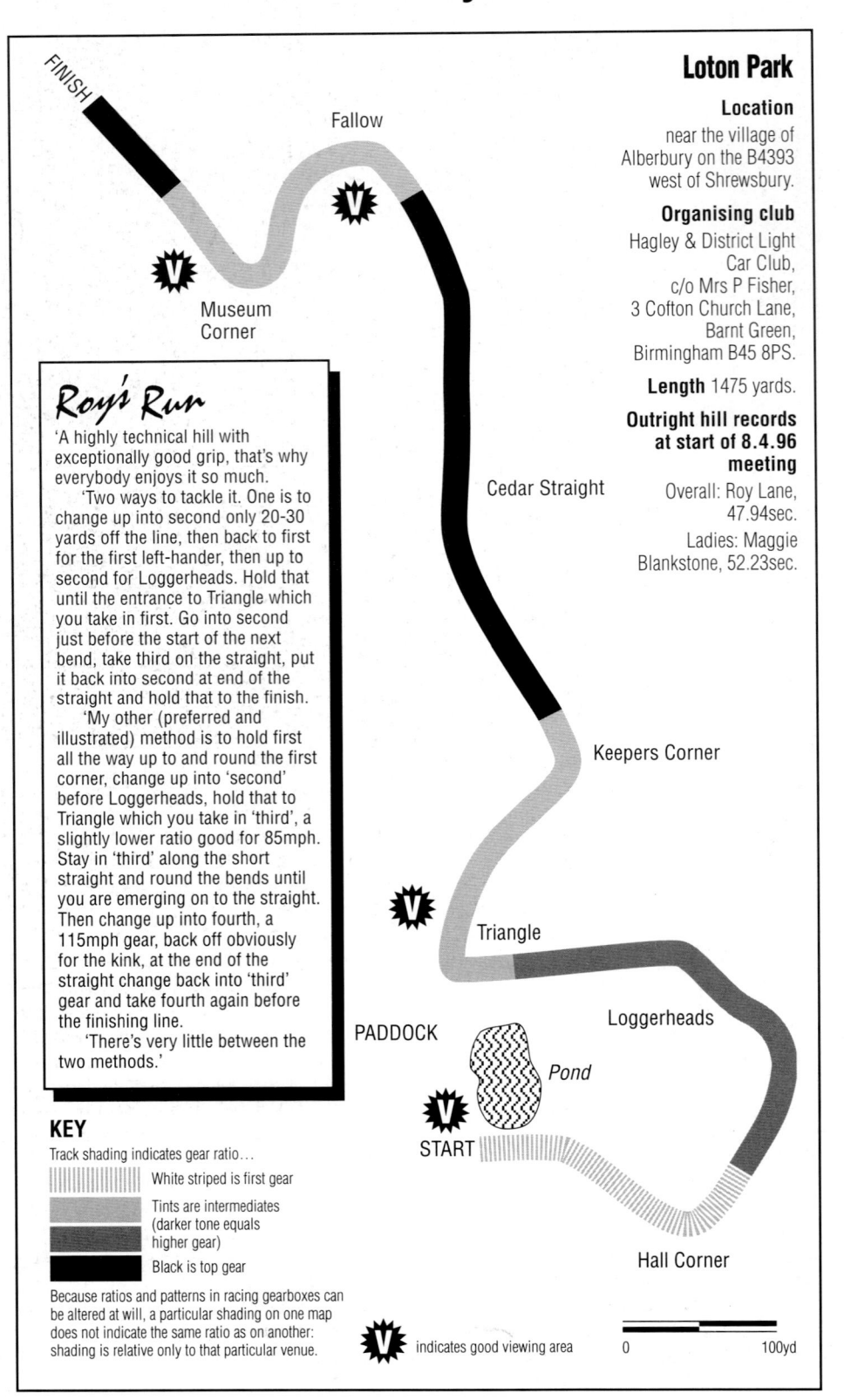

Loton Park is a curious place. Some British hillclimb venues consist of the drive up to some extravagant and gloriously situated country mansion owned by a car nut, but when you approach Loton Park on the B4393 west of Shrewsbury you wonder if you're within 30 miles of the place, because from five miles out the land all around looks quite flat. And even when you get nearer, there's no mansion in evidence as you drive in through the gate, just a paddock immediately inside.

The house is not far away — just over the road in fact — but it's far enough to make you wonder what the road which now constitutes the hillclimb was built for.

The answer is surprising. This 300 acre estate, the property of the Leighton family, was used as a storage depot during World War II. A network of roads was built, twisting around the hillsides, to service the many buildings scattered around under the trees, each nicely separated from its neighbour to minimise vulnerability to bombing. A more obscure place to hide machinery and munitions would be hard to imagine.

The buildings are nearly all gone now, but the bases remain, sections of hillside levelled by cut and fill to provide ideal bases for spectating, marshalling, or filming. Perhaps because of this background the estate, beautiful piece of English countryside though it is, seems to lack the genteel charm of some of its fellow venues.

Roy describes it as 'technically a very difficult hill — everyone falls off here sometimes and if it happens a lot, the meetings can take ages to get through'.

At 9.45 on this particular Sunday morning there is no sign of life in the Lane camp, even though others are out and about. So I walk the hill.

In hillclimbing circles walking the hill is a cross between a religious rite and a hallowed tradition. So much so that some drivers feel positively deprived if they get up too late to do it (your best chance is before the first practice of the day). Yes, it makes for pleasant morning exercise, but it is much more than that. Hillclimbing is such a precise, in-

CHAPTER 2

The paddock on Sunday morning.

tricate sport, that the smallest variation in surface condition or track dampness can make a vital difference. There's no substitute for being there, seeing it, *feeling* it underfoot.

It's about mental preparation as well. To stand there in silence, looking up a gently rising, curving stretch of narrow tarmac, and to realise that next time you see it you will be travelling at the best part of 100mph and it will seem steeper, twistier and much, much narrower, is to realise what you came here for. You either conclude that you need your brains tested or you come back down the hill focused and determined to get on with the job.

This particular hill is really two hills. The lower section consists of a curving loop around a small hill, which ends in a short straight and a hairpin. Carry straight on at the hairpin, known as Triangle, and you find yourself back in the paddock. Negotiate the hairpin and you enter the upper section, a longer stretch which climbs through the S-bend of Keepers Corner and on to Cedar straight, leading to the long left-hander at Fallow. A short straight, a sharp right-hander (Museum Bend) and another short straight lead to the finish.

When originally opened to motor-sport in 1960 by the Severn Valley MC, only the upper section was used. In the late '60s the lower extension was added and since 1970 the site has been administered by the Hagley & District Light Car Club.

As I climb I notice that Cedar Straight isn't really straight at all, but has a steady curve to the right, followed by another to the left. Moreover, there's an evil little dip in the middle which looks nothing from a distance but is enough to ground a car, as the scrapes on the tarmac prove. The best vantage point looks to be near the top.

On the way back down I meet Norman Kittle going up. He doesn't know me, but this stocky Irishman with big fur-lined jacket and shock of thick dark hair is not one to let unfamiliarity stand in the way of conversation. I find it hard to reply at first, for his strong Ulster brogue takes a while to adjust to, but his openness wins you over.

This morning Norman is not a happy man. His Metro 6R4 is entered in Class G (Sports Libre cars over 2000cc) but it's not going anywhere, least of all up Loton Park. An expensive engine rebuild culminated in expensive tinkling noises the first time the motor was fired up; apparently the cutouts in the pistons were not large enough to accommodate the valves and every one is bent. I'm glad I wasn't on the other end of the phone when he relayed that piece of news to the engine builder. (We learn later that the problem was traced to a camshaft timing glitch).

Family honour will therefore rest on the performance of brother Andy in Class L with the big boys; Racing Cars over 2000cc.

LIVING WITH SPEED

Tony Southall in the Reynard Vauxhall ends his second run with a spin.

Down at the Steel King trailer Roy has emerged from his motor home. We push the car out and generally get things organised. 'Very hard to get everyone going this morning' he observes, as though it's the start of the season and he isn't really geared up himself yet.

Appearances can be deceptive, however, for although Roy is in motorsport for pleasure rather than profit he nevertheless takes it *very* seriously. In preparation for this season he has lost a stone in weight and all winter long this former potential British Olympic cyclist has been keeping fit by pedalling, 500 miles since the New Year to be precise. He's not a man to make a big deal about such preparation, he just does it.

Indeed, there isn't much that he does make a song and dance about, for despite his sporting record he remains a highly approachable and, in the nicest sense, ordinary bloke. A little taller than average but no Gerhard Berger. Average build. Wavy greying hair, thinning at the front. Spectacles.

He could be any young child's grandad, except that this grandad can drive a 580hp racing car quicker than practically anyone else around. Only the absence of flab and the quickness of movement tell you that there's more to Roy Lane than meets the eye.

The result of this self-discipline is that the grandfather from Warwick was fastest in yesterday's practice and is now the man to beat.

Next to him are three guys who aim to do just that: George Ritchie and Roger Moran sharing a brand new Pilbeam MP72, powered like Roy's by a Judd engine, and Patrick Wood's MP58, a similar chassis to Roy's but with a hybrid Cosworth DFZ-R.

George and Roger had engine problems in practice while Patrick was plagued with spongy brakes. Overnight he has rerouted a brake pipe under instead of over the gearbox in an attempt to eliminate a high spot which he suspected was causing an airlock.

Roy, on the other hand, has had a pretty straightforward time. Gearing is his main concern: the remapped engine is giving so much more torque that on first practice, using the same ratios as last year, he was over-revving. For second practice he dropped the gearing by two ratios and produced a run which 'felt quicker but was actually slower'.

He ascribes the fall-off to the drop in temperatures at the end of the day; even a one degree drop in track temperature can mean the difference between success and failure. Nirvana is a warm dry track for grip and cool dense air for power, an understandably rare combination.

Patrick has seen all this before, for Roy's ability to put in a fast time 'straight out of the box' is legendary.

Although Patrick's overnight work has effected an improvement, he's still not happy with the brakes. Nevertheless this most cheerful and approachable uphill racer finds the time to show me what makes his car unique — the telemetry.

Traction control may be banned on the circuits but it certainly isn't on the hills. Benetton electronics wizard Richard Marshall lives near Patrick and to counter his frustration at having his ingenuity circumscribed by F1 regulations has applied his knowledge to the MP58 as a spare-time project.

There are sensors everywhere, comparing wheel speeds, measuring suspension loads, recording every nuance of every run. 'All I need now is no job — no job and loads of money — so I've got time to analyse the data' grins Patrick. This is his third season with traction control and everyone is watching anxiously to see if the latest version of this unique system gives him a vital edge.

Roy jokes that the weight of black boxes alone should be worth half a second to the rest of the field, and in truth Patrick's car *is* heavy, but not because of Richard's input. The villain of the piece is its Cosworth engine, which weighs substantially more than a Judd.

As the action starts I take station on the hill to watch the fun. With so many championships and classes running in parallel, hillclimbing offers something for everyone, from a vintage GN to a roadgoing TR6 or practically any age and size of single-seater. There are dozens of private battles being fought out there.

One of them is clear enough though, for in the Modified Production Cars over 2000cc (Racing), Tony Lambert and Mark Waldron are all set to continue their ding-dong battle of last season. The contrast between Tony's Ferrari 308 GT4 and Mark's TVR Tuscan is fascinating; two slick-shod V8s, very closely matched yet utterly different in concept. The turbocharged red Ferrari howls up the hill, its sophisticated mid-engined layout rewarding precision and tidiness.

CHAPTER 2

The growling yellow TVR is utterly different, a car which only gives its best when it's trying to get away from him and when Mark is just — but only just — managing to stop it. So far today poke has the edge over pedigree, with Tony messing up his first run and Mark rubbing salt into the wound by breaking Tony's two-year old record.

Among the fast men, current champion Andy Priaulx shows that he intends to continue this season as he ended the last by producing a first run of 49.39, just ahead of Roger Moran on 49.55, whose practice gremlins are now clearly sorted. Roy can only manage third, on 49.61. Patrick is a little further back but, ever the optimist, he spots a chink in the clouds and puts his slicks out to cook in the sun.

In the historic category Graham Galliers thrusts the fearsome Brabham BT21 Quattro up the hill, only to stop on Cedar Straight. The reason becomes clear in the paddock at lunchtime, where frantic activity is centred around the front of this unique four-wheel drive racer.

Graham has persuaded the 4.2 litre Oldsmobile V8 to give more grunt over the winter and as a result the front differential has cried enough and broken away from its mountings just in front of the driver's ankles.

'On the way up I looked down at the diff and thought, that's funny, it seems

Above: Hectic lunchtime activity as Graham Galliers converts the Brabham into 2WD and (right) back in action as a result.

19

LIVING WITH SPEED

Mac Hazlewood throws the Ram D Type into Museum.

Mum may be a racing driver but a little girl's needs still have to be met. Ann Goodyear with daughter Hanna.

nearer to my feet than usual', he explains. His tone is totally matter of fact, the voice of someone who's got halfway back from Sainsbury's and noticed that a carrier bag has fallen onto the floor. The fact that he's been within a few seconds of having gear teeth fired at his testicles with all the velocity that 320bhp could muster seems not to worry him at all.

A broken diff sounds pretty fundamental, but the man is indomitable. Remove the front-to-rear driveshaft and the front driveshafts, talk nicely to the scrutineers, and have a second run in two-wheel drive, that's the theory.

The front driveshafts need a little persuading to part them from the hubs and a helper is despatched to the Steel King trailer to beg a large hammer. He returns with a distinctly well worn device amid much ribaldry about the relative standards of preparation of Roy's cars and Roy's hammers. I find myself as Chief Spanner Holder during the whacking ceremony, which duly sees the Brabham robbed of two driveshafts and nearly half its traction footprint.

'Go and find me a black plastic bag for the bits' Graham asks.

'Why black?' someone asks.

'To put over my head. I'm going for a fast one!'.

Since he's probably never driven the car in 2WD before, let alone in anger, his desire to shut his eyes and hope for the best is understandable. The afternoon promises to be interesting.

In the event Graham, eyes apparently wide open, makes two respectable runs and salvages something from the day, though it's not enough to lift the Brabham off last in class.

Over with the Modified Production Cars Over 2000cc, Mark Waldron looks set for an easy afternoon. Tony Lambert falls off on his first run and fails to beat Mark on his second, so the TVR pilot has nothing to prove when he starts his second run — he's already broken Tony's class record and no one else is within a second and a half.

But he's going for it anyway. There's a glorious roar, a flash of yellow through the trees, and the TVR emerges out of Fallow on a very fast run. 'It's a bit of a handful this car,' enthuses the commentator, 'but he's mastered it'. Seconds later, the Curse of Murray Walker descends: he gets the power on fractionally too early at the exit of Museum, gets one wheel on the dirt and executes a neat 180 right in front of us. Waldron's new class record has become Waldron's 'fail'.

In hillclimbing, the margin between success and failure is small indeed.

Tension builds as the top 12 run-off approaches. For while after two prac-

CHAPTER 2

Car on the Hill

MG MGB

Alastair Crawford, Modified Production Cars Over 2000cc

As an object lesson in what can be achieved on a strictly amateur basis, with no sponsorship whatsoever, Alastair Crawford's MGB is hard to beat. It's fast, it's fun, it didn't cost a fortune to build and it's capable of regularly notching up points in the Leaders Championship.

The car was conceived when Alastair's 1973 MGB GT ('I've always had MGs') had an accident at Knockhill during an MG Car Club two-lap sprint in 1989. Three years of racing with the B GT ended there and then: 'The car looked quite solid but when it hit the tyre wall it just disintegrated. So we took all the good bits from that and reshelled it in this roadster, because the roadster's obviously a lot lighter.'

It would have been possible to echo the design of MG's own V8 models, but in view of their deficiencies — they tended to be nose heavy and lacking in traction — there was no point.

'This is our own installation', explains Alastair. 'We moved the engine further back and further down compared to the factory MGB V8s.

'We've actually hung the engine mounts off the suspension crossmember because you can then have vertical engine mounts, which are much easier to get at than the originals. Also on the original cars, the exhausts go out, follow the block round, through the chassis and out. It's very restricting because you haven't got much room there.'

The best thing would be to take the pipes out through the inner wheel arch, but that entailed making new holes in the structure, which was not on. 'The RAC production car regs don't let you alter the basic unitary construction between the wheel centres.'

It was the exhaust manifolds which suggested a solution. The unit is taken from a TVR Tuscan so 'we modified the Tuscan exhausts and brought them forward out of the engine' — like the ones on Mark Waldron's car — 'then out through the inner wings ahead of the front axle centreline. The pipe disappears just behind the headlamp pods, goes over the front tyres and then meets up and goes out the back.'

More ingenuity is evident in the chassis.

'Suspension wise, again we worked around the production car regs. We've kept the double wishbone arrangement which the B had, but we've optimised the pick-up points and we're using Ralt RT30 uprights and wheels and brakes.'

This is permissible because the configuration's the same as the B, namely coil spring and double wishbone. 'The only thing we've altered is, we've ditched a kingpin and trunnion for a conventional single-seater upright, the idea being to put ball joints top and bottom and put anti-dive in the front, because the B's got a horrific amount of dive in the front suspension. Allan Staniforth did the design and geometry for me and it's *very* stable under braking.'

Despite a claimed 400bhp (the Tuscans boast 380bhp) the car will not be a contender for outright victory in the Leaders this year — Alastair has found the pace too hot for that. 'I've competed in the MG Car Club Championship for many years and since '92 I've always won one of the two championships or won the class. But the step up to the Leaders is huge'.

Ultimately Alastair, an electrical engineer by profession, would like a Pilbeam, possibly an MP43 to avoid the costs associated with the big V8s. As a halfway house a Megapin might fit the bill — he's taken a shine to Allan Staniforth's example. If he goes single seat, it will be the end of a 10-year association with MGs which started at Baitings Dam hillclimb in Yorkshire in 1986, his first taste of competition.

In the meantime, however, we are likely to see a lot of this very rapid MG.

Shelsley Walsh, August meeting.

---

tices and two runs most entrants are beginning to load up their trailers, the real work is only just beginning for the fastest 12 runners of the day. They are eligible for the RAC Championship run off, an extra two runs which alone will decide who gets points in this year's championship.

Judging by the afternoon's runs, the top spot will go to one of five drivers: Roger Moran, Andy Priaulx, Roy Lane, Patrick Wood and Andy's father Graham who shares his car. But there will be no new hill record today: the tarmac is too cold.

At 21 years old, Andy has an obvious advantage over all the other top runners. Hillclimbing may reward experience more than most motorsports, but it takes a whole lot of experience to make up for 20 years of wear and tear on mind and body.

He's a very personable man, exhibiting all the confidence that comes from knowing you have youth and natural ability on your side, but none of the arrogance which so often comes with it. In 1995 he won the British Hillclimb Championship on a maximum 100 points, something which had not been achieved since Roy Lane did it back in 1975.

Today though, he has something to prove, for Roger Moran was fastest in the afternoon runs by nearly a second.

After the first runs, Andy's back on top, by just 0.01 seconds from Roy, with Roger just 6 hundredths behind that. All three improve on their second runs, but Andy's improvement is dramatic. From our vantage point at Triangle, it's clear he's trying very hard indeed. He's markedly quicker to get back on the power after the hairpin, so quick that he surprises himself, finds himself coming into the Esses too fast and loses time getting the Pilbeam straight again. Despite this, he wipes 1.24 seconds off his time and

21

LIVING WITH SPEED

Championship Top Tens after Round 1

RAC
1. Andy Priaulx 10
2. Roger Moran 9
3. Patrick Wood 8
4. Roy Lane 7
5. Graham Priaulx 6
6. Tim Mason 5
7. Justin Fletcher 4
8. Malcolm Orme 3
9. Peter Harper 2
10. John Moulds 1

Leaders
(only nine points scorers)
- =1 Andy Kitson 9
- =1 Clive Kenrick 9
- =1 Mark Waldron 9
- =1 Alan Thompson 9
- =1 Rob Stevens 9
- =1 Mark Coley 9
- =1 Mark Lawrence 9
- =1 Paul Shipp 9
- =1 Justin Fletcher 9

Andy Priaulx receives the spoils.

0.2 off Roy's outright hill record, set just a few months before.

A buzz goes round the paddock. To break the hill record on a cold April day, after making a mistake, he must have had one hell of a run everywhere else. Maybe it's only 0.2, but it's a very telling 0.2. The Priaulx winning machine is still in business.

Roy seems a little subdued. He finishes fourth, behind Roger and Patrick. His daughter Julie and I both reckon Roy was slow getting the power down after Triangle, the very point where Andy shone. He takes it on board, but is philosophical. 'It's only the first event of the season,' he muses.

By his standards it has been a mediocre start. But there is still a long way to go. And the word on the hill is that Roy is not a man to be underestimated.

Man on the Hill
Steve Owen

A conversation with Steve Owen is an echo of his approach to racing. It veers off in all sorts of directions, explores all sorts of avenues, is driven on by sheer energy. There are blind alleys, the occasional unfinished sentence, but there are also many successes and innovations.

Now 37, Steve Owen has made his mark through hard work and infectious enthusiasm. He wants his cars out there, on the track, providing feedback, and it's not unknown for him to offer OMS drivers petrol money to encourage them to turn out.

He built the first OMS around 1986 following a long-standing interest in karting and racing cars, but didn't go full-time on his own until 1991, by which time he'd worked as a metalwork technician in a school, in the fibre-optics industry and for an American automotive firm doing laser wheel alignment and engine diagnostic equipment.

Most of his early cars were aimed at the 500cc class — 'one's in Cockermouth car museum' — but latterly he has concentrated on the next notch up, the 1100 class. There isn't really a standard OMS, since Steve is always keen to move on and try new ideas, but the closest thing to a production model is the spaceframe version of his aluminium monocoque design. 'I got talking to a chap one day and he said he'd buy one if it was a little bit cheaper, so I made him a spaceframe version and it went great. I sold about 15 of them after that.'

There's also a newer design based around a carbonfibre tub, but the spaceframe design remains the best seller. Both share the same suspension geometry and most of the suspension parts.

Sturdy independence and a willingness to tackle anything have become the hallmarks of his enterprise. He works entirely on his own and is totally self-financed, wary of getting too deeply embroiled with the bank manager.

'The bank thinks I make model cars', he laughs. 'I went one day to see him about some cash and he looked at the books and said to me on the way out: 'For a minute we thought you made real cars but we've realised they're models.'

'I was about to correct him but then I thought it wasn't worth it, so I said "that's right" and walked out. He never knew any different'.

He still doesn't — unless he reads this — and Steve is confident enough now not to worry if he does.

Although his cars are more often seen on the hills than anywhere else, he is by no means dedicated to one branch of motorsport.

'We made some cars for the 500 circuit championship and won — more on reliability than anything else because everything else seemed to fall by the wayside at the time. And one guy's got one of the sports cars in South Africa on the road.' He also made some trials cars, which have inevitably become confused with hillclimb cars in the eyes of the non-motorsport minded. Hillclimbing has an unfortunate name, he feels, but 'there again, what else can you call it?'

He also makes components and tackles one-off projects — recently for instance he produced some parts for a historic Formula 3 Argo.

The bodywork for the scooter which tackled the Scooter Land Speed Record is an OMS creation, and 'the Spondon bike that you see in the advert for Chris Richards, I did the bodywork for that.'

'I'll make anything for anybody, generally racing parts but it doesn't have to be. These days there's not a lot of people around who'll do oddball stuff.'

Although his name is now synonymous with bike-engined cars, it was not always so. Around 10 OMSs have used car-derived engines, including one with a 2.5 Hart and another with a Sierra Cosworth Turbo. Steve himself won the FTD Championship at Harewood in a car-engined design.

But it's the bike-based packages which sell. 'You can offer a whole package that people can afford and it's going nearly as quick as people could ever want to go. So they buy them. You've got to spend a awful lot more on a car-engined car to make it viable.'

'I'd love to be doing the car-engined cars; I think there's a hard-core who'd never buy a bike-engined car, because they don't like the look of the chain, they don't think it's quite a car.'

He's been considering building a car around Ford's Zetec engine. But other than that 'there's only a few directions you can go, like the K Series or the Vauxhall.

Doune, September meeting.

Things like the BDA you can't really use any more because they're just not reliable enough.'

For someone who prides himself on producing every part of the car himself apart from the power unit, the ultimate goal is inevitably to produce that as well. 'We were in the process of making a V8 bike-derived engine. It would have been the complete package, we'd have been making everything, brilliant.'

'Unfortunately those things do take that little bit more money. I'm self financed on everything and there comes a point where I just couldn't raise that bit more. The thing with Britain is, everybody tells you what a brilliant job you're doing but it's very awkward to get anybody else to chip any more money in to give you a hand.'

He hasn't given up on the idea though. 'One day we might get the V8 thing going and it would be great.'

23

LIVING WITH SPEED

'In the clearing stands a Cobra' — Wiscombe Park

KEY
Track shading indicates gear ratio...
- White striped is first gear
- Tint is intermediate
- Black is top gear

Because ratios and patterns in racing gearboxes can be altered at will, a particular shading on one map does not indicate the same ratio as on another: shading is relative only to that particular venue.

⚡ indicates good viewing area

0 — 100yd

House

START — BOTTOM PADDOCK
Wis Corner
Wis Straight
← Bunny's Leap
The Gate
The Esses
Martini Hairpin — Castle Straight — Sawbench Hairpin
TOP PADDOCK — FINISH

Roy's Run

'The grip varies at Wiscombe: they resurfaced it out of Sawbench up to where the old bridge used to be and on that section there's now no grip at all. You used to be able to exit that corner so quickly. Maybe it will come back again as the surface wears.

'I always start in a very low gear because the first corner goes back on itself: it's more than 90°. So you want to come out of there very quick and very clean. Round the first corner, change up. Hold that 'second' gear (a 118mph gear) all the way over Bunny's Leap to the Gate.

'Bunny's Leap is a strange place, you've got to make sure you angle the car correctly as the approach is all important. You skim the boards on the left and make sure the car comes down flat and square. Any sign of it coming down touching the grass on the right hand side, you're going to be in trouble — you'll be off into the field on the left. 2 litre cars can just about get over there flat but we don't.

'Approaching the Gate, you brake at the last minute, change across the box into 'third', and hold that all the way through to Sawbench. Back into first — you've got to be clean out of that corner, no hesitation whatsoever — change back up into 'second', back into first for Martini and to the finish.'

Wiscombe Park

Location
just over one mile from the village of Southleigh near Honiton in Devon.

Organising club (spring meeting)
Woolbridge Motor Club Ltd, c/o Linda Briant,
8 Brookside Close, Preston, Weymouth, Dorset DT3 6DW.

Organising clubs (autumn meeting)
Five Clubs, namely Bristol MC & LCC, Burnham-on-Sea MC,
Haldon MC, Plymouth MC & Taunton MC.
Meeting secretary Peter Adams,
14 Marguerite Close, Newton Abbot, Devon TQ12 1PA.
Tel 01626 52230.

Length 1000 yards.

Outright hill records at start of 28.4.96 meeting
Martyn Griffiths 34.65sec.

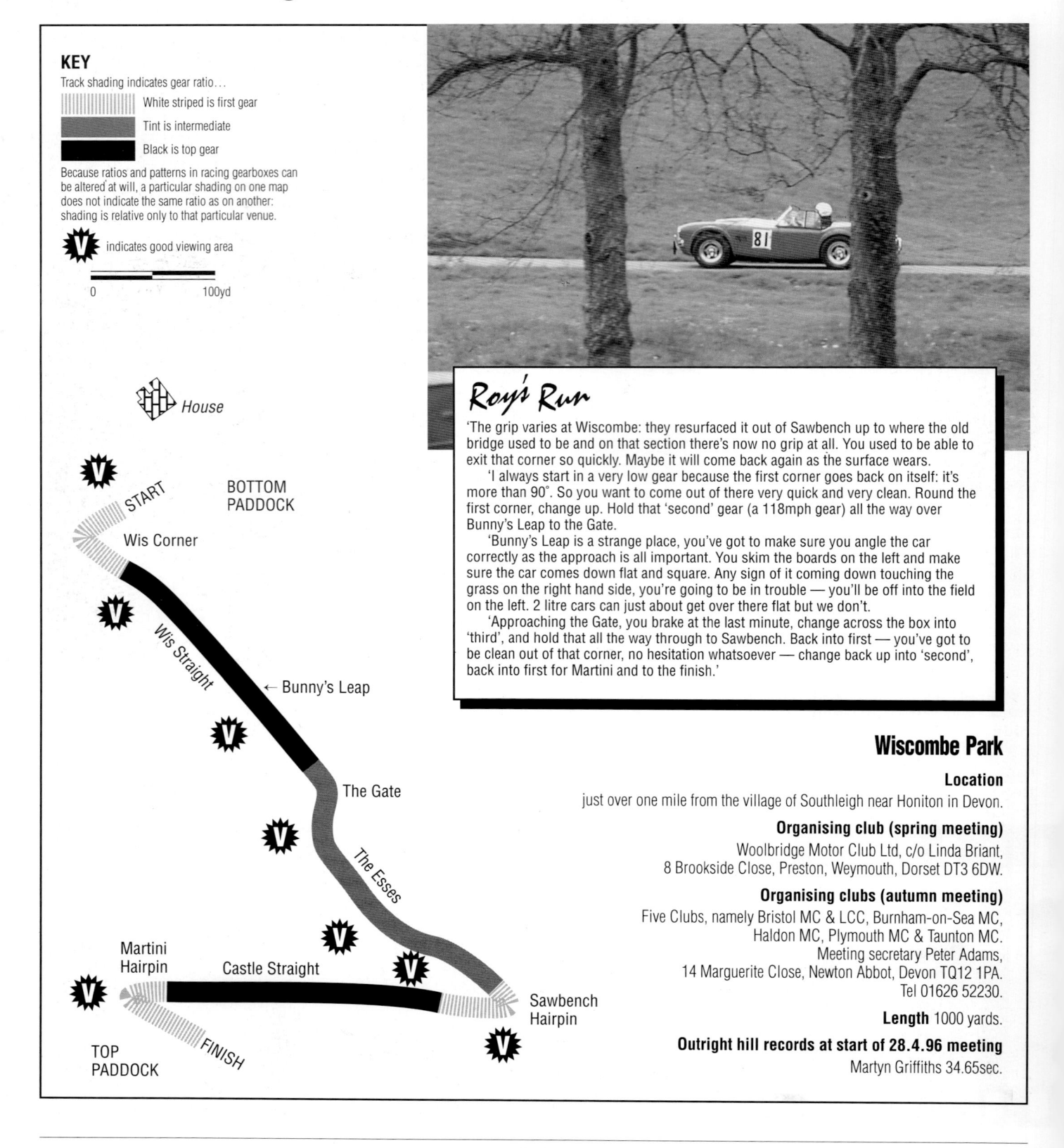

CHAPTER 3

Simon & Garfunkel didn't write exactly these words, but maybe if they'd been hillclimbing at Wiscombe Park in the early '70s they would have done. For then as now, speed events at this most picturesque of West Country venues are regularly graced by the magnificent AC Cobra of Paul Channon.

Not many cars find their way on to the gravelled drive of the front garden of the elegant old house, but the Cobra is an exception. There's nothing keeping the others away, no chains or signs, but nevertheless most stay respectfully in the paddock immediately outside, in the magnificent grounds of the Wiscombe Park estate, almost as if they recognise what sacrilege it would be to spoil such a perfect classic-car coffee-table book cover with their presence. And since local Vauxhall dealer E Channon & Sons is a principal sponsor of the event, no one is going to accuse Paul of parking where he shouldn't.

Time was when there was regularly another red car on the gravel, a 1950s single-seater HWM. Shared by Wiscombe owner Major Chichester and his friend Major Lambton, the Jaguar-engined car — its original Alta ditched in the interests of reliability — could regularly be seen storming up the hill in the hands of one or the other. In the '60s and '70s stories abounded about heady Saturday night parties in the old house, of midnight sorties in the most unlikely machinery to get fresh supplies for the bar, and of drivers in less than 100% fettle the morning after, setting some strangely inconsistent (but not always slower!) times.

How many of these tales are true and how many apocryphal is debatable, but there is certainly a kernel of truth in there somewhere.

These days the HWM is elsewhere, having been sold over a decade ago, and the two majors not quite so much in evidence on race days — hardly surprising since they are now in their 80s.

The beautiful old house, however, looks just the same except that it's benefited from a fresh coat of paint recently. Roy remembers staying in one of the upstairs rooms and recalls that nothing was ever changed for the sake of it: furniture and decor had altered little in 200 years and no one had ever attempted to make the place into a showpiece — it was just a family home, complete with rows of dusty bells in the kitchen to summon long-departed servants, and phone numbers scribbled on the wall.

Despite the picture-postcard setting, no one should make the mistake of thinking that the Cobra is only there for the sake of photographers. It is in fine condition, but it is not concours and Paul makes no apology for that: now as always, the car is there to compete, to be enjoyed as Thames Ditton and Carroll Shelby intended. Never much bothered about championships, Paul simply wheels it out of the Vauxhall showroom whenever an event comes along that he fancies. Sprints and hillclimbs are its principal diet, which the 325hp machine consumes with relish. Today it is on road tyres and attracts the attention of Mike Shepherd-Smith, the only other man in the Modified Production Cars Over 2000cc so equipped. He admires the AC, wonders if fear of damaging it adds several seconds to every run.

The Ginetta G33 driver is openly apprehensive about damaging his own car, which is in pristine condition. 'I don't know quite what possessed me to find myself suddenly in a class with Mark Waldron and all the rest' he muses. 'Last year I was in a Dutton and although I'd have been very sad if I'd hurt it, I'd have been able to explain it to my wife. But if I prang this one I'm going to be in trouble.'

Paul doesn't seem to labour under any such domestic constraints, but he is similarly aware of the tyre disadvantage. 'I normally have this thing on 10 inch

Wiscombe icons: The house, Paul Channon with Cobra, Wiscombe director Richard Brown in Ralt.

25

LIVING WITH SPEED

slicks and what does surprise me is that the steering's far heavier on these. I don't notice it on the road, but my God, I haven't half got to work at it to get it round Martini.'

Whatever their tyres though, neither Mike's G33 nor Paul's Cobra can hope to take the class: that will go to one or other of the battling duo of Mark Waldron and Tony Lambert, with Geoffrey Kershaw's twin-turbocharged 4WD V6 Sierra an outsider.

The track is set in a valley, with the paddock on one side, the start nearly at the valley bottom and the hill climbing up the other side. A start straight of just a few metres leads to the 90° left-hander of Wis Corner, which rarely witnesses serious incident. That privilege belongs to the next hazard, Bunny's Leap, a deceptively difficult hump in the middle of the main straight. Only the very brave or the grossly underpowered take this flat out, and most of those who do find themselves landing awkwardly on the other side, all crossed up and wrong-footed for the approaching right-hander at the Gate.

The Gate is not as sharp as it appears, but it is daunting nonetheless because it marks the start of the dense woods which shroud the rest of the course. Wiscombe punishes mistakes severely, with numbers of very solid trees right on trackside. There are straw bales at strategic points but there's never any doubt about who would come off worst in the event of a mishap.

Paul can confirm this, for although he's managed to keep the Cobra between the trees for most of its 20 year racing career, he admits to 'stuffing it about four times', the worst incident being here at Wiscombe. 'About 10 years ago up through the Esses I went into the trees and took the whole nearside out.'

The Esses wind from the Gate to the hairpin at Sawbench. After Sawbench drivers blast up the steep flat-out Castle Straight to Martini, the final hairpin. Martini looms up at you very fast and it is all too easy to brake too early. 'Of course what you tend to forget,' explains Paul, 'is that the hill's quite steep there.' (1:6.9 to be precise). 'Immediately you lift off, the speed drops of its own accord to a certain extent. But if you do lock up, you mustn't try and get round. Forget it, scrub the run and go straight on'. There's an escape road at Martini that takes you straight to the top paddock.

The Steel King team changing ratios.

Despite its idyllic setting, Wiscombe is not every driver's favourite venue, not only because of the lack of run-off areas but also because of its unpredictable weather. Locals say that the valley in which it nestles gets around twice as much rain per annum as places just 10 miles away — something about the topography just seems to suck the rainclouds in.

Today, however, the weather is glorious. It is destined to cloud over during the afternoon, but the dry forecast will prove correct. Although the surface is breaking up a little at the Gate, the track is generally in good condition and times were fast yesterday, during Woolbridge MC's club event which many drivers (but not Roy) used as a warm-up for today's championship round. Everyone is looking forward to an all too rare, dry Wiscombe.

Everyone except Tim Daniel that is. He got a little too warmed up yesterday in his Mallock Mk24 and rearranged the bodywork at the Gate to the point where he is strictly a spectator today. This is particularly galling for Tim because he is now out of the very class which he sponsors, Clubmans Sports Cars. His only consolation is that it was his last run of the day, not his first.

He puts on as cheerful a face as can be expected in the circumstances. 'If you don't crash occasionally you're not trying hard enough' he asserts firmly, though you get the impression that the person he is most hoping to convince with this statement is himself.

Normally he is a serious contender in the class, which today will see fellow Mallock pilot Martin Groves just miss out on breaking Colin Pook's hill record of 38.70 seconds with a 38.90 best. Colin himself, also in a Mallock, will be a few tenths behind on 40.62, with the Vision of the Goodyear family — Mark and Ann — a further two tenths distant.

A few metres away in the paddock is a man who last year would have been up there with them, former Clubmans competitor Basil Pitt. This year he's taken the plunge into 'proper' single seaters with a Ralt RT3 in the 1600cc Racing Car Class and is enjoying it immensely. 'The handling's so different with the engine at the back, far more responsive. The cars turn in a lot better on the corners, you can take them quicker. But I'm inclined to think that when this breaks away it breaks away for good, whereas with the Clubmans you can

Cleaning the tyres on Stewart Bayliss' Jedi Mk1.

CHAPTER 3

Approaching the start line, Wiscombe Park, September meeting.

Inset: Andrew Russell.

Both photos: Norman Burr

Car on the Hill

Ginetta G15

Andrew Russell, Modified Production Cars Under 1400cc

Apart from the fact that it smells of Castrol R, there's little to set Andrew Russell's Ginetta G15 apart from any of its Imp-powered rivals. So why has it been notching up class wins all season with monotonous regularity?

No doubt it has something to do with the driver, a 38 year-old transducer engineer from Worcester, who has owned the car for 14 years and knows it inside out. Drivers in that situation mesh with their cars so intimately that they frequently achieve results which they could not approach even in a theoretically superior car, purely because their confidence is so high.

But the car *is* quick. Its Hartwell-tuned engine is opened out to 1100 cc by boring and stroking and using an offset-ground forged crank. 'You can get them out to 1200, but this one revs like a 998. It will pull about 9000 when I get carried away, but I try not to go up there too much! Touch wood, I've not had any engine trouble this year.' Whether the Castrol R has anything to do with this reliability he isn't sure, but that's what the engine builder recommended and he's not arguing. 'If it's not broken, don't mend it.'

The only thing he has had to mend this year is the gearbox. The transmission is a known weakness with this car, hardly surprising as it was designed for around 50bhp and now has to transmit around 130. To make matters worse, the rear-mounted engine gives the G15 excellent traction off the line, so the transmission can't even seek relief in wheelspin. Indeed, the G15 has been timed at 2 seconds for the first 64ft at Prescott, which represents around 1g and is as good as the smaller single-seaters. In this situation 'something's got to give' observes Andrew.

This example has slightly more rearward weight bias than standard, because to save weight Andrew has removed the radiator (normally mounted in the nose) completely. 'It only runs for 40 seconds at a time, so I just pump the water round the engine.'

The rest of the car is surprisingly standard. Suspension is lowered and stiffened, with slightly higher rate springs on the front and much higher on the back. Adjustable dampers complete the roadholding department. The bodyshell is mostly original, 'apart from a few stone chips' and even the original orange paint is for the most part the factory finish — remarkable for a hard-used 1971 car. The chassis is a steel ladder affair, simple but relatively heavy compared to the rival Clan with its glassfibre monocoque. The G15's weight approaches 550kg: 'The Clans should be a little quicker than this'.

He used to drive the Ginetta to work but 'it got more and more modified and more and more undriveable so I ended up trailering it.' It's the only car he has ever competed in as a driver, his previous motorsport consisting of navigating on night rallies in an Imp, an experience he describes as 'frightening'.

It seems unlikely that this very effective Ginetta will be for sale in the near future. 'I'm fairly happy with this machine; I occasionally look at single seaters but they're so dreadfully expensive for something that's half competitive. This thing's half competitive already.'

LIVING WITH SPEED

Man on the Hill

Justin Fletcher

Now rated at one of the hottest young drivers on the hills, Justin Fletcher has been tempted to follow in Andy Priaulx's footsteps and turn to Formula Renault Sport circuit racing in the hope of pursuing a full-time racing career. But despite a succession of stirring drives which have seen his Pilbeam MP62 mix it with the V8s and often beat all but the top four or five of them, Justin has his feet too firmly on the ground to make the plunge yet.

'I would like to take it on further but I'm now 25 and I've got a career. Last year I wanted to go testing in Formula Renaults but I decided that I'd started a new job and didn't want to go and mess it all up.'

He works in recruitment consultancy, finding accountants for companies in the City, and admits that working with financiers is not half as interesting as driving up Wiscombe with 300bhp behind your backside. If there was such a thing as a professional hillclimb driver 'I'd be here like a shot I can tell you.'

This is his second year with the MP62, which he shares with his father Nick. That year his quickest rivals were Roger Moran, Tom Brown and Tom's father Richard. This year Roger and Richard have moved up a class but into the picture has come longtime competitor Tim Thomson who is proving quite a threat. So Justin will have his work cut out to win his class regularly, let alone the Leaders Championship which he covets.

Although Nick Fletcher started his competition career a long time ago, driving Sprites and Lotus Cortinas in the '60s, 'there was a gap of about 10 or 15 years while we brought our children up'. By the time he was ready to return to the hills to which he had been introduced all those years ago, courtesy of a night rally which had its final stage at Loton Park, son Justin was there to spur him on.

Shelsley Walsh, August meeting.

'Justin and I started more or less together. We built a Caterham Seven in about 1989 and ran that for a couple of seasons', recalls Nick.

Shelsley beckoned, Justin having his first experience of it in a 1071 Mini Cooper shared with his twin brother Adam. 'They did quite well but Justin had an unfortunate incident at the Esses and comprehensively wrote the car off. We then bought a March 79B which was a lovely car, ex-Barry Groombridge. It had done very well at Wiscombe hillclimb and still holds an up to 1600 record there. Justin and I ran it for two seasons, then we decided we wanted to have something lighter and we bought this MP62.'

Do they fancy a V8? 'I think not really. We've shall hang in here with the 2 litre engine. Justin's doing very well and I'm enjoying it'

But he admits that these things tend to acquire a momentum of their own. 'If you ask me in a year or two's time it could well be that we've got a V8!'

---

bring it back again. Very interesting though! I'm already quicker on the three hills I've been to with the Ralt' he explains, but there is obviously much more to come.

The car is actually quite elderly, having been produced in the early '80s, but has been well cared for and remains competitive. Last season, in the hands of previous owner Simon Ashley, it won every event it entered bar one. Proof that you don't need a '90s design to worry other competitors on the hills. Power comes from a Cosworth BDA with around 210 bhp.

Like many speed competitors, Basil is in the automotive business — he's an after sales manager at a VW-Audi dealer. In fact Tony Fletcher, co-ordinator of the RAC Hillclimb Championship and the man who probably knows more hillclimbers than anyone else, reckons that some 60% of competitors have motor industry connections. Of the others, farmers are the largest group.

But there can be few drivers whose livelihood places them as perfectly as Roy's. Not only does he rebuild and develop cars, he teaches hillclimbing one day a week at Prescott, makes competition silencers which are widely used on — surprise — hillclimb cars (and many others) and is an agent for AP racing components. He's also located in the right part of the country: living near Warwick in the Midlands, he's not only centrally placed for any venue, be it Scotland, Devon, or anywhere in between, but is also just 38 miles from Prescott and 40 from Shelsley Walsh.

This morning I find him discussing the engine tune with John. It feels a little strange at the bottom end, hunting between 2000 and 3000 rpm. 'There was a big hesitation over the yump' — Bunny's Leap — 'I couldn't get my power back in, felt like I was overgeared. Perhaps it was just me, the first thing in the morning, waking me up!'

'What do you think, are we too lean or too rich, or is it the ignition timing?'

'Too rich', opines John, who proceeds to take a read-out of the telemetry.

Despite these minor concerns, Roy's in good spirits today, fresh from an outright win with a new course record at Curborough sprint the weekend before. To add icing to the cake, Antony came home fourth with the new Ralt — 'quickest car off the line I've ever seen, it really is'. A win today would be particularly sweet for Roy, for it would see him equal Martyn Griffiths' record of 67 RAC Championship round wins.

He swaps practice experiences with Patrick Wood. 'Generally, I think the track's in the best condition I've ever driven it. There's more grip than I've ever known here', Patrick reckons.

'I bet you've got Jean Alesi's old front tyres this weekend, or Michael Schumacher's ex rear ones. I got tremendous wheelspin out of Sawbench.'

'Yes my traction control was working overtime there, really overtime.'

CHAPTER 3

Brian & Adrian Moody's Ginetta G12 is not only pretty but also highly effective.

'Perhaps I ought to have traction control! Do away with my right foot!'

'Actually it was slower on the top 12 runs at Curborough than everyone else. We set it up for what we thought was the optimum likely start but the start was so good, with so much grip off the line, that when the electronics brought the engine revs back to 5000, which normally is enough to give me wheelspin, it just bogged the engine down.'

This F1-inspired electronics is all very well, but in F1 you have a team of engineers back in the pits to analyse the data as it is generated. All Patrick has is his girlfriend, her son and a folding chair in the back of the trailer.

I leave the pair to their paddock banter and wander over to Simon Durling, who is busy playing with his tyre pressures. At partner Tim Barrington's suggestion, he is dropping the fronts from 14psi to 12. Simon knows all about the subtleties of tyre pressures, not least from his involvement with sporting trials, with which he fills the winter months when the hills are closed.

Back at the start, a gaggle of cars is coming back down the hill from second practice, among them Bill Morris, who for some unknown reason has his silencer in his arms. Whatever caused it to migrate can't have slowed him down much, for his second practice was an improvement to 39.55, well adrift of Justin Fletcher's 37.19 but in touch with Justin's father Nick in the same car, on 39.45, and Mike Lee on 39.19. Mike's car is a Lyncar 79B, while both the others are Pilbeams, Bill's an MP54 — highly modified by McBeath brothers Simon and Andy — and the Fletchers' a newer MP62. Clearly Justin Fletcher is the man to watch in this class, with every prospect of a Top 12 position at the end of the day.

In the next class up, Graham Priaulx is the man on form. He is currently two hundredths ahead of Roy and one tenth ahead of son Andy. Since he had a big moment at Martini, locking up and only just managing to get round, and is also slower off the line than Roy, he will really fly if he gets those two things right.

But first it's time for lunch. Lunch in the sunshine. Engines are killed as participants and spectators alike enjoy what is probably their first chance of the year to laze about on dry grass. After the hustle of the morning, it seems strangely peaceful. The commentary is replaced by *A Whiter Shade of Pale*. A father picks up his toddler by the hands and swings him round in a circle. A young couple snooze on the grass, wrapped in each other's arms. The smell of burgers wafts across from the mobile kitchen. The old house looks on, approvingly. This may not be big time motorsport but it beats the hell out of huddling in front of the telly watching Sunday Grandstand.

As the afternoon runs start it's time to climb up to Martini and watch the action. Sports Libre up to 2000cc are running as I walk and I reflect on how much poorer British motorsport would have been had Major Mallock not begun to build racing cars. Besides providing countless drivers with a mount in the Clubman's Class (would there even *be* one without the Mallock, one wonders?), the same chassis also provides competitive motoring in the Sports Libre division, where engine regs are more liberal. Today, Bournemouth driver James Forsyth is proving the point, taking an emphatic class lead to prove that his win the day before was no fluke.

Sports Libre over 2000cc provides a lot of spectacle as the machinery is extremely diverse. Today a shared Metro 6R4 is in evidence, plus Duncan Stewart's V8 Dutton and Paul Parker's huge Royale, which is a real handful on a track as tight as this. Paul is not having the

'My dad's exhaust pipes are bigger than your dad's.'

29

best of days, having suffered the ignominy of running out of petrol on his second practice. Yes Paul, we know the 6.2 litre Chevy is thirsty, but this is ridiculous. A whole tankful between the start and the Gate?

The Dutton is outclassed in this company, but the others are closely matched, as Paul proves by splitting Andrew Fraser and Tim Painter in the Metro. The 6R4 drivers were a well known single-seater pairing in the '70s and have shared the charismatic 4WD machine in recent times, to good effect it seems.

At the top of the course Mike Lee's Lyncar finishes its afternoon's work with an engine blowup that deposits oil at Martini, forcing a break in the proceedings.

When the fun restarts, Graham Priaulx continues his morning's form with a superb 35.99, the only man under 36 seconds. Roger Moran is close on 36.24, Roy rather out of touch on 37.29, despite dropping first gear by one notch and third by two in an attempt to match the engine's rev range better to the hill. Roger's run will be his last as far as the class runs are concerned, as he and George Ritchie opt to scratch their second blast to give them time to fix a clutch problem before the Top 12 run-off at the end of the day.

One of the appealing things about following a whole season of RAC Championship climbs is that the class list varies from meeting to meeting, so you rub shoulders with cars and drivers you wouldn't normally see. Here there are special classes for Ginettas and Kougars, the former producing a large and diverse field ranging from Imp-engined G15s to the V6 G21 of Steve Fidler, the latter attracting five of these handsome Jaguar-engined Allard-esque roadsters. And it's a Ginetta which shows how Martini should be tackled, Adrian Moody taking the G12 round in a beautifully controlled slide which helps him to second in class.

You can see a lot from Martini. Like

Dramatic sequence showing (left to right) Graham Priaulx getting on the grass on the exit of Bunny's leap and sliding into the trees.

30

CHAPTER 3

the sheet of flame which spits out of Gerald Prior-Palmer's Integrale on the overrun. Or the Most Lurid Slide of the Day, the award for which surely goes to Chris Briant in the Lotus Sunbeam with a special bonus for recovering sufficiently to cross the finish line still travelling in the right direction. Worst Approach Award goes to Rodney Thorne in the TR8, who locks up first one wheel, then the other, looks thoroughly out of the control the whole time but somehow manages to scramble round. Air of Detachment Award goes to Graham Chard, not for looking cool but for losing his Westfield's bonnet on the approach, the offending metal hanging on by the right-hand hooks and waving hello to the marshals as it passes. Best Aroma Award goes to Andrew Russell, whose very quick G15 leaves a nostalgic whiff of Castrol R.

In the now very competitive 1100cc Racing Car class, the battle between the new record-holder Phil Cooke and Ian Chard is resolved when Ian's Jedi runs wide at Martini and ends its run embedded in the bank, fortunately without serious damage. What was that Paul Channon said about not attempting to get round?

Biggest drama of the day, however, is reserved for Graham Priaulx, whose attempt to improve on his storming first run ends at Bunny's Leap, where he gets it wrong, puts a wheel off the track, loses it completely and ends up in the shrubbery near the Gate. The car is a mess and Graham is taken to hospital for a check up. Poor Andy sees his chances of FTD evaporate through no fault of his own, but has the consolation of knowing that his father has nothing worse than concussion.

This reduces the Top 12 to a Top 10, as neither Priaulx can now take their place on the start line. Running order is in reverse order of qualifying, which gives Roger Moran the advantage of being last off the line and knowing exactly how much he has to do. Particularly pleased to be in there is Justin Fletcher, who has earned his spot by setting a 2-litre Racing Car class record.

Suddenly Roy, having not looked like a winner all day, finds something more and shaves a full second off his best to put him ahead after the first runs. At 36.23 he's still a quarter second off Graham's best, but it's the run-off that counts for Championship points and that might still be enough to win the round. The class runs in the afternoon determine who gets into the Top 12 and in what order they run, but as far as times are concerned the slate is then wiped clean. If you do brilliantly in the afternoon and screw up on the Top 12, you get no points.

Patrick Wood and Roger Moran tie for second on 36.40, so after the first runs Roy is the man to beat. Second time out he fails to improve, while Patrick manages to find less than a tenth. So now the pressure is on Roger to find something extra on the very last run of the day; only he can snatch the lead from the Steel King Pilbeam.

Standing at Sawbench, I hear the orange MP72 howling through the trees. That Judd is certainly working for its living. It looks fast, and it is, but it's not fast enough: 36.34. The old master has done it!

The presentation back in the paddock is an emotional moment for Roy, a moment when he writes another page of hillclimb history. Sixty-seven wins, equal with Martyn Griffiths' record. And this from the man who said in 1975 that he would retire once he won the championship.

As we push the Pilbeam into its trailer, I ask him whether his improvement was due to the engine running better, or the gearing changes?

'Oh it was me. I just wasn't going fast enough.'

Above right, Graham, in orange overalls, thanks the marshals before (top right) a marshal stands in the cockpit as the wreckage is towed away.

Championship Top Tens after Round 2

RAC			Leaders		
=1	Roger Moran	17	=1	Justin Fletcher	18
=1	Patrick Wood	17	=1	Mark Waldron	18
=1	Roy Lane	17	=3	Tom New	15
4	Tim Mason	12	=3	Phil Cooke	15
5	Andy Priaulx	10	=5	Martin Groves	13
6	Justin Fletcher	7	=5	Peter Hannam	13
=7	Graham Priaulx	6	7	Tony Lambert	12
=7	Bill Bristow	6	8	Graham Priaulx	11
9	George Ritchie	5	=9	Andrew Russell	10
10	Simon Durling	4	=9	Andy Priaulx	10
			=9	Paul Parker	10

31

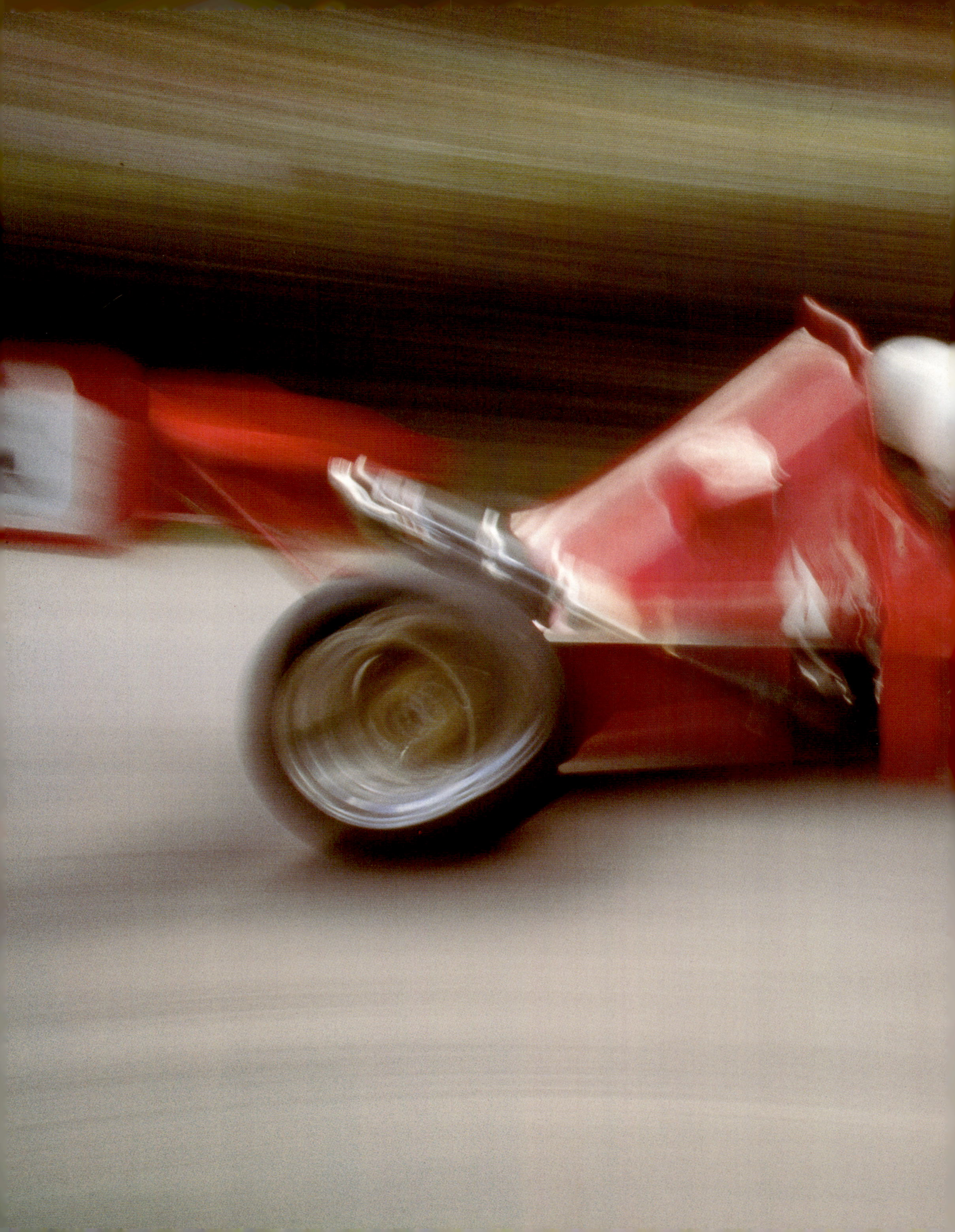

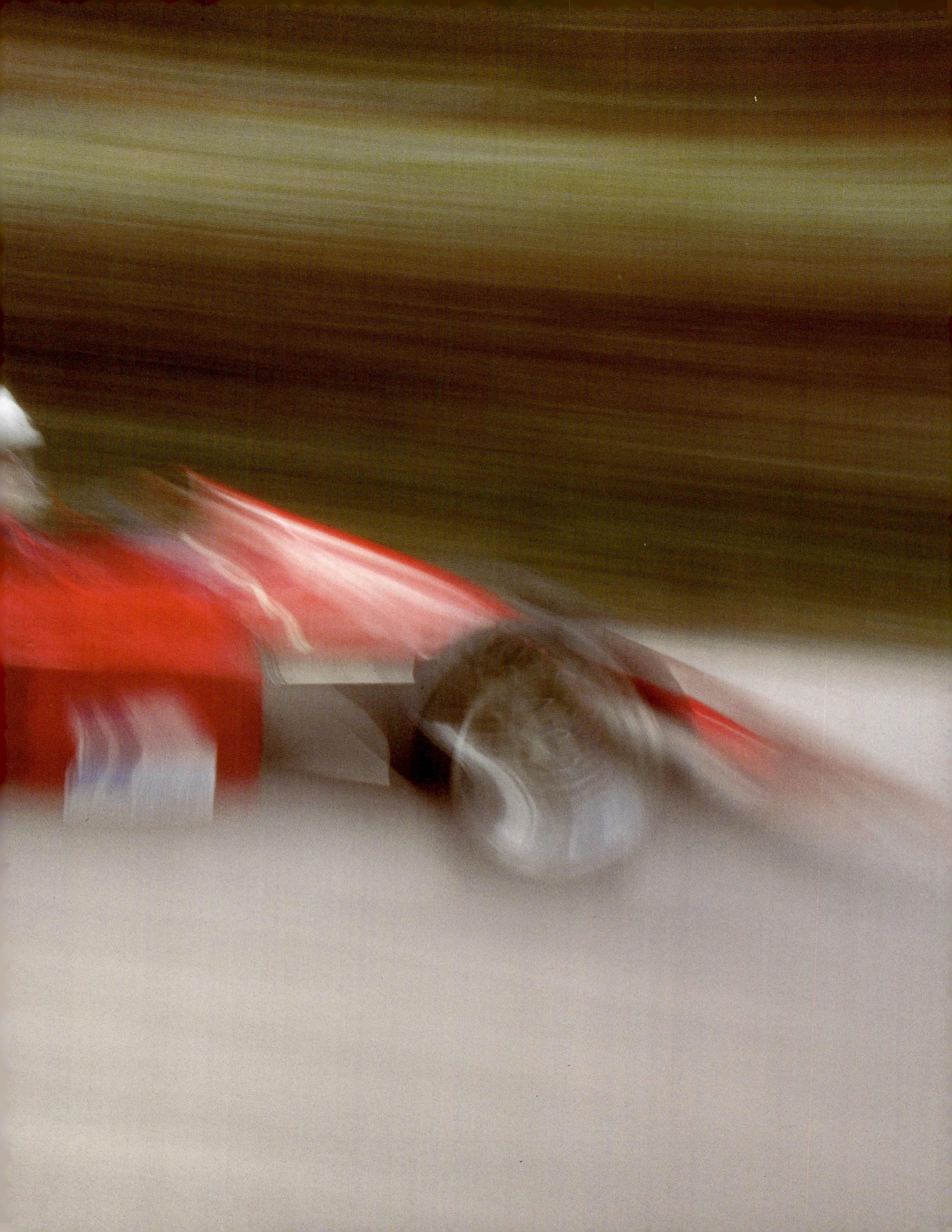

LIVING WITH SPEED

'He had no need to do that, but he still went for it'

Prescott

Location near the village of Gretton approximately six miles east of Tewkesbury.

Organising club Bugatti Owners Club, Prescott Hill, Gotherington, Cheltenham, Glos GL52 4RD. Tel 01242 673136; fax 01242 677001.

Length 1127 yards (Long), 1132 yards (Cross-Over), 880 yards (Short).

Outright hill records at start of 5.5.96 meeting
Overall, Long Course: Roy Lane, 38.04sec. Ladies, Long Course: Maggie Blankstone, 42.11sec. Overall, Cross-Over Course: Mark Colton, 38.35sec. Ladies, Cross-Over Course: Maggie Blankstone, 42.91sec.

KEY
Track shading indicates gear ratio...
- White striped is first gear
- Tints are intermediates (darker tone equals higher gear)
- Black is top gear

Because ratios and patterns in racing gearboxes can be altered at will, a particular shading on one map does not indicate the same ratio as on another: shading is relative only to that particular venue.

V indicates good viewing area

Roy's Run

'At Prescott the grip is still very good. The original course was the short one, while the cross-over course is now not used at all. The cross-over was easier to drive because the approach speed was slow in and fast out, which is always quicker than the opposite.

'Now I go first off the line (a 70mph gear), towards the bridge, and change up (a 115mph gear). On the approach to Orchard you back off to about 85-90, then back on again hard, up to 110 on the approach to Ettore's. This first part is the fastest part of the course. At Ettore's, back into first, round the corner (it tightens on you so the first section is the quickest), back into second on the exit (100mph on this bit), then on the approach into Pardon change across the box into 'third' which is a gear about halfway between the first two.

'In 'third' you can reach 95mph before you get to the right hander at the start of the Esses. In most setups you hold that all the way to the end of the Esses where you change into 'fourth', which is 7mph lower than 'third'. As you run up towards Semi-Circle you push the lever forward into third gear spot and go all the way to the finish, reaching about 100mph over the line.

'It is also possible to do the course using just two ratios, which is the approach I took at the second meeting of the year.

'I know *exactly* where I'm losing against the day I got the record. It was a nice warm June weekend, ideal conditions, and as I turned to go into the blind corner at the start of the Esses I was absolutely flat. I gently braked, turned across the kerb — just put two wheels on the edge — and then absolutely floored it, so much so that I had a job to stop it. And that's where all the time came. I've tried to do it many times since and it ain't half difficult! I don't know whether I'll have the bottle to do it again!

34

CHAPTER 4

Prescott

Depending on who you talk to, the spiritual home of British hillclimbing is either Prescott or Shelsley Walsh. Shelsley has been going longer, but Prescott is the only full-time permanent racing venue, unencumbered by being part of a working estate, farm or whatever.

'When you're at Prescott, you don't talk about Shelsley Walsh. And when you're at Shelsley, you don't talk about Prescott' is how Roy sums it up. Roy himself has to be a little circumspect, since he adores the atmosphere of the Shelsley paddock but has been well served by Prescott over the years, where he earns money every other Wednesday teaching hillclimbing to all comers in all types of road vehicles.

The venue was bought by the Bugatti Owners Club in 1937 when the estate of which it formed a part came up for sale. The BOC had for some time been running hillclimbs at various minor venues but longed for a permanent base. With the Bugatti even then being the favoured car of the rich enthusiast, the club had far more money at its disposal than most motor clubs and was able to buy the site outright. The result of this farsighted move is that the club has been able to develop the site steadily, without having to worry about keeping the landowner happy or fitting in with the land's everyday role.

All around you the fruits of this happy independence are there to see. Seating at strategic points on the hill. Proper toilets. A club house. A Bugatti museum. A permanent pedestrian bridge over the track. A permanent map to help visitors find their way around. A play area for the kids. A scout hut for the marshals, who have their own SWB Landrover and trailer to take them to their stations on the hill. The marshals, incidentally, are noticeably more numerous than at other venues, numerous enough to have formed their own club.

Ettore would have been very proud of it all. Even the marshals' Landrover is painted an appropriate shade of blue.

At some hillclimbs the entire paraphernalia of motorsport disappears so soon after the last car leaves the paddock and so completely that you could return next day and wonder if you had dreamed it all. Not so at Prescott. This place lives and breathes speed, that's all it exists for.

Spectators don't only get reasonable facilities, they also get unrivalled viewing. The local topography ensures that there are plenty of vantage points from which a good proportion of the track can be seen. Combine that with a beautiful Gloucestershire setting and you have the recipe for a good family day out.

This morning things are moving slowly at RTL110, the Lanes' luxurious mobile home, due largely to grandson Christopher's predilection for snuggling into bed with grandma and grandad first thing in the morning. So with the shades still drawn at 9:20, I decide to take advantage of the lull and walk the hill.

It's quite a complex track as it can be arranged three ways: full course, short course and cross-over course. The full course blasts under the bridge to a sweeping left-hand curve and thence to the long 180° right-hander at Ettore's, so long that the road ends up doubling back on itself, enabling Ettore's to be cut out altogether (short course) or taken in the reverse direction (cross-over course). Today we are using the full course.

Whichever you drive, you next arrive at Pardon Hairpin, a climbing left-hander which leads into a straight. Next come the Esses (has anyone ever counted how many motorsport venues have an Esses?), a short straight, a long right-hander called Semi-Circle and finally the

Above: Norman Kittle warms up his Metro 6R4 after…
Immediately below: …'making a few wee mods'.
Bottom: Business end of the beast. No gas struts, they add weight — a stick is good enough.
Facing page: Roy receives the spoils.

35

Tony Croft's magnificent Ronart SP125 at the start.

Prescott paddock: Where better on a fine day?

CHAPTER 4

finish. Semi-Circle looks the most hairy point to me: not a lot to stop you sliding off and a long, long drop if you do.

Unlike most other venues, Prescott has a return road, so the action can continue without interruptions for batches of cars to come back down the hill. This has three advantages. Spectators like it because the non-stop action builds up the atmosphere. Entrants like it because the organisers can accept larger 'grids' than other venues. And it's a boon for drivers, who can get straight back to the paddock and make the most of the time between runs. Frustration for a hillclimb driver is to have a misfire or other curable problem on your first run and to find that you're first into the top paddock. Your tools are at the bottom, you're at the top, the clock is ticking and you have to sit there fuming for 20 minutes until a whole batch of cars has built up and you are finally cleared to roll back down.

Down in the paddock things are stirring. Roy and Betty sit and enjoy the morning sun as 187 racing drivers and their cars come to life. It has been unseasonably cold overnight and there is a possibility of cloud later, but right at this moment, from where we are sitting, the world looks a mighty fine place.

We watch Norman Kittle, 'making a few wee mods you know', his engine now in fine fettle after its problems at Loton Park. The car is standing on four sets of rollers while it warms up in gear. It's not a particularly elegant noise, but it's certainly hard to ignore. 'All the rallycross boys do that you know', Roy remarks. 'It's probably worth 15-20 bhp to them to warm the transmission up'.

Roy, it turns out, is very familiar with the 6R4 as he did quite a lot of development driving on the car for Rover. 'The engine was derived from the Rover V8 with the back end chopped off. For the actual first engine, which had to be maximum of 3 litres normally aspirated to fit in Group B, they took a Rover engine and literally cut two cylinders off the back and welded a plate on. In fact I know someone who's got one of those cars with that engine in. They also used Rover heads, again with the ends cut off. Then after they'd built about 10 of those and they kept blowing up and had proved totally unsuccessful, they built the genuine engine.

'The car I had and developed for them, at Gaydon on the test track, was in fact one with a special Cosworth engine. They built two engines like that for Tony Pond to do the Manx and I took one car to Shelsley in August 1986. It was ever so quick. All the top nobs from Austin Rover came to watch. But I was trying to drive a single seater the same day, because I was in with a chance of the Championship, and it wasn't the right thing to be doing. Good fun though!

'Do you know the most exciting bit of all? Taking it out on the road in the morning to warm the transmission up. Me and Antony took this car out for about 10 or 15 miles round the lanes — and there's some lovely lanes round Shelsley. My God, did it go!'

We're still chewing the automotive cud when Norman makes his first run of the day. 'I bet he's changed gear four times by the time he gets to the bridge' says Roy. And sure enough he has.

When Roy starts to busy himself readying the Pilbeam, I wander off to learn a bit more about the smaller single seaters, for it is the two smallest classes, up to 500cc and 1100cc, which have seen the greatest changes in the last few years. Ten years ago, a typical 500cc car was what would now be classified as a historic machine, complying with the immediate postwar F3 and powered by a motorcycle engine of similar vintage. Even the quickest 1100s were based around obsolete FF2000 circuit cars powered by Imp, Ford pushrod or, in the case of the most effective machines, expensive Cosworth 4-valve units.

Then in the mid '80s two quite separate things happened within a year or so of each other: the Trakstar and the Jedi. One was to prove a fascinating dead end, albeit a thought-provoking one, the other highly influential.

Effectively a hillclimbing kart, but incorporating rudimentary suspension as required by the regulations, the tiny Trakstar with its two-stroke engine — initially from Yamaha and later Rotax — was despite its roots and appearance eligible for the small racing car classes. Aided by excellent power-to-weight ratio and phenomenal manoeuvrability, it was soon posting success after success in the hands of Dick Foden and Phil Jefferies — and producing cries of 'foul' from many competitors in conventional cars. After a few years the rules were changed to effectively outlaw kart-based designs, but the lesson was not lost on racing car builders, who by then had started to look long and hard at the potential of two-stroke and other motorcycle engines.

For inspiration they had not only the Trakstar but a car which actually predated it by a year or two and which was to prove far influential in the longer term — the Jedi. Designer John Corbyn had noticed the number of '50s Cooper-JAPs still on the hills and concluded that their formula of chain drive and motorcycle power unit remained as valid in the '80s as it had been 30 years earlier. The result was the Jedi, a modern-looking, modern-handling racing car which, thanks to its use of a complete bike power train including clutch and gearbox, could be built for dramatically less than any single seaters currently available. No Hewland gear sets needed here!

John was not the only constructor to make the motorcycle connection, but he is certainly one of the most successful. A glance at today's entry list shows that every one of the eight entrants in the up to 500 class is driving a Suzuki-engined Jedi, total production from the Wellingborough, Northants, concern now approaching the 60 mark.

The marque also figures in the next class up, though here there is stiff competition from OMS and Hi Tech.

Searching for a Jedi to look at in more detail, I find Paul Crocker just back down from his first run and nursing a cracked nose — the car's not his. While his friends tape up the damage, I ask him about the car.

This one has an 1100cc Kawasaki ZZR four-cylinder watercooled engine, which develops 146 bhp in standard tune. Fitted to a road bike this power

37

LIVING WITH SPEED

Above, centre: They also serve who only sit and watch: repairing the nose on Paul Crocker's Jedi and (above left) back in action at the Esses.

Richard Marshall and traction control Peugeot.

unit is staggeringly fast yet beautifully flexible: open up the bike from standstill and first will take you to over 70. At this point you can drop it all the way into top (sixth) and have enough grunt even at these lowly revs to lift the front wheel. Not surprisingly, the ZZR unit is a popular choice amongst hillracers.

'Yesterday in practice we came across problems with the rear uprights twisting, because they were fabrications made out of aluminium,' he explains in his soft West Country burr. 'Previously the engine in this car was a 350 two-stroke pumping out about 95bhp, but this engine produces 146. So we reverted to the original Jedi steel uprights'.

However, there was no time to set up the rear suspension properly. Unbeknown to Paul the back wheels were toeing out too far, a fact which he discovered the hard way when he attempted to tackle the first hairpin.

Despite the duct-tape on the nose the six year-old white and red Mk1 Jedi is a delightfully pretty car. It's tiny, but every inch a proper racing car, almost as though someone had taken Roy's Pilbeam and reduced everything to two-thirds size. No matter what kind of motorsport you like, if the sight of a Jedi doesn't make you want to leap in and try it, not even a *little* bit, then it's time you bought an anorak and took up bird-watching. The thing's got 'drive me' written all over it, metaphorically anyway.

Only one item looks slightly incongruous; drum brakes all round, a rare sight on a competition car. 'I find them more efficient than discs', Paul says. 'We used to run an Imp-engined Harrison and had a lot of trouble with the discs not warming up properly. But these twin leading shoe Mini brakes do the job quite proficiently. After all, you haven't got time to get brake fade!'

He reckons the whole car could be built to this specification from scratch for the right side of £15,000, including the £600 needed for a set of tyres. While this is a lot of money for someone to fork out on what is basically a hobby, in motor racing terms it is peanuts — a competitive single-seater racing car for the price of a well-specced Mondeo.

He sees Mark Lawrence and Phil Cooke as the men to beat in the class. Phil also has a Jedi but with a modified chassis and a highly tuned Suzuki GSXR 1100 motor, while Mark has opted for an OMS chassis but with a similar engine to Paul's, albeit in a higher state of tune.

This means that Paul has a softer engine than either of them, but he does not find this as big a disadvantage as it might seem. The hills are so tight that torque and driveability go a long way to counteracting outright power. With a mildly tuned engine you might not win but if you can drive accurately and aggressively you'll not be far behind. Put yourself in the same situation on a circuit and you'll be lapped.

Car on the Hill

Target Pilbeam MP58-04

Patrick Wood, Racing Cars Over 2000cc

Barbon, May.

Traction control details: above, wheel sensor and below, control box.

One thing sets Patrick Wood's Pilbeam apart from every other single seater on the hill: traction control. And the system is wholly and unreservedly the work of one man: Richard Marshall.

Richard works for the Benetton F1 team and has been responsible for much of their sophisticated engine management and telemetry. Not surprisingly, many elements of Patrick's system parallel the Benetton approach, but Richard is at pains to emphasise that Patrick's car was not built on the back of his employer. If anything it was the other way round: his interest in the subject — of which the Target Pilbeam and his own Peugeot 205 are practical manifestations — came first, the professional application later.

In common with a number of top runners, the Target Pilbeam has a data logging system on board, to enable the car's performance to be analysed after each run and hopefully improved. Unlike the others, however, this data logging is linked to the engine management in such a way that the information can be used immediately to modulate engine power and inhibit wheelspin.

'There are three ways of controlling the power from the engine', explains Richard. 'You can use an ABS-type system, where you actually brake one of the wheels that's spinning, you can try to control the throttle by some means, or you can spark cut. Of the three, spark cutting is by far the most effective since it's a very direct action, much less of a problem from a control point of view. People have tried combinations of the three but in general spark cutting is the only real way to do it, and that's what this system does. It interrupts the signal to the spark box from the ECU'.

The result is a deliberate misfire which even now prompts some ill-informed commentators to conclude that there is something wrong with the engine. Richard laughs. 'The Peugeot had a misfire for three years before people realised what we were doing. I was running the system on the Peugeot before anyone had actually raced it in F1, so it was very new ground for everyone, myself included. I learned a lot in the first year, had a few fluffed starts, and took some time to get an algorithm that really worked properly, which it now does. You don't have to worry about it, you just switch it on and use it.'

That algorithm, and the software of which it is part, is the heart of the system. The most critical input is from wheel sensors, which on Richard's installations are fitted to all four wheels, although he acknowledges that this is something of a luxury. It is not vital to measure the speed of rotation of all four wheels, merely 'advisable'.

'You need a fair number of teeth as well. Standard datalogging systems typically use two teeth per revolution, but if you work that out into distance travelled per tooth, it's rather too long a distance for a system like this to work.'

Having measure the wheel speeds, you know fast each corner of the car's going and can thus calculate slip. 'Then the clever bit is to decide how much to cut the engine, when to cut it and when not to cut it. The most difficult thing is to get the car off the line without bogging it down — I've certainly managed that a few times in the Peugeot!'

'It's not just a question of slip' he admits. Obviously other parameters like engine revs also need to be fed into the software, but precisely which parameters they are he does not reveal.

However, with conditions varying from hour to hour, the system clearly needs to draw from quite a few sources and have plenty of feedback if it is not to be caught out. 'There's a fair number of parameters in there, some saying: "this engine's getting out of control, let's cut it" and others: "if you cut it now it's going to bog down".'

The datalogging side of the system is not unique, though it is unusually comprehensive, necessarily so if the traction control is to be used effectively. 'If you can't tune it, you've got no idea whether the thing's performing to its best.'

Lateral and longitudinal acceleration are monitored through cockpit-mounted sensors, throttle position is recorded, and potentiometers on all four corners of the car record what the suspension is doing.

'There are three different categories of data: things the controller uses, things the driver can use to adjust the way he drives the car and things you might use for developing the car in the longer term. Even if it doesn't seem relevant at the time you always collect the data, because in six months time when you're sitting in front of the telly in the winter thinking "what are we going to do to improve the car?" you can go back and ask yourself what happens if we change this or that.'

Has it really made a difference to Patrick's times? Patrick himself is noncommittal, explaining that he made other changes to the car at the same time as the system was fitted, making it hard to isolate the effect of the traction control.

The jury is likely to be out on that particular question for some time yet, as other competitors don't look like getting the chance to try it for themselves. Despite lots of interest, Richard has no plans to offer the system for sale. 'It would probably too expensive to build commercially'.

Prescott, September meeting.

Man on the Hill

Stormy Fairweather
Flag Marshal

Call him Roger Fairweather and no one on the hills will know who you are talking about. Mention Stormy and you get instant recognition.

For in a marshalling spectrum which goes all the way from turning out once a year for the local sprint, to single-mindedly dedicating almost your entire leisure time to helping others enjoy their sport, Stormy belongs indisputably at the serious end.

He's no stranger to competition himself. During his many years in the army he rallied in military Land Rovers and since joining civilian life he has piloted a Rover SD1 2600 up Gurston. Does he prefer marshalling or driving? 'A lot of it's a question of cost, but I do like marshalling though.'

You only have to look at him to realise that. Not for him the dazzling dayglo of the occasional helper: Stormy's overalls have seen service in countless ditches and verges, have sheltered behind numberless straw bales in every conceivable type of weather, have pulled drivers out of stricken cars in the most desperate circumstances — and it shows. In his belt is an evil-looking knife, ready to cut drivers out of their belts in an emergency. On his battered beany hat are pinned a dozen badges. This is a man who is proud of what he does.

He has never marshalled north of the border, nor much in Northern England except at Harewood. But from his home near Salisbury this 51 year-old motor mechanic travels to practically every motorsport venue in the Midlands and Southwest, be it used for circuit racing, hillclimbing, rallying, or rallycross. A typical year will see him working at 70 to 100 events. 'I try to marshal at least one day every weekend.'

'I've gradually worked my way up through the gradings scheme,' he explains. 'I started as a novice, then went to course marshal, fire marshal, and now flag marshal; I'm training to be an observer.'

After that there are two routes open to him and he is at present unsure which to take. He could go for examining observer, 'which allows you to grade and sign other peoples' grading cards if they're on post with you. But I'm thinking about trying for the RAC Rescue Licence.'

There are of course many other marshals who take their motorsport every bit as seriously as Stormy, a fact for which every driver must be thankful. Motorsport is blessed with hundreds of enthusiasts who get as much pleasure from organising as others do from competition.

But very few have overalls with quite the same patina.

A bigger disadvantage for Paul is that he has not competed at Prescott for 10 years, having restricted himself to events in the South West in the meantime. Now this dark-haired thirty-something is having to learn the subtleties of the course all over again.

In the event Paul finishes sixth out of 10 starters. As he predicted, top men Cooke and Lawrence post the best times, 42.03 and 42.53 respectively, with no less than four drivers in the 43s. Unfortunately for Paul he's the last of the four, just nine hundredths behind fifth place Brian Robbins in a Hi Tech Yamaha. Maybe if he'd not blown that first run he'd have pushed a little harder in the second, but driving the hills is like serving in tennis: miss the first and you're disinclined to take chances with the second. Nobody wants the embarrassment of falling off twice in one day.

Up on the hill Dominic Pilbeam has just sent his first serve crashing into the net, or rather on to the grass on the inside of the exit to Pardon hairpin. He gets crossed up on the way out and heads for the infield, fortunately stopping before he reaches the trees a little further down the hill.

Unsurprisingly his mount is a Pilbeam, for today the Bourne-based concern is here in force. Brothers Dominic and Ciaron share the driving, father Mike watches from the paddock, chief mechanic Mick Howlett looks after the car and acts as a mobile advice centre to any other Pilbeam driver with a problem or query. I'd seen Mick at earlier meetings but hadn't realised his significance. With pony tail, roll-up, old jeans and long beard, he looks more like a roadie for ZZ Top than a factory chief mechanic. Only the very British beany hat spoils the Texan image.

I catch Mike Pilbeam in the paddock after the car is retrieved and ask him why Alister Douglas Osborn's name is painted on the side. Although he doesn't compete regularly now, Alister is one of the very best hillclimbers of the last 20 years (he was RAC Champion in '77) and no hillclimb programme is without his name somewhere in its record table.

Mike explains that Alister is Pil-

40

CHAPTER 4

Pete Griffiths prepares for his next run.

beam's works development driver. 'This is our works development car and we were invited by the Australians to take the car out there to compete in the Australian hillclimb championship, which is a four-day weekend affair. The two drivers were Alister and Peter Finley — he's an Australian hillclimb champion himself.

'The two of them were first and second in the 2 litre class and second and fourth overall, so they very nearly won the Australian Championship — just seven hundredths of a second off it. We would have done it but we lacked local knowledge really. And this was unlimited capacity — the car that actually won it was much more powerful — so we were pretty pleased with that.'

Mike Pilbeam's a grey haired, quietly spoken man in his 50s, the sort of character who weighs his words carefully before he speaks. Perhaps because he doesn't regard words as cheap, he's no extrovert, but if you take the trouble to make the opening he'll chat for ages.

And he has no shortage of stories to tell, as his motorsport roots go right back to the BRM days at Bourne in Lincolnshire, where his own premises are still based.

Although Mike is clearly very proud of the dominance his cars currently enjoy in the larger single-seater classes, construction of hillclimb cars is something of a sideline for the Lincolnshire concern, which among other things is heavily involved in the Honda touring car campaign. For the Pilbeam family, a day on the hills is something of a day out.

Hillclimbing attracts all ages of machinery, new and old, but by following the RAC championship rounds we are only glimpsing the classic and vintage scene, as it is large enough to have a momentum of its own and tends to be concentrated at separate events.

But this is Prescott, owned by the Bugatti Owners Club, where no meeting would be complete without at least a sprinkling of Ettore's creations to add a little French blue to the proceedings. So at this venue there is a tantalising peep at the world of wonderful and irreplaceable machinery whose exhaust notes regularly reverberate around the Gloucestershire hills.

Four *Bugattistes* are obliging us today, one of whom catches my eye as he seems to be suffering a fuel pressurisation problem in his 1926 Type 35T and has to drop back off the start line to sort it out. It's Hugh Conway, a name which anyone even slightly familiar with Bugatti lore will recognise, for his late father, also confusingly called Hugh, was a renowned Bugatti fanatic, a disease which is clearly hereditary.

In addition to his love affair with the machines from Alsace, Conway Senior was a very fine engineer, occupying a senior management position in Rolls Royce Aero Engines. In the late '60s when Concorde's engines were being developed, machinists in the development shops at Bristol would frequently joke that the design of Olympus turbine blades bore an uncanny resemblance to Bugatti pistons.

(I know, because I was there, a fly on the wall, or rather a greenfly, as apprentices were known on account of their green overalls. Once, but only once, I was overtaken by a glorious blue Bugatti streaking down the Gloucester Road, its driver clad in leather helmet and wearing an expression which can only be described as a mixture of intense concentration, pure joy and manic enthusiasm. I have never forgotten the sight of the wind tearing at his clothing as he hunched slightly over the wheel, nor the feeling of ordinariness with which he left the rest of us. At that moment he was

The end of Dominic Pilbeam's first run.

LIVING WITH SPEED

Healeys queue at the paddock exit. The Frogeye is John Passmore's.

on another plane, one which most of us would be lucky to experience even once in our lives.)

For ordinary mortals at that time, a secondhand Mk1 Sprite was as good as many could manage. A few years earlier — 1963 to be precise — Roy Lane himself had started his racing career in a Frogeye derivative, an ex-works Sebring Sprite, and there are a couple of Frogeyes here today. John Passmore's green wire-wheeled example looks a gem, but as I admire it I am intrigued and strangely comforted to discover that despite its excellent condition there is still a rust bubble emerging at the base of the scuttle where it joins the sill, in exactly the same place where mine went...

It is part of a well supported classic car class for vehicles over 600cc built before 1971. The range of machinery is enormous, everything from a Frogeye to a Brabham BT21B, so the handicapper's skills are much to the fore. Austin Healeys and Lotuses make up most of the entry, and of these one Lotus in particular catches my eye, the well cared for and very original Lotus 7 Climax of Tom Clapham. It's very rare to see a Seven with the original cast magnesium wheels. Many of the cars are road registered and running on road tyres, so the handicapper's job must be fearsomely difficult.

Sometimes the most incident prone corner teaches you less about technique than a less dramatic spot. The Esses at Prescott, for instance, do not witness as many spins and offs as Ettore's or Pardon Hairpin, but they demand a lot of technique if an inch-perfect line is to be achieved. Observation of different drivers' techniques can be very illuminating.

CHAPTER 4

Roy Standley looks good in his TVR Tuscan, clean and aggressive. But one driver in his class (Modified Production Cars over 2000cc, Racing) looks *much* quicker than everyone else — Mark Spencer in the Escort Cosworth. The car wonderfully controllable, the driver utterly in control — all the more creditable as the car is a roadgoing vehicle, apart from having slicks. Anyone who wonders whether the term 'classic' can really be applied to a modern car has not witnessed an Escort Cosworth being driven full tilt up Prescott.

His efforts earn him fifth in class, behind the battling Waldron/Lambert duo, the Porsche 911 Turbo of Richard Jones and Standley's Tuscan.

Among the single seaters in the 1600cc Class, Jim Bassett looks tight and tidy in the Ray FF2000 without producing anything spectacular by way of a time, while Peter Whitmore's Chevron B49 is only slightly quicker despite — or perhaps because of — locking up on the approach.

Trying even harder is Paul Shipp, his OMS-Suzuki outgunned for sheer power by the Pilbeam-BDA of eventual class winner Tony Tewson but coming home only seven tenths behind thanks to some very hard charging which takes him wide — much too wide — on the first Ess. Watching Paul nearly turn Esses into SOSs, it's easy to understand how he acquired a reputation for providing good entertainment value.

Third in class goes to Willem Toet, an aerodynamicist with John Barnard's Ferrari design team. Today he is having a day off from motor racing and has decided to go motor racing himself. He might have made it a Pilbeam one-two had he not hit the dirt on the way in and lost time.

Tewson's time turns out be only one tenth outside the class record, good enough to get him into the Top 12 run off despite having only 1600cc. For a driver in the small capacity classes to get to mix it with the big boys at the end of the day is a real accolade. And of course on a practical level, it gives him another two cracks at the hill.

One class up, Pete Griffiths is looking very good indeed, equalling the best effort of winner Justin Fletcher's state-of-the-art Pilbeam MP62 with his 17 year-old Chevron and only missing the class win by virtue of a slower aggregate time. But neither of them is a match for Tewson today.

He goes on to better the Class record in the run off, but by that time attention is really being focused elsewhere. For history may be made here today; will Roy Lane take his 68th Championship win, an all time record, or will Prescott-loving Patrick Wood pull something out of the bag on one of his favourite courses?

The scene is set for a nail-biting climax. Roy has already won his class and thus has the luxury of running last. After the first runs he leads again, on 38.53, so far the only Top 12 run under 39 seconds. As the second runs proceed, driver after driver fails to break into the magic 38s. Now only Patrick can deny him his place in the record books.

As Patrick scorches away, traction control working overtime, a buzz of excitement rises in the crowd round the start line, as they watch the timing board and listen to the commentary. 'To stop Roy becoming that history maker, Patrick Wood has to beat 38.53. Nineteen... twenty seconds and he's clear of Pardon! Well I think Patrick's saved the best for last... if he can keep it going this could well be well in the 38s... it may not be over yet... Patrick's so quick up into Semi... yes he does stop it... 34,35... he's out of sight... he's in with a good chance... can he do it? Oh! he's missed it by a tenth of a second — 38.65!'.

Roy Lane, already waiting on the start line with 4 litres of Pilbeam rumbling behind him and no digital clock in sight, has no way of knowing whether he has already won or whether he must pull something even better out of the bag this time up. Unless, that is, a member of his team gives him a signal.

The Steel King crew has been down this road many times before and knows exactly what to do. Some days Roy likes to be told the situation, others not. Today he does.

Daughter Julie has been watching the clock with all the single-minded intensity of a schoolgirl desperate to see the end of a Latin lesson, and with just as much desire to see the figures move fast. The moment Patrick's score comes up, she races over to the fence by the start line and waves an upturned thumb in her father's direction. It's enough to tell him that this is now his day, no matter how fast he drives this time up.

'Will this be a victory run, or is he going to go for the record? He would love to take the British record of the most number of wins with a hill record but maybe, just maybe, conditions aren't right, but I don't think anybody's told Roy that because he at the moment appears to be going for it... eighteen, nineteen seconds and he's out of Pardon!... he is on a flyer, can he possibly add another record to his incredible tally today, the first ever sub 38 second climb of Prescott... he's going for it, he's out of sight, the clock is ticking away... 36, 37, no he's just missed it — 38.46, but it is still the fastest time of the day. He'd already won the meeting, he had no need to do that, but he still went for it, and tonight Roy Lane is the leader of the RAC British Hillclimb Championship in association with Autosport by one point from Patrick Wood and two points from Roger Moran.'

The words of commentator Robin Boucher round off the day aptly and as Roy takes another run up to acknowledge the crowd, friends and family gather round in the paddock waiting for the presentation.

Only one member of the family is absent: Gilly the cocker spaniel, safely out of harm's way in the motorhome. But I *know* she is wagging her tail.

Championship Top Tens after Round 3

RAC			Leaders		
1	Roy Lane	27	=1	Justin Fletcher	27
2	Patrick Wood	26	=1	Mark Waldron	27
3	Roger Moran	25	3	Phil Cooke	24
4	Tim Mason	19	4	Martin Groves	22
5	Andy Priaulx	10	5	Tom New	21
=6	Bill Bristow	9	6	Andrew Russell	19
=6	Simon Durling	9	=7	Tony Lambert	18
=6	George Ritchie	9	=7	Clive Kenrick	18
9	Justin Fletcher	7	=7	Rob Stevens	18
=10	Graham Priaulx	6	=7	Mark Coley	18
=10	Derek Young	6			

43

The Cumbrian hill was the venue for Tim Mason's first ever RAC Championship win.

Barbon Manor

Location
in the village of Barbon off the A683 approximately 4 miles north of Kirkby Lonsdale, Cumbria.

Organising club
Westmorland Motor Club Ltd, c/o Mrs L Idle, 48 Bellingham Road, Kendal, Cumbria.

Length 890 yards.

Outright hill record at start of 11.5.96 meeting
Overall: Patrick Wood, 21.04sec.

Roy's Run

'Only two gears are needed at Barbon. I fit a slightly higher first than normal to get me up and around the first corner and to avoid hitting the rev limiter over the finish.

'Immediately out of Crabtree corner change up on the approach to the next left-hand kink, about 20 yards this side of it. Your top gear for the straight has got to be a 120mph gear — if you are brave enough, because it is quite bumpy up there.

'At the approach to the hairpin, change back into first and hold it to the finishing line.

'The critical part is Richmond Bend, where the oak tree is. Drive that right and you get a slingshot effect up the straight.'

KEY

Track shading indicates gear ratio...

White striped is first gear

Black is top gear

Because ratios and patterns in racing gearboxes can be altered at will, a particular shading on one map does not indicate the same ratio as on another: shading is relative only to that particular venue.

V indicates good viewing area

0   100yd

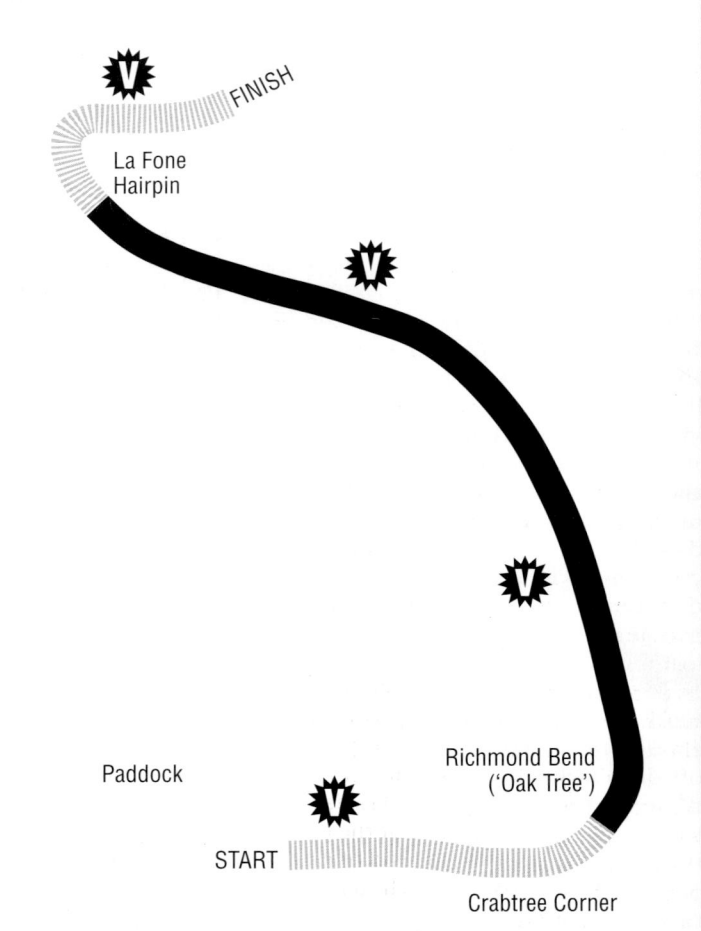

CHAPTER 5

'It is God's law that you will have a couple of bad results.'

Barbon Manor

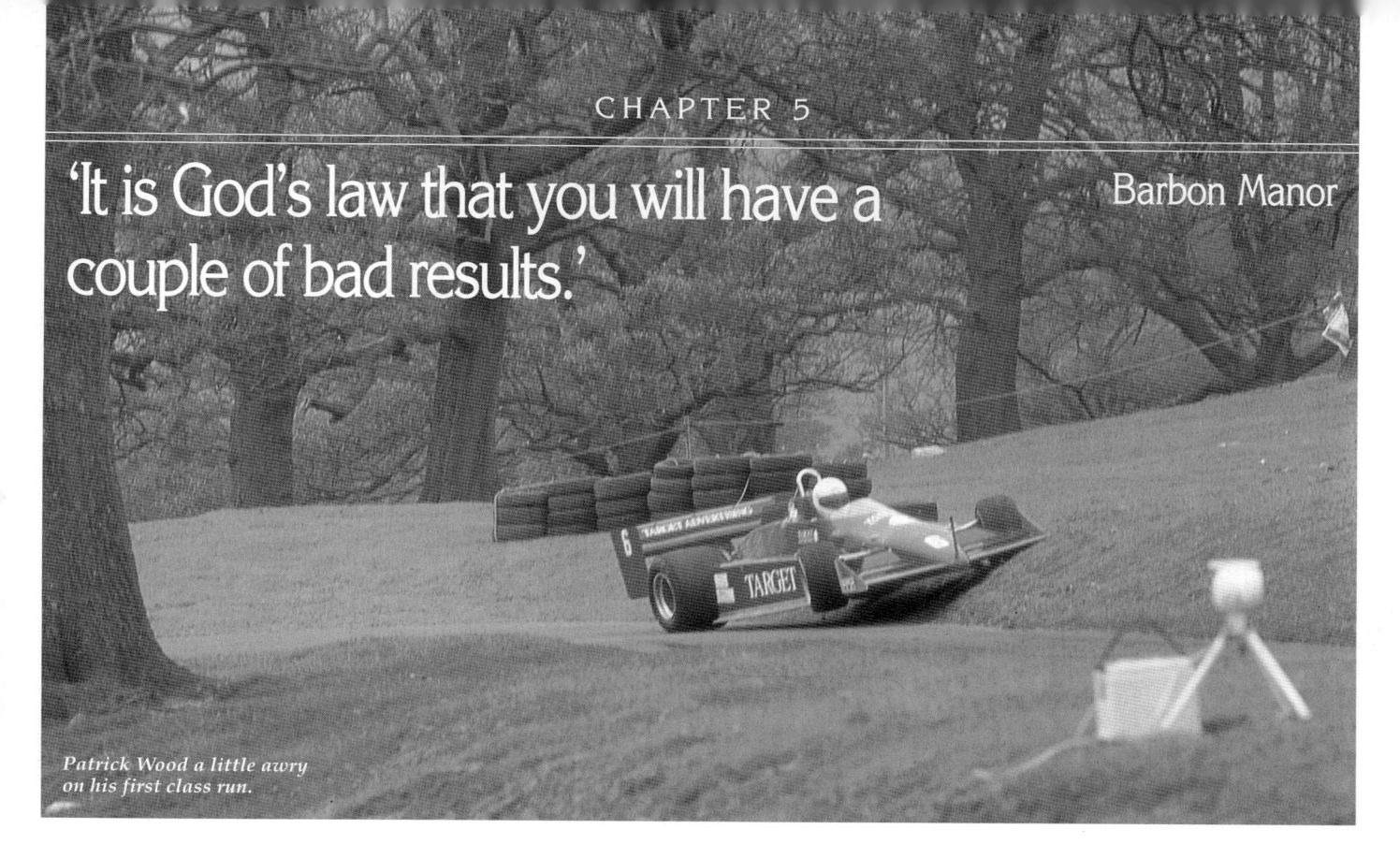

Patrick Wood a little awry on his first class run.

Barbon is a curious mixture. For the competitor, the drive of Barbon Manor is one of the shorter, less interesting courses and because meetings there are always one-day affairs, the trek north to the Cumbrian hills can seem hard to justify.

The need to squeeze practice and competition into one day inevitably makes the paddock numbers noticeably smaller than at Prescott. And the fact that there is no return road does not help the organisers swell the numbers.

For the spectator, however, it exercises a powerful appeal. Despite being in a relatively thinly populated part of the country, crowds the size of Prescott's are far from unknown. And its splendid location, in a stunningly beautiful valley a few miles north of the famous old Cumbrian town of Kirkby Lonsdale, makes it a fine day out even for those who don't really know much about motorsport or even about cars. If you get tired of the action, just sun yourself on the hill and enjoy the view.

For those who *are* in the know, Barbon represents a rare opportunity to witness top class machinery and drivers without travelling halfway down the M6. In an area starved of motorsport (ask yourself how many racing circuits there are in the North, Oulton Park excepted) Barbon hillclimb and the RAC Rally represent the two highlights of the local motorsport year.

The combination of these two factors ensures that Barbon retains the support of the public year after year.

Despite the shortness of the course (the hill record stands at only 21.04, to Patrick Wood) and the fact that some Southern and Midlands drivers give it a miss, by 1995 entries had swelled to the point where the organising club, the Westmorland Motor Club, decided to expand the traditional two meetings per year to three. The motorcycle meet in July and the RAC Championship round in May remain but the latter is now oriented more towards single-seaters and modern competition cars, while a new June meeting looks after historics and club competitors.

Given that most hillracers are as much in the sport to have fun as to win, one part of the attraction must be the Barbon Inn. Not many hillclimb venues have a pub within walking distance, but the bottom of the Barbon course is just a short stroll from the Barbon Inn, as olde worlde and convivial a watering hole as you are likely to find anywhere in the county. Many an off-track excursion or off-colour time has been laid at the door of mine host's hospitality the night before and the subsequent difficulty in distinguishing tent from racing car.

Though no stranger to the festivities himself, this morning I find Roy thoroughly sober after a quiet night. He's well briefed on the gossip though, as Julie apparently felt no such inhibitions. For Roy, this is no time for indiscipline: he's leading the championship after the first three rounds, with every prospect of a good finish today.

It's a nothing sort of a day, overcast and rather cold for the time of year, but dry. Drivers are slow at coming out for practice, hoping for a bit of sun to warm up the track. There is unlikely to be a new hill record today, nor any sunbathing at the top hairpin.

Nevertheless top hairpin is still be the favourite viewing point, as it allows spectators to see all but the first corner of the course. The start leads into a tight left-hander, followed by a straight and the long, fast left-hander at Oak Tree. From the hairpin you can see the exit from the first bend, the approach to Oak Tree and the whole of the main straight which follows it. This leads into the very tight top hairpin and the short, straight blast to the finish.

Barbon has never been Roy's favourite hill and he has only ever won here twice, in 1989 and 1991. On the first oc-

Malcolm Wishart in his Mallock on his way to fourth in class.

casion his winning climb included a glorious power slide all the way round the top hairpin, the like of which I have never seen before or since, from him or anyone else. Having watched many drivers struggle to judge the hairpin — the road curves gently into it and then tightens, so the temptation is to slow down early, if only because the armco and the stone wall behind are screaming at your instincts of self preservation — it's easy to conclude that the climb is won or lost on this bend.

Easy but wrong. 'It's all lost round Oak Tree in the middle,' says Roy. 'At the first corner, there could be a little bit that pays dividends, the hairpin a little bit, but in the main it's the piece in the middle. That is the vital part, because you get a slingshot effect on the straight. If you're not a brave man with big balls you don't go through there quick enough and I don't go through there quick enough half the time. You've got to have the right feel for the car on the day.'

Near the Steel King motorhome in the paddock are a thirty-something couple with a little girl. I've noticed them and their blue Clubman's Class Vision V86 at every round this year, so I decide to learn a little more about them. Mark and Ann Goodyear hail from Martley in the Midlands and bring three-year old Hanna to all the championship rounds. They count hillclimbing as a large part of their social life as well as a form of motorsport.

Hanna attended her first hillclimb when she was seven days old, much to the disapproval of the midwife, and is now thoroughly at home in the paddock, totally unconcerned by the noise and hubbub and on first-name terms with many of the drivers. Roy, whom she adores, is Grandad Roy. Ian Stringer (Racing Cars over 2000cc) is Uncle Ian. But confusion sets in when she sees Ian's co-driver Tim Mason driving the same Pilbeam, which leads little Hanna to the conclusion that Ian's daughter Grace has 'two daddies'.

The Goodyears only bought the car on the understanding that they would both drive it, Mark feeling that it was unfair to spend so much time and cash on something only one of them enjoyed. But he need have no worries on that score: Ann clearly gets just as much out of competing as her husband does.

'I set her a target in my mind of getting under 30, and she just did a 29 on the first practice,' Mark laughs. 'So I'm going to revise the target now!'

Mark is realistic about his own chances. 'I'm a little bit off the pace; it's only my second year with the car really, and the first full year I've had. But it's coming, which is nice. And the car's good.'

His first effort was a disappointment at 27, due mainly to the engine being too hot at the start. 'We have to mess around here, doing noise checks and everything, and I left the line at 90°, which was too hot really — the engine was popping and banging. It wants to be around 70° ideally. But then as it got up the straight

CHAPTER 5

and the air started coming in, it cooled down and got back to full power.'

Theoretically all cars should conform to RAC noise limits but not all cars are checked at every event — some venues enforce the regulations more tightly than others. Many cars use purpose-built repackable aluminium-cased silencers, manufactured by none other than Tech-Craft (prop: R T Lane).

'Last year's Midland Champion Martin Groves is the man to beat in the Clubman Class today', explains Mark, 'but it's his first time here.'

Martin's main competitors in the Leaders Championship, Richard and Alan Thompson, tend to compete only in the Midlands so Martin could rack up some useful points today unless the on-form Chris Merrick can do something about it.

In the event, he can't. Despite his unfamiliarity with the hill, Martin Groves goes on not only to take a comfortable win but a new class record on 23.62, with Merrick only managing a best of 24.39. Mark Goodyear is well content with a 25.29, good enough for third, while Ann is not far behind on 27.44.

The Leaders Championship, introduced in 1970 and now sponsored by engineering group Ricardo, adds a lot of spice to the hillclimb scene and provides drivers in some of the less glamorous classes with a real incentive to compete strongly and regularly. Drivers get points for their class performances, so drivers from all kinds of backgrounds and cars of all types find themselves jostling for position on the Leaders leaderboard. All RAC-based classes are eligible, from Modified Production Cars up to 1400cc to Racing Cars over 2000cc.

Entry in a class does not automatically enter you in the Leaders, you have to consciously sign up. Some drivers, who only compete occasionally and drive for personal satisfaction rather than out of any hope of winning, don't bother.

One such driver is John McCartney, a craggy-faced man of around 60 who is here today with a Chevron B48. I ask him who he regards as his principal opposition.

'Anno domini,' comes the sanguine reply, 'without a shadow of doubt. I don't know who the rest of the class are to be honest with you!'

He's had the Chevron some 10 years now, before which he had BRMs and Coopers. I ask if there are any changes to the car this year.

'Nope. None at all. It's totally original, the same as it was last year, the year before, and five years before that. It was originally designed as a Formula Atlantic, Formula 2 chassis and it was one of the first cars done by Chevron after Derek Bennett was killed in his hang gliding accident and Chevron got hold of Tony Southgate, who was designing Arrows Grand Prix cars at the time. If you look at the Arrows 01, this is a miniature version — it's got the same sidewings, the same rear suspension. It wasn't very successful as a circuit car largely because Derek Bennett wasn't there to do the development work on it, but it's not a bad car. I've had it fitted with a 1600 Formula Pacific engine — a Brian Hart version of the BDA. It's got inboard front suspension and a Hewland FT200 box.

'Do you change the gearing between rounds?'

'No! I'm too lazy to do that! The car would be a lot quicker if you changed the driver rather than the gear ratio. This is a younger man's sport in spite of Roy Lane, who's the glorious exception.'

Despite this observation, it is undoubtedly true that the average age of competitors on the hills is higher than in many other branches of motorsport. Hillclimbing only happens in short bursts, so it is not physically arduous. This facet of the sport certainly helps it attract a wider age group than, for example, circuit racing.

Typical of the younger end of the sport — indeed epitomising it — are Steve and Lynn Owen. Lynn is a dental technician, Steve builds racing cars — OMS racing cars. The name is derived from Steve's initials turned backwards, presumably because a car called a Smo would somehow lack paddock cred. Together with the Jedi, it is the OMS which has turned around the smaller capacity single-seater classes in the past few years. At Prescott I talked Jedi. Now it is time to learn about its Leeds-based rival.

I find Lynn standing by the little OMS S/C sports racer which she and Steve are sharing today. Slightly built, dark-haired, quietly spoken, she's the kind of person who would make the dentist's chair seem that little bit less daunting. The Owens are unlikely to be much challenged here, since they are the only two in Sports Libre Cars up to 1400cc. This paucity of competition is partly a reflection of the fact that although they make both open-wheeled and sports racing versions of the OMS chassis, the former are by far the most popular and account for some 45 of the 50-odd OMSs produced to date. Both versions use the same wheelbase, but drivers like the simple bodywork of the open-wheeler, which they can remove single-handed and work around easily in a garage.

Lynn feels that 'if the bike engines hadn't come along the classes would have died out, because there aren't that many car engines now to use in these classes. What attracts customers is the cost of the engine. You're looking at about £1000 — maybe £1500 for the newer engines — but you get the engine and gearbox, it's all there and it's highly competitive in standard trim before you even start running it on Mikuni carburettors or perhaps methanol.'

'You're wedded to Suzukis are you?'

'Not especially. We have a single-seater that uses a Kawasaki ZZR. Mark Lawrence has had his ZZR tuned a little bit at TTS but in our carbonfibre single-seater we run it as standard, but with Mikunis on methanol. The methanol keeps the engine temperatures down — it does get a bit hot with two of you driving.'

'But methanol-fuelled engines need a lot more rebuilds don't they?'

She laughs. 'Well we've never actually rebuilt engines as such — apart from Steve who's blown up two Suzukis. This one now is on its second season and we've never touched it — it just went straight in from the bike. And the Kawasaki in the single-seater likewise. But as

47

LIVING WITH SPEED

Man on the Hill

New and old(er) Toms and Sevens at Barbon: Tom New and (opposite) Tom Clapham. The latter photo was taken around 1992 but it could just have easily been 1996, or 1976.

Gurston Down, August meeting.

Tom New

One of the fastest of the current crop of young drivers, motor mechanic Tom New is a self-effacing individual who prefers to get on with the job first and talk about it later.

His actions certainly speak for themselves. His immaculately prepared Caterham Seven is the envy of many competitors and was assembled and developed by Tom himself. Although the fact that he works in the motor trade is obviously a great help — Tom has worked for his present employer practically since he left school and describes him as 'very understanding' — the fact remains that when you admire Tom's Seven, you're not admiring a cheque-writing exercise so much as a lot of very hard work.

And he knows how to drive it: in only his third season of competition driving he is now challenging hard for the Leaders Championship, helped by father Terry, who crews with him.

It was his father who gave him the idea, for though not a competitor himself, he often went to Gurston as a spectator and took his son along. So from the age of 15 Tom has been exposed to racing cars. Since Terry had always admired the Seven, the choice of car was obvious.

'We decided that we'd go to Caterham's and bought a kit.'

The Seven did service as a road car for a couple of years, fitted with a 1700 pushrod Ford. Initially this pumped out around 140bhp, but the temptation to go for 'a little bit more power' was irresistible. 'At the end I suppose it had about 160bhp.'

The big jump came in 1995 when Tom decided to switch to Vauxhall power. With typical attention to detail, he made the engine stronger than it needed to be, with an all-steel bottom end. 'I decided if I developed it as much as I could to start with, I wouldn't have so far to go to actually get some more power out of it.'

Output is currently 240bhp but there is more to come next year.

'I'd like to put full management on it. We're going to put some different cams in as well, hopefully maybe see another 15 brake at the top end and a bit more driveability through the mid range.'

He's not dissatisfied with the driveability now, but on a Seven more is always welcome, especially when it rains. 'I rely on the grip. In the wet there's nothing much over the back end and it's just horrible.'

He chooses his words carefully when asked about the relative merits of the Caterham and its Westfield cousin which now outnumbers it on the hills, but he is clearly happy with his choice.

'I think with the right engine it's the better car to have. It's a stiffer chassis.'

Despite his good showing to date, he regards 1996 mainly as a learning process. 'This year all I wanted to do was do all the climbs. I'd done Shelsley and Loton and Prescott all last year and the year before, I wanted to go to Barbon and Harewood and Doune.'

Barbon he describes as a driver's course like Loton, with lots of places you can lose time. He agrees with Roy Lane that the speed around the Oak Tree is critical.

'Somebody said to me "how are you going round that?" I said "I'm going in second." "Oh no, you've got to go in third," I was told'.

Next run he tried third and found they were right. 'You can put the power in and it digs in and you carry on going.' He ended the day 'a couple of seconds' quicker than he started it.

At 24 he may still be learning, but he's learning very fast.

---

people start to tune them, yes they do wear.'

Steve started building in 1986 and went full time some five years ago. He builds everything himself — nothing is farmed out except the painting and even that used to be done in house until pressure of work forced a rethink. Fibreglass, chassis construction, suspension components, all are made by Steve, to his own design, as are the unique-to-OMS wheel centres. 'We couldn't get wheels', Lynn explains.

'This our life, doing this. It's all-consuming. And we've got one or two people now like Paul Shipp who we can work with very well, who give good feedback and who can develop the cars.'

Some drivers, especially those in the bigger classes, look askance at the OMS. Too light, too small, not enough to pro-

CHAPTER 5

Lotus 7 Climax

Tom Clapham, Historic Sports or Racing Cars manufactured 1953-1960

Seek a car synonymous with Barbon and one vehicle stands out immediately — Tom Clapham's Seven. Not only was Barbon the venue for Tom's first ever hillclimb, way back in 1952 with a modified MG TC at only the second event ever staged there, but the Lotus he now owns was bought new just seven years later and has seen practically continuous service at Barbon ever since. Until 1965 Tom and Seven pursued a very active hillclimbing career right across the country, highlights being FTD at an Oulton Park sprint in 1963 and FTD at Loton Park in the rain in 1965. And he holds in perpetuity the Unlimited Sports Car record at the now defunct Rest and Be Thankful.

After this the Lotus was seen mainly at Barbon until 1989, a loyalty explained by the fact that Tom now lives in the village just a stone's throw from the paddock. Since 1989 the car has been back on the national circuit again.

Originally it was a road car used also for competition but early in its life, during 1961-62, the car shed paraphernalia like headlights and spare wheel and was developed for speed events, at which point Tom found himself with a serious 1500cc Sports Racing car and stopped taxing it for the road. Now the car is classed with the historics, which is why he can continue to compete with no rollbar or seatbelts.

But though its categorisation may have changed, the car itself is almost exactly as he developed it back in the early '60s. Even the original blue cellulose ('a Morris Oxford Traveller colour') still shines.

Tom acquired the Lotus as a rather incomplete box of bits consisting largely of chassis and front suspension. 'I think it was a kit they robbed bits off to complete other kits'. There was no back axle, so he took advantage of the omission to build his own unique rear suspension. One look at the radius arms bolted to the sides of the cockpit will tell you that this is no ordinary live-axle Seven. This one has an independent rear end, using a Lotus 11 Le Mans diff housing, ZF limited slip diff, lower wishbones and a fixed-length driveshaft in place of an upper wishbone. Tom describes it as 'rather more crude but just as effective as the subsequent Lotus-made 7X'.

Under the bonnet is an FWA racing spec Climax engine linered out to the 1220cc capacity of the roadgoing FWE, which according to Tom gives you the best of both worlds, the power of the 1220 and the strength of the FWA. 'Even now I rev it to 8000', he admits. Breathing is via two 45DCOE Webers which draw from an airbox linked to the passenger footwell, the idea being to breathe still air and thus avoid the tuning complications which result from venturi effects across the mouths of the carbs.

Transmission was originally through an Austin A30 box, but 'after consuming several sets of second-gear pinions' this was replaced by a Sprite box with straight-cut close ratios.

Completing the package is a set of original mag alloy 'Wobbly web' wheels, as fitted to the Lotus 16 GP car. These replaced the original wires early in the car's life. Still no slicks though — back in '59 they were a thing of the future.

Having a car which has scarcely changed a jot in 35 years gives Tom the chance to measure how his driving is changing with age. And as far as he is concerned, it is not deteriorating at all: at 67 his times are every bit as competitive as when both car and driver were in their youth.

Later that season Tom would dramatically underline this premise by setting his fastest ever time at Shelsley Walsh, in the low 37s.

Clearly, both car and driver are enjoying their renaissance on the hills.

Shelsley Walsh.

Car on the Hill

---

tect you if you make a mistake. But the entry lists speak for themselves and the Owens' commitment is acknowledged even by those who are never likely to be their customers. Ann Goodyear, for instance, doesn't particularly like motor-cycle-engined cars, but she acknowledges that when you buy an OMS 'you don't just buy a car, you buy Steve Owen'.

One of the best known cars at Barbon is 73 JAB, a fearsome silver Porsche 911 Turbo now owned by Richard Jones from Stroud. Richard has only had it for a couple of seasons, having swapped his AC Ace Bristol for it, and the car still bears the registration of the man he got it from; local driver Tony Bancroft, from Skipton.

Like most Porsches it doesn't look particularly exciting under the lid, only the huge turbo dangling beneath the skirt giving it away, but in Tony's hands the car developed some 600bhp running on nitrous oxide injection and held the class record at Barbon for several years. Although it is destined not to regain it today — Richard's best time was 25.73, against 24.99 of new record-breaker Mark Waldron — it is still a blisteringly fast car, especially considering that Richard has been known to use it on the road, as did Tony.

Tony, meanwhile, has completely rebuilt what was already a good Ace-Bristol into a pristine example of what is perhaps the most desirable of all '50s British sports cars. And it is here today, all red leather, silver paint and triple Solexes. Along the way he has become thoroughly obsessed with the model to the point where he is now something of an expert on it. Not only is he Ace-Bristol registrar of the AC Owners Club, he also rebuilds them for a living.

Made redundant from a textile company a few years back and now in his 50s, he spent some time looking for a new mission in life. Then he took Richard's car to bits, enjoyed putting it back together, and decided that he'd found a new *raison d'etre*. A slim, balding man with a quick, slightly nervous way of speaking, he will talk with authority about anything Ace, given the smallest spark of interest.

Today his car is one of only two competitors in Historic Sports or Racing Cars manufactured between 1953 and 1960. The other, Tommy Clapham in his nimble Lotus 7 Climax, is sure to win. But it's good to see the Ace being used in anger, even though today it sounds decidedly off-colour — the result, Tony is to discover later after many frustrating hours of tinkering, of nothing more sinister than a partial fuel blockage.

Meanwhile the fast boys have been busily working out who will constitute the Top 12 and the Championship run off is about to commence. Roy has been fastest in the afternoon event on 21.69, the only driver under 22 seconds, and thus will run last in the run-offs.

But this counts for nothing in the championship. It's the better of the two run-off times that determines the points in the title chase. And in the first of them three drivers throw down the gauntlet by posting sub-22 second times. Roger Moran leads on 21.71, Tim Mason is just behind on 21.76 and Patrick Wood is threatening on 21.88. Roy has it all to do.

He sets about doing it with a vengeance. A real balls-out effort round the Oak Tree sends him flying up the straight and into the top hairpin fully half a second ahead of anyone else so far today. And then, as he tries to select a gear for the short blast to the finish, he finds himself with a boxful of neutrals. Rolling to a halt, he throws his hands up in the air, despondently. No time on his first run.

Inspection back in the pits reveals an eye joint in the gear linkage has broken, the result of the hole being drilled off-centre originally and the pin gradually wearing through the eye. 'That's just about the only part of the car we've never had apart since we bought it' Roy observes ruefully. 'But it is God's Law that you will have a couple of bad results during the season'.

With the gear linkage buried deep inside the monocoque, out of sight has been out of mind — until today. Though the problem is not major, it cannot be fixed quickly because linkage parts so rarely fail that no one carries spares. Had it broken on the second run he would have been assured of at least a few points. As it is, he has won the class but scored a big round zero in the championship — a big disappointment on a day which had seemed to be going well.

Consolation comes from knowing that his problem has helped Tim Mason take FTD and his first ever RAC win, a popular result in and out of the paddock.

Championship Top Tens after Round 4

RAC
1	Patrick Wood	35
2	Roger Moran	33
3	Tim Mason	29
4	Roy Lane	27
5	Simon Durling	16
6	George Ritchie	15
7	Bill Bristow	13
8	Andy Priaulx	10
9	Tim Barrington	9
10	Justin Fletcher	7

Leaders
1	Mark Waldron	36
2	Phil Cooke	33
=3	Justin Fletcher	31
=3	Martin Groves	31
5	Tom New	30
=6	Tony Lambert	24
=6	Jim Robinson	24
8	Ian Fidoe	22
9	Mark Lawrence	21
10	Andrew Russell	19

After a frustrating day, the photographer's attentions are not always welcome.

CHAPTER 6

'A tremendously challenging place'

Lerghy Frissel

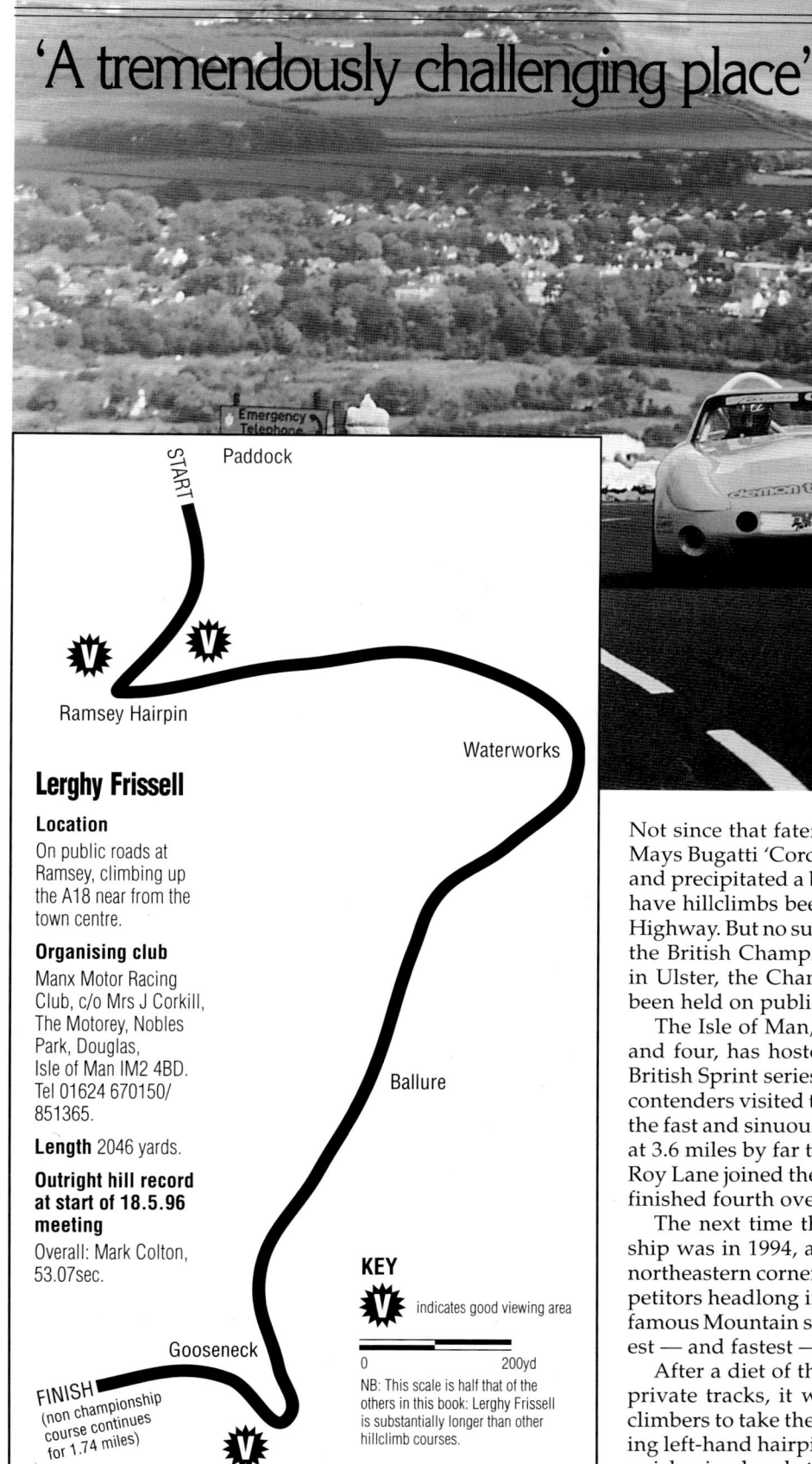

The Isle of Man RAC round is run on the lower part of a 5km course which is used in full for another hillclimb event the day before. Here Mark Waldron storms up the upper part of the course on the Saturday before the championship round.

Ian Henderson

Lerghy Frissell

Location
On public roads at Ramsey, climbing up the A18 near from the town centre.

Organising club
Manx Motor Racing Club, c/o Mrs J Corkill, The Motorey, Nobles Park, Douglas, Isle of Man IM2 4BD. Tel 01624 670150/ 851365.

Length 2046 yards.

Outright hill record at start of 18.5.96 meeting
Overall: Mark Colton, 53.07sec.

KEY
V indicates good viewing area

0   200yd

NB: This scale is half that of the others in this book: Lerghy Frissell is substantially longer than other hillclimb courses.

Map labels: START, Paddock, Ramsey Hairpin, Waterworks, Ballure, Gooseneck, FINISH (non championship course continues for 1.74 miles)

Not since that fateful day in 1925, when Francis Giveen's ex Mays Bugatti 'Cordon Bleu' hit a wandering spectator at Kop and precipitated a ban on public road speed events in Britain, have hillclimbs been permitted to take place on the Queen's Highway. But no such restrictions exist 'across the water'. Since the British Championship began in 1947, qualifying rounds in Ulster, the Channel Islands and the Isle of Man have all been held on public roads, closed for the duration.

The Isle of Man, that haven of motorsport on two wheels and four, has hosted many hillclimbs — and rounds of the British Sprint series — over the years. In 1968 RAC Hillclimb contenders visited the Island for the first time to do battle over the fast and sinuous Tholt-y-Will climb at the base of Snaefell, at 3.6 miles by far the longest course the series has ever seen. Roy Lane joined them for their one and only return in '69, and finished fourth overall in his Tech-Craft Buick…

The next time the island hosted the hillclimb championship was in 1994, at Lerghy Frissel. Based in Ramsey on the northeastern corner of the island, the new climb pitched competitors headlong into the start of the motorcycle TT course's famous Mountain section. At 2406 yards (2.2km), it is the longest — and fastest — round since Tholt-y-Will.

After a diet of the mainland's relatively short and narrow private tracks, it was something of a culture shock to hillclimbers to take the main road out of town into a open, climbing left-hand hairpin, before launching into the series of ever-quickening bends to begin the climb up the mountain. Much

51

LIVING WITH SPEED

faster than Craigantlet's bumpy Belfast outskirts or Jersey and Guernsey's tortuous coast roads, this is fast, open-road motoring where the quicker cars soon build up to the 130-140mph mark — and stay there.

Organisers Manx Motor Racing Club are anxious to gain European status for Lerghy Frissel Mooar, the even longer course for Thursday's 'Bid for Europe', the curtain-raiser to Saturday's British Championship event. For this the climb continues through sweeping, open bends towards Snaefell for another 2.8km, by which time speeds have become breathtakingly fast.

Last year, Peter Harper and the Vision Viper made hillclimbing history here with the first 100mph average — from a standing start, remember — ever seen at a British hillclimb. No F1 V8 powered machine this, but a 2.5-litre 4 cylinder Hart-derived unit. The feat was matched again this year too, — by Peter Griffiths and the 2-litre Chevron-Millington...

In this rarefied atmosphere there's little margin for error. Stone walls on one side and a wire fence on the other that offers little to bar unscheduled progress by an errant motorcycle — or hillclimb car — down the steep, rolling hillside.

Patrick Wood made the Manx trip in 1995. 'It's a tremendously challenging place. The trouble is that each successive time you go there you're going to get closer to the limit until you eventually overstep the mark. In a V8 single seater that's going to be at very high speed and there's just nowhere to go'.

It's unclear whether it is that notion, or the not inconsiderable cost of crossing the North Sea with motorhome and trailer (the longer the rig, the higher the ferry charge) that has kept Patrick and the majority of the top British contenders away from the event today.

Whatever the reason, it has left the door open for an enthusiastic bunch of runners in less powerful machinery. The entry includes 2 and even 1-litre machines and the faster sports cars, all their drivers eager to have a real stab at championship points — many for the first time — on what many consider the most charismatic hill in the series.

Much modified Rover engine sports a Chevrolet-based crank and sits well back in the engine bay with the exhausts exiting forward and then looping back.

Bill Bristow, lying seventh overall as the series entered its fifth round, is the highest placed championship contender to put in an appearance. The former motorcycle racing mechanic is no stranger to the island's classic road circuit: 'After coming here so many times with the bikes it's just a fantastic opportunity to be able to race here. We've competed at Lerghy Frissel since 1993, first with the Caterham, then with 4-cylinder Hart power in the Vision and the RT36 — wouldn't miss it. We managed eighth overall last year but we're hoping for better things this time...'

Come the run off, only Andy Kittle's MP72 and Paul Parker's Royale can boast eight-cylinder power, and some of Andy's horses are nobbled by a persistent top-end misfire which he only manages to trace at a late stage in the proceedings.

Foremost among the four-cylinder runners are five drivers in three cars; Pete Griffiths in the Millington-powered Chevron, Bristow and Russ Pickering sharing Bill's Ralt RT36, and father and son Richard and Tom Brown doubling the RH430, a hybrid machine originally based around an earlier Ralt chassis by Adrian Hopkins.

The rest of the Top 12 features drivers who would normally be packing up to go home at this stage of the proceed-

Car on the Hill

TVR Tuscan
Mark Waldron, Modified Production Cars Over 2000cc)

Mark Waldron's fearsome TVR Tuscan has been developed into one of the most potent cars on the hills during the past two years. His first acquaintance with the car was in the 1994 season, when Barry Lines offered to share it with him. Mark recalls 'I tried to restrain myself from answering *too* enthusiastically, and then bit his arm off at the elbow.

'We had a good season sharing it' but at the beginning of the next season Mark bought the car outright and started to develop it into the car it is now. 'It's still a yellow TVR Tuscan but it's somewhat different from when we originally had it'.

That is something of an understatement. The engine is still a Rover block but it is now heavily reworked. Capacity is out to 5 litres, courtesy of a steel Chevrolet-based crank, while the standard gearbox has been ditched in place of a Quaife 4-speed dog box. The differential is unique to Tuscans and consists of a Maserati Biturbo casing with Quaife and GKN internals. 'Typical TVR part' grins Mark, 'I don't think anybody else would come up with that combination.'

'We're told we have 450bhp, about as much as we can use with a front-engined rear-wheel-drive set up.'

Maybe he could use more if he wasn't restricted to 16" rims. 'We'd like to go to the 18" rims that they use in the TVR Challenge, because they'd allow us to put the bigger brakes on, but we can't get soft enough rubber.'

He's not short of adhesion at the back though, using 12" wide slicks 'whereas the Challenge cars use 9.5" rubber'.

Various aerodynamic tweaks, some subtle and others less so, complete a formidable package.

52

CHAPTER 6

Man on the Hill
Bill Bristow

Bill Bristow has the reputation of being a hard charger, a driver who will always give 110% even at the risk of falling off.

It's a description he doesn't argue with. He thinks it probably stems from the days when he first competed on the hills, in a Caterham Seven.

'I started with a 1700 crossflow when everybody else was using twincams; I move up to twincams and everybody else has BDs, and so forth.' He always found himself needing to try that bit harder. 'I just always want to win'.

He admits that his win at Lerghy Frissell 'was basically down to people not supporting the Isle of Man' events, a situation he feels quite strongly about.

'I've always had the philosophy that if you're going to do a championship you should do every round. This dropping scores is a dreadful thing. We have a situation whereby people pick and choose rounds. If it was less rounds with all rounds to count, maybe that would be different.'

'Having said that, it was a good time!'

This is his second season with the Ralt. 'We ran it with a 2.5 Hart last year, this year I've got a very special 2.5 off John Beattie. It's not a Hart block, it's mainly down to John's own work. The cylinder head is Hart, but the block and the crank and the rods and the pistons are not.'

Bill is extremely pleased with the unit and gives it most of the credit for his improved performance this season. From 11th in the championship last year, he has every prospect of a top ten placing in 1996. 'Of course there's a learning curve in the car as well, it was the first year in a proper single-seater last year'.

Despite his satisfaction with the engine, he now finds himself firmly back in the must-try-harder situation he remembers so well from his Caterham days. The Beattie is giving 333 bhp, well down on the V8s, but the overall weight is not proportionately lower, 460kg compared to 5-600 for the V8s.

Bill knows he can't beat 'em, so he intends to join 'em. His existing Beattie 2.5 has to go back to its builder at the end of the season, so Bill needs a new engine for '97 and has his eyes fixed firmly on a V8.

'Initially I would be quite happy with a small V8. I'd want a competition V8 as opposed to a road-derived V8 but perhaps an F3000 engine would suit' — a Judd rather than a Cosworth, because he prefers gear-driven cams to belt driven.

Bill is a projects engineer who works for a company making highspeed labelling machines. There is no real opportunity for sponsorship through his job and it is a measure of his single-mindedness that he is willing to go the V8 route despite the lack of outside finance. 'I don't do anything else but go hillclimbing and sprinting, I spend all week doing the car and all weekend travelling.'

He is far from on his own, however, for Bill is never seen at a meeting without his partner Joan, a dedicated motorsport enthusiast in her own right. 'I've known her to disappear off and go and watch qualifying at a grand prix on her own.

'She is very into motorsport, loves it as much as I do. You're very fortunate when you've got people like that, when you've got people behind you.'

It's not only the competition that brings Bill and Joan back year after year. 'We have a fantastic social life at the hillclimbs. My head's telling me last night was a bit too social! It's a travelling circus really.'

'Everybody's so helpful as well. If you've got a problem you'll be working on it and another pair of hands will appear from the side. You'll look over your shoulder and it'll be somebody like Jim Robinson. I'll never forget Barbon two years ago when I was running in the Sports Libre Class and I broke a diff. I'm *frantically* trying to change a diff and this magical pair of hands appears — it's Robbo. My main competitor in the class rolls his sleeves up, gets stuck in, and helps me change a diff. The sport is populated with people like that, it's fantastic for that.'

Bill Bristow makes a point of competing at every RAC round. Here he is at Loton Park in April.

Championship Top Tens after Round 5

RAC
1	Patrick Wood	35
2	Roger Moran	33
3	Tim Mason	29
4	Roy Lane	27
5	Bill Bristow	23
6	Simon Durling	16
7	George Ritchie	15
8	Tom Brown	12
9	Andy Priaulx	10
=10	Tim Barrington	9
=10	Peter Griffiths	9

Leaders
1	Mark Waldron	45
2	Phil Cooke	33
=3	Justin Fletcher	31
=3	Martin Groves	31
=5	Tom New	30
=5	Tony Lambert	30
7	Jim Robinson	24
=8	Ian Fidoe	22
=8	Peter Griffiths	22
10	Mark Lawrence	21

ings — men like David Flanagan and son Daniel, who just sneaks the little OMS into the bottom of the run off, and Glyn Sketchley in the Megapin CFM9.

Bill runs last, thanks to a class-winning 58.50 that is approached only by 2-litre record-breaker Griffiths (58.70) and Kittle (58.71). All three improve in the run-off, but Tom Brown improves more than anyone to rocket himself into second overall thanks to a meteoric second run that shaves over a second off his previous best.

It is not quite enough, however, to prevent Bill from taking his first ever Championship win on 57.16. Often in the points, invariably a hard trier and an entertaining driver, lack of sheer power has always kept him from the top — until now.

Maybe the fast boys did give it a miss. But victory smells pretty sweet nevertheless. And what better place for an ex-biker to achieve it than the Isle of Man?

LIVING WITH SPEED

'The banana yellow machine looks strangely naked'

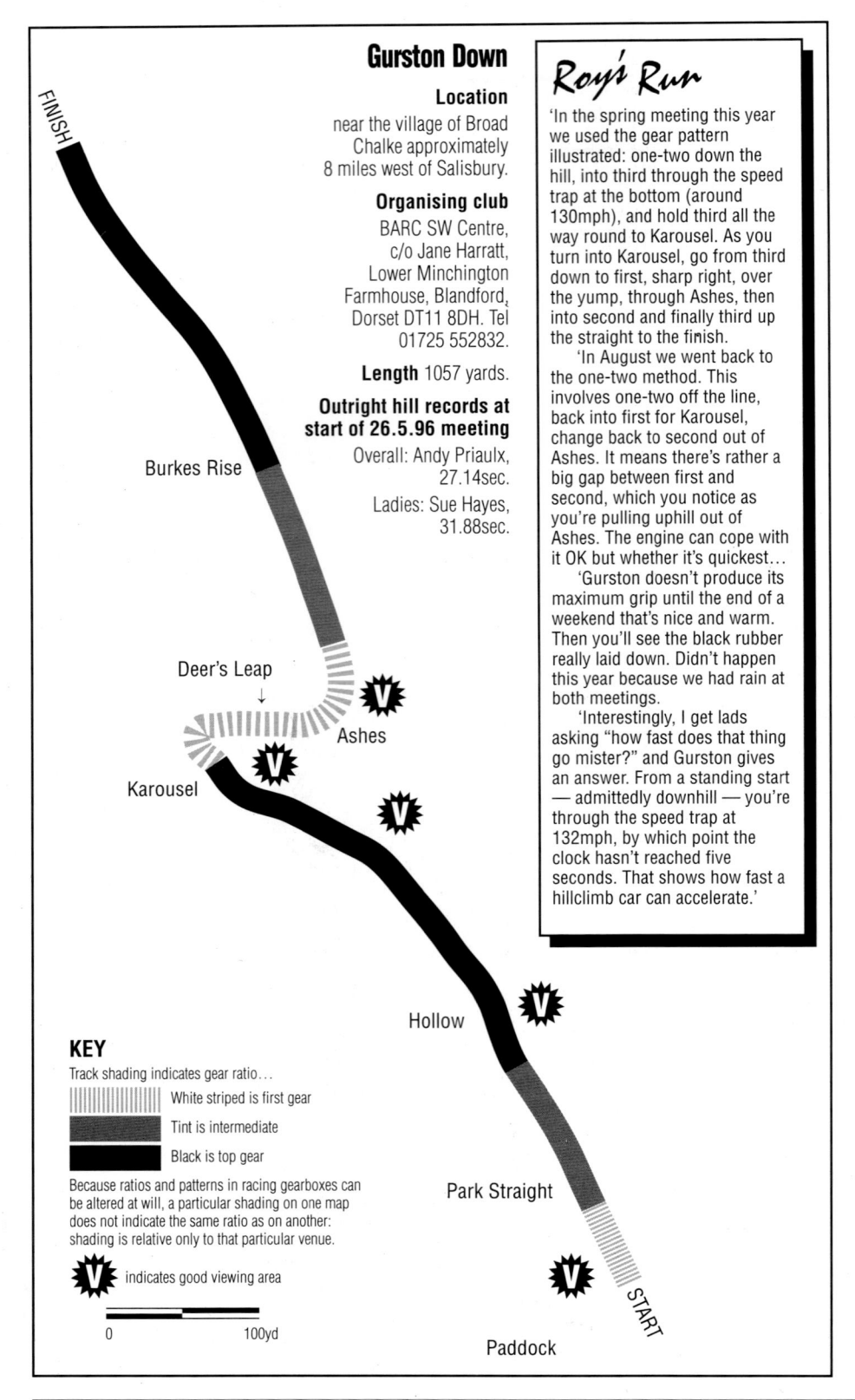

Gurston Down

Location
near the village of Broad Chalke approximately 8 miles west of Salisbury.

Organising club
BARC SW Centre, c/o Jane Harratt, Lower Minchington Farmhouse, Blandford, Dorset DT11 8DH. Tel 01725 552832.

Length 1057 yards.

Outright hill records at start of 26.5.96 meeting
Overall: Andy Priaulx, 27.14sec.
Ladies: Sue Hayes, 31.88sec.

Roy's Run

'In the spring meeting this year we used the gear pattern illustrated: one-two down the hill, into third through the speed trap at the bottom (around 130mph), and hold third all the way round to Karousel. As you turn into Karousel, go from third down to first, sharp right, over the yump, through Ashes, then into second and finally third up the straight to the finish.

'In August we went back to the one-two method. This involves one-two off the line, back into first for Karousel, change back to second out of Ashes. It means there's rather a big gap between first and second, which you notice as you're pulling uphill out of Ashes. The engine can cope with it OK but whether it's quickest…

'Gurston doesn't produce its maximum grip until the end of a weekend that's nice and warm. Then you'll see the black rubber really laid down. Didn't happen this year because we had rain at both meetings.

'Interestingly, I get lads asking "how fast does that thing go mister?" and Gurston gives an answer. From a standing start — admittedly downhill — you're through the speed trap at 132mph, by which point the clock hasn't reached five seconds. That shows how fast a hillclimb car can accelerate.'

KEY
Track shading indicates gear ratio…
- White striped is first gear
- Tint is intermediate
- Black is top gear

Because ratios and patterns in racing gearboxes can be altered at will, a particular shading on one map does not indicate the same ratio as on another: shading is relative only to that particular venue.

V indicates good viewing area

After the historical curiosities of Loton Park, the quintessential Englishness of Wiscombe, the buzz of Prescott and the grand vista of Barbon, it's a bit of a let down to find yourself driving into a farmyard. A farmyard with lots of exciting cars in it, and set in pretty Wiltshire countryside, but nevertheless a farmyard.

Mind you, this less than ecstatic first impression could have something to do with the fact that it is bucketing down with rain, as though the whole place is for ever just failing to overtake some invisible 44 tonner on a celestial motorway. True, the weather is varying a bit: sometimes it rains like there is no tomorrow, sometimes it rains like tomorrow has already come, sometimes it just plain rains, but it remains wet, utterly, absolutely, miserably wet. The kind of wet that seems as though nothing will ever be dry, ever again. The kind of wet that has the kids paddling through red mud on their way through the gate into the spectator area and the adults finding ever more circuitous ways of entering without doing the same, as the red squelch gets steadily larger.

From the drivers' point of view, there are worse places to have rain. Barbon, Loton Park and Wiscombe to name but three. For unlike all of those, Gurston Down has a multiplicity of barns and sheds to provide shelter and storage. It is still very much a working farm and competitors have to be prepared to share a pit with this year's combine harvester, or last millennium's rusty old trailer, or anything in between. But that's a small price to pay for keeping dry.

The course is not particularly long — just over 1000 yards — and on a map does not look particularly interesting, as it consists basically of two straights with a group of bends in between. On the ground, however, it's another matter, not least because this is one hillclimb course that starts not by climbing but by dropping — steeply, down Park Straight to a tricky, off camber left-hand kink at Hollow, the start of another very long, gently climbing left-hand sweep. This ends at Karousel, a complex of fast and climbing right-hander, very short uphill

CHAPTER 7

Gurston Down

David Grace, launching the new Ralt over Deer's Leap on its first day out.

straight and hairpin right. A short, steep climb then leads to Ashes, a 90° left hander, and then to Burkes Rise, a long, climbing section — far from straight in a faster car — that takes you to the finish.

The main spectator points are at the start, at Hollow (which catches out a surprising number of drivers), and at Karousel/Ashes. The latter is a great favourite with photographers because the steep climb out of Karousel flattens out suddenly before Ashes at a brow known as Deer's Leap, where cars as well as deer get airborne and provide lots of dramatic shots.

This morning it's the saloon drivers who are having the last laugh. The others brave the elements as best they can, some with the help of sodden assistants who hold an umbrella over the cockpit until the last possible moment, others by tossing their own brolly unceremoniously on to the trackside just as the green light comes up. Fortunately, there is no obligation to go immediately the green emerges; hillclimb drivers can start in their own time, within reason. It's the breaking of the timing beam which sets the clock going, not the extinguishing of the red.

Considering the conditions the drivers are staying on the tarmac remarkably well, but inevitably there are exceptions. On his first run Westfield driver Jim Whiteside spins off in dramatic fashion at Hollow, first to the left, then after an overcorrection to the right, and finally backwards into the banking. The track is left muddy, as indeed is the car, but otherwise it's mainly the driver's pride that is hurt. The car is extricated and Jim proceeds to trickle up the hill, a grass skirt dangling inelegantly from the Westfield's rear end.

Marshals spend a long time trying to clean up the track but it's impossible to

Streaming wet conditions as Simon Drake sets off on a run in the Van Diemen RF85 which he shares with Mike Reed.

LIVING WITH SPEED

Maurice Ogier and Kevin Prevel enjoying themselves at Hollow.

remove all the mud, which may be why Paul Gwinnett leaves the track at much the same point in dramatic fashion a few minutes later when the weather is at its very worst. Mind you, he has the very best of excuses: he has no wet tyres with him, and a slick-shod turbocharged Talbot Sunbeam Lotus cannot be the easiest of vehicles to cope with under such conditions.

That honour has probably already gone to the Escort Cosworth. In a dramatic demonstration of the benefits of four-wheel drive, Mark Spencer's second practice saw him take the Ford up in a blistering 37.50. This meant that at the end of practice he was faster than every other competitor at the meeting — even those in the big racing cars. A fantastic achievement in what, tyres apart, is basically a road-legal car.

Every other driver bar one, that is. The one? Roy Lane, the same man whose motorhome I've been sheltering in. It's a big plush American Winnebago, boasting everything from a turbodiesel to a kitchen sink, central heating and a built-in TV above the windscreen. I don't think I would trust myself with such a device. 'And why did you run off the road sir?' 'I was watching Coronation Street, officer'.

Right now it's the central heating which is most welcome, as I try to dry my sodden clothes. Roy's wife Bett takes one look at my bedraggled appearance and, in a masterly piece of timing, puts the kettle on.

As the first runs proceed the rain eases, finally stopping at 11:40. By the time we emerge ready for Roy's first run, the track is, if not drying, as least no longer streaming wet. Times begin to tumble and the Escort's advantage is eroded. But Mark still ends the day with a fine class win on 36.87, nearly a second ahead of Geoff Kershaw's 4WD Sierra. Today the Fords are king in Modified Production Cars over 2000cc; the regular class leaders, Messrs Waldron

CHAPTER 7

Left: Paul Gwinnett struggles through Karousel in his Talbot Lotus. Above: scars of an off-road excursion bear witness to the difficulty of driving on slicks on a day like this.

and Lambert, simply cannot get the power down.

Today, for the first time this season at an RAC Championship round, there are classes for motorcycles and three-wheelers, which add a lot of colour and interest to the meeting. Unlike the car driver, ensconced in cockpit or bodyshell, the body language of the biker is visible to all. As Mike Shorter rockets out of Karousel, leaning forward for all he's worth to stop the Triumph entering an uncontrollable wheelie at Deer's Leap, we can see him working the bike, willing it to stay on the ground despite his right-hand resolutely screwing the throttle open. Great stuff.

Even greater stuff is the entertainment value which the sidecars and three-wheelers provide. The latter consist predominantly of motorcycle front ends and a lot of home-brewed and often very polished engineering at the back end. At present the crew to beat seem to be Jon Warren and Jo Lumley on their 900 Kawasaki trike.

As with the sidecars, it's the presence of passengers which makes them such a favourite with the crowd. The antics of the man — or woman — on the back make for great spectating.

For proof of just what can happen to passengers, one need do no more than talk to Guernseymen Maurice Ogier and Kevin Prevel. They are here today with their Windle sidecar outfit, a frantic 500cc two-stroke JPX engined device with full racing fairings.

The hills attract a wide variety of types of motorcycle and motorcycle-derived machinery, some which would clearly be at home on a circuit, others which would be happier in an enduro, still others which are basically road bikes.

Maurice and Kevin's outfit is an out-and-out racing design, with the rider crouched down inside a fairing in a position which makes it totally impossible for him to look behind. On more than one occasion, apparently, he has reached the top of a hill only to find that Kevin has been centrifuged onto the tarmac some 400 yards back. If by definition everyone who competes in motorsport is slightly mad, then sidecar passengers suffer from a peculiarly intense brand of lunacy that is all their own.

Today Kevin reaches the top of the hill

57

still attached to the rig, much to his relief but to the secret disappointment, I suspect, of many spectators. The pair are delighted with their trip to Gurston, not just because they are both still in one piece and within 400 yards of each other, but also because they have managed no fewer than seven climbs over the weekend.

Two practices and two timed runs are the norm in hillclimbing, but many clubs try to fit in extra practices if the schedule permits, to give competitors value for money.

Here, with the BARC's Southwestern centre in charge, five practices is unusually generous and can only be achieved by slick organisation. It makes the trip from the Channel Islands well worth while.

Unlike the car drivers, who almost universally wear racing overalls, bikers and their crews wear all sorts of gear. Some opt for overalls, but others retain their traditional leathers while still others opt for anoraks and Barbour trousers.

With the hill continuing to dry, morale increases and the paddock starts to buzz as the small single seaters warm up for their second runs.

Paul Shipp feels the temperature of his OMS's Yamaha engine as co-driver Angela Hewitt waits in the queue. Stewart Bayliss' two-stroke Suzuki-engined Jedi, with its distinctive four chromed exhausts, is smoking much more from the offside upper pipe than the other three.

Mark Coley's Jedi isn't smoking at all, much to the frustration of Mark and crew who exhaust themselves pushing it up and down the paddock in a frantic effort to get it to fire up. And when it does, Mark can only manage fifth out of six in the class, a poor result for Gurston's 500cc Racing Cars record holder. Local man Rob Barksfield bags first spot.

With the track drying, times start to tumble and successive classes find themselves posting fastest time of the day on their second runs, eclipsing the efforts of more powerful cars in the rain. Had he been registered for the overall Hill-

Deer's Leap on two and three wheels: Kawasaki-powered Jon Warren and Jo Lumley (above) and KTM-mounted Paul Jeffery (right).

climb Championship, Phil Cooke's class-winning 33.52 in the Jedi 2/27 would have put him firmly — albeit temporarily — in the Top 12 despite his car having only 1074cc of Suzuki power.

As we move up the classes, driver after driver shaves huge chunks off his first-run time, making what is always a knife-edge sport even tighter. Effectively, today there is only one competitive run.

Driver after driver finds himself in the Top 12 at the expense of much more fancied names who have yet to run, only to be gradually pushed down on to 'the bubble' — 12th out of 12 — and out the bottom as the fast boys come out for their second run.

Two drivers, however, make a more permanent mark on the scoresheet. Justin Fletcher produces a storming 31.01 in his Pilbeam MP62 to take the class by nearly a second from Tom Brown, who is himself nearly a second ahead of Pete Griffiths. Considering that the track is still far from fast, to produce a time only 0.87 away from Roger Moran's class record of 30.14 is nothing short of remarkable.

The other driver who can hardly fail to attract attention is David Grace, a famous name making a welcome comeback to the hills after missing the first part of the season for the very good reason that he had nothing to drive.

David, second in last year's title chase and champion in '93 and '94, is here at Gurston for the first airing of a new Ralt Gould which was not completed until 5.30am this morning.

Sean Gould and father David have been working 7am till 7pm for weeks to finish this car, which had literally not turned a wheel before it started its first

CHAPTER 7

Man on the Hill

Robin Boucher

If Tony Fletcher is the Bernie Ecclestone of hillclimbing, Robin Boucher is the Murray Walker — without the ridiculous gaffes. And he's been at it about as long, for his soft West Country accent was first heard over the microphone as long ago as the mid '60s.

A typesetter by trade, he never had any intention of becoming a 'voice'. Although he'd attended one or two of the very early meetings at Wiscombe Park, his present involvement with motorsport can be traced to a $1/32$nd scale model car racing club, which included quite a few enthusiasts from the North Devon Motor Club.

Someone said 'you ought to come to the Winckley Sprint' and when he did he found a sport let down by its presentation. 'All that was happening was that somebody was reading times out,' Robin recalls. 'We said at the end of the day: "needed a bit more atmosphere didn't it?", to which came the reply "We can never find anybody to commentate, why don't you do the next one?" I said "I'll give it a go", and that's really how it started.'

He's been giving it a go ever since. At first he concentrated on South Western events but before long he was in demand from Cornwall to Scotland. He has the gift of being able to inject urgency into his voice in just the right measure to bring an event alive; add that to an encyclopaedic knowledge of the sport and a typesetter's ability to marshal information — he frequently works out class positions before the organisers, while simultaneously talking, smoking and drinking tea — and you have a commentator of rare ability.

His trade is more relevant to this than it first appears. 'When you're holding a mike in one hand and a pen in the other it's very difficult to write the times in most programmes. I spend a lot of time typing up much bigger score sheets on the computer. As you're typing it up you're noticing everybody that's there and formulating ideas of what's going to happen.' The rest of it comes entirely from his head: 'When they're running a car off the line every 15-20 seconds, you haven't got the time to go through commentary sheets, unless they send them to you beforehand.'

What is it about commentating that gives him such a buzz?

'I don't know. But I very much like facts and figures and mathematics. I try and aim my commentary not at the hillclimb enthusiast but at the general public. You probably say a certain amount of the same things each week, but you are talking to a different audience, outside of the paddock. I've always taken the guideline that if we charge spectators to come in and entertain them, we must give them the best we can. They could pay their money and go to the safari park or whatever, there are so many leisure activities. The vast majority aren't motorsport enthusiasts, they're just there for a day out. They've perhaps seen it advertised that there are Formula 1-engined cars — something you won't see now in circuit racing in this country, not at club level anyway.'

He gets annoyed if he feels the public are being short changed and points to the Westmorland MC as an example of what can be done. 'At Barbon there are one or two little displays, something for people to walk round and have a look at. They've *tried*.'

The epitome of what he doesn't like is the scene he once witnessed at a club sprint at Three Sisters.

Robin at work, Gurston Down.

John Hayward

'The circuit owners were charging people five quid to get in and I'm sitting there thinking "this is despicable". All they're seeing is car after car going round the circuit. They haven't got a clue what's going on and even the drivers don't know. In the fullness of time somebody would amble over from the timekeeper with a piece of paper and eventually scribble on a board, sometimes half an hour after some competitors had done their runs. The most important thing about commentating a hillclimb or a sprint is times, and as soon as the competitor's finished a run.'

Delaying tactics by drivers also annoy him. 'Some people in the Top 12 don't appreciate the marshals, the organisers and particularly the spectators. I think a Top 12 that takes an hour and 10 minutes is completely and utterly out of order. One thing we insist on in sprints is an in-depth enquiry if a Top 12 takes more than 30 minutes.' He would like to see a countdown clock automatically triggered by the departure of the previous car. Exceed your time limit for coming to the line and you miss your run — automatically, not (as happens at present) when the Clerk of the Course finally loses patience.

His commentary box offers an unrivalled view of everything that is happening and has given him strong views on how events should be run. Increasingly he is putting these ideas into practice, this year taking over the running of the RAC Sprint Championship in a parallel manner to Tony Fletcher's stewardship of the Hillclimb series. He also runs the Midland Speed Championship, which offers a mixture of sprint and hillclimb events with affordable road-oriented classes, to bring new names into the sport, rather along the lines of the Scottish model which fostered Graeme Wight Jnr and George Ritchie. 'Look at the Leaders Championship, you've got to have a full-race machine to do any good at all.'

He worries that too many of today's up-and-coming drivers are the sons of existing competitors: 'I think the hillclimb classes now need looking at because unless we start getting some new people in at the bottom end, we're going to be struggling in 10 years time.'

However, there is more to Robin than words, be they over a Tannoy or in a committee meeting. For although he's never owned a racing car he's driven over 50 different vehicles in speed events over the years, from 850 Minis to the F5000 McLaren of then sprint champion Dave Harris, back in the '70s.

His most serious seasons were 1988-89 when he shared a 2 litre Chevron Hart with Steve Jewell, but he rates his most enjoyable drive as a climb up Loton in Barrie Lines' full-race Renault Alpine A110. 'It was a very strange car to get used to', he recalls, 'if you didn't wring its neck you frightened yourself silly with that rear suspension, which was exactly what I did on the first run, going gently. Got halfway up the straight in top and it wasn't sitting down hard enough, gave me a real shaky moment through the kink. Then I realised what I'd done and next run I did it flat in third. It just sat down and went through like it was on rails.'

His ambition is to commission somebody with the necessary engineering expertise to build his own top level hillclimb car, a popular route with hillclimbers in the '50s and '60s. David Gould's British Championship winning Gould-Hart, driven by Chris Cramer, was an exception in 1985 but the privately built machines at that level are a rarity nowadays due to the influence of Mike Pilbeam. 'The known quantity is to go to Mike with a cheque. You know you're going to get a car that's going to work well, out of the box. Nobody is prepared to take the plunge any more.'

He looks with interest at what rallycross competitors do with Metro 6R4s and Ford RS200s and reckons that part-time four wheel drive is the way to go, automatically switched through electronics. Another route might be a cross between a Jedi and an MP62 with a motorcycle-derived engine. 'At the moment we're only scratching the surface with bike engines — 300hp from 1500cc engines is the norm in the States.'

Even if he never realises his ambition, competitors and spectators alike are sure to hear a lot more from Robin Boucher in the years to come.

59

LIVING WITH SPEED

Jedi Suzuki GSXR
Phil Cooke, Racing Cars 500-1100cc

Drivers of small-capacity racing cars can be divided fairly equally into two groups: Jedi and OMS. Each is fiercely loyal to its chosen marque and drivers do not often change camps.

Phil Cooke's Jedi breaks this tidy rule. Built in 1991 as a Suzuki-engined 500 in standard bike tune, it was used in this form for two seasons and then re-engined with an ex-works GP engine from the early '80s — 'it probably would have been used by someone like Barry Sheene', Phil reckons.

It produced about 124bhp, not bad for a 500, and gave Phil 'a couple of good seasons, a few records here and there, some of which are still standing. I still hold the Brighton half-mile 500, Barbon, and Wiscombe.'

Then for the 1994 season Phil did an unheard of thing. He took his Jedi to Steve Owen at OMS to have honeycomb sides put in, sacrilege to Jedi enthusiasts schooled in the virtues of space frames and aluminium panelling. 'We cut out the cross-members of the sides and the floor, put in inch honeycomb, riveted and bonded it from the outside and then glued it.'

Does John Corbyn approve of the modifications made to his creation by his arch rival? All Phil will say — with a wry smile — is 'he's not making any like this at the moment'.

For 1995 Phil kept basically the same chassis apart from a few mods from suspension guru David Gould. 'It's quite a bit stiffer than most and doesn't run anti-roll bars'.

Most attention went on the power unit as Phil moved up to the 1100 class courtesy of a Suzuki GSXR, watercooled unlike the earlier oil-cooled designs. Phil reckons watercooling enables the unit to run at higher compression — currently around 13:1 — 'but it's quite cammy, we tend to gear it short and change gear a lot. Not as often as on the 500 though, which had a six speed box and you used all of them, up and down.' He acknowledges that the performance of the car owes much to Silverstone-based engine builder TTS.

This year he has been rewarded with several new records, including one here today. He goes particularly well at Gurston and won the hill championship here in 1995.

Phil Cooke, The Esses, Prescott, September meeting.

---

run today. Indeed, details were still being completed in the paddock.

The banana yellow machine looks strangely naked — it's so new, there hasn't even been time to put the stickers on — and because David did not get to Gurston in time for practice proper, his first run is regarded as practice and only his second will count for position. No one expects him to win with such an untried car; even a competitive time will be an achievement.

In the event David produces a stunning second run of 30.03 on a still-damp track, good enough to net him second in class to Roy Lane's 29.50 and provide him with two more valuable proving runs in the Top 12.

For Roy, this is food for thought in more ways than one. To have a challenger of David's calibre back in action will clearly hot up the title chase, for with only the best 10 scores to count out of 16 rounds, David must still be regarded as a serious title contender despite his late start.

But his emergence is more significant than that, for there are marked similarities between the yellow car and Roy's new Ralt, which he has yet to drive in anger (though son Antony and son-in-law John have competed in it at non-championship events). Both use a carbonfibre Ralt tub, both use a similar type of rear suspension (Roy's is from a Pilbeam MP72) with horizontal inboard springs. The principal difference is the engine: a Judd for Roy, a Cosworth taken from an earlier car for David. All season Roy has been torn between a desire to try something new and a conviction that he should stick with the well-proven Pilbeam for as long as it remains competitive. Being able to watch a similar car will give Roy to some extent the best of both worlds: valuable information without risk to his championship chances.

Significant by his absence is Graham Priaulx, his Pilbeam still not mobile again after its serious accident at Wiscombe. He's on the entry list though, which is a good sign. Not on the entry list, nor likely to be for the rest of the season, is son Andy, who since his father's accident has been signed to drive on the circuits in Formula Renault Sport. Contractual restrictions mean that from now on his presence on the hills will be limited to the paddock.

With so much hanging on just one run, there's a real buzz on the hill, a buzz which had seemed inconceivable in the miserable conditions of the morning. Commentator Robin Boucher senses the mood and makes his own contribution to it in the way that all commentators

CHAPTER 7

Championship Top Tens after Round 6

RAC
1 Patrick Wood 43
2 Roger Moran 42
3 Roy Lane 37
4 Tim Mason 35
5 Bill Bristow 24
6 Simon Durling 21
7 George Ritchie 18
8 Tim Barrington 13
9 Tom Brown 12
10 Andy Priaulx 10

Leaders
1 Mark Waldron 48
2 Phil Cooke 42
3 Justin Fletcher 40
4 Martin Groves 35
5 Tony Lambert 34
6 Tom New 32
7 Andrew Russell 28
8 Mark Lawrence 27
9 Peter Griffiths 26
10 Pete Hannam 25

That awful moment when you know you're going to hit something and there's not a damn thing you can do about it. David Flanagan heads for the bank at Ashes in his OMS and (right) marshals help him out of the cockpit, unscathed apart from his pride, though the same can't be said for his front suspension.

should but so few do — analysing, interpreting, questioning, informing.

As drivers come and go in the Top 12, he keeps constant track of who's in, who's out and who's going fast at the speedtrap at Hollow. 'And now it's Roger Moran on the bubble, 34.44, the man who was quickest at the end of the first runs, so he's got some work to do. But here's Roger Moran on a fight back, 125mph down into Hollow... big wheelie as he goes over the Deer Leap, now around the Ashes, heading up towards the finish, sprinting up to 120, 130 miles an hour — this is going to be quick from the unlimited capacity class newcomer, but will it be the fastest time of the day for Roger Moran? Yes it is! 30.07, three O point zero seven, and now the man in trouble is Tony Marsh...'

Then rain threatens again and Boucher uses the uncertainty to add to the tension, to spur the meeting on. 'I know what the drivers will want to do in a situation like this, *they'll want to get on with it*'.

Today we are hearing Boucher at his best.

Justin Fletcher's meteoric run has ensured him a place in the Top 12, the only 2-litre runner to make it. Roy will run last, David Grace second to last, Roger Moran third from last, Patrick Wood fourth. A few spots of rain fall — not enough to make any difference but enough to add urgency to the situation. Times continue to tumble but after the first runs Roy still has the edge on 28.69 with David the only other driver under 29 seconds, on 28.91. Come the second runs, Roger shaves a full second off his time and Patrick nearly as much, to equal Roy's first effort. David improves, but not by much, to 28.71, slipping to fourth.

This leaves the championship points hanging on the last run of the day, a fitting climax to an event which had started on a desperately low key and is ending in complete contrast. If Roy manages to beat Roger's 28.57 he wins and takes his third championship round of the year. If he doesn't improve, he's equal second.

An article in *Autosport* a year or two back reviewing top hillclimbers said that Roy was at his best when under pressure. And so it proves today: he sends the crowd home with something to talk about as he storms to Fastest Time of the Day; 28.25 and his 69th win.

I'm sent home with a vastly higher opinion of Gurston than I started, and with the feeling that 1996 could be a vintage year for the Steel King team.

61

Roger Moran.

Shelsley Walsh

Location
near the village of the same name approximately 10 miles northwest of Worcester.

Organising club
Midland Automobile Club (Est. 1901) Ltd,
c/o Mark Joseland,
Woodbridge, Upper Sapey,
Worcester WR6 6EX.
Tel 01886 853411.

Length 1000 yards.

Outright hill records at start of 2.6.96 meeting
Overall: Richard Brown, 25.34sec.
Ladies: Joy Rainey, 28.32sec.

Roy's Run

'Grip is the problem at Shelsley. It's now down to 50-60% of its best, everywhere. This affects the way you set the car up.

'I have tried using three gears to the Esses but at all meetings this year I have stuck to two. First change comes just before Kennel: settle the car nicely, try and give it another bootful going into Kennel, although these days it has lost a lot of its grip and it's a big understeering moment if you try to do it too quick. You need a lot of aggression there because all the momentum you gain there —whether it's one, two or three extra mph — is speed you'll carry all the way to the Esses.

'First gear is probably 70-ish. Second gear is a 120mph gear; I hold it all the way through Crossing, through the speed trap, up towards the Esses, and then cross the box into 'third' (approximately a 90mph gear), to go through the Esses. Turn left, turn right, floor it as hard as you can, then change up into fourth which is about a 140mph gear.

'Once you could go out of the Esses and floor it, you'd be away. Now you just get wheelspin: sometimes it pays you to let it spin to get some temperature in the tyres again, then she'll grip and away you go. This year I managed the fastest I've ever pulled over the line, 139mph.'

KEY

Track shading indicates gear ratio...

White striped is first gear

Tints are intermediates (darker tone equals higher gear)

Black is top gear

Because ratios and patterns in racing gearboxes can be altered at will, a particular shading on one map does not indicate the same ratio as on another: shading is relative only to that particular venue.

V indicates good viewing area

0 — 100yd

CHAPTER 8

'A brave man at the end of the day.' Shelsley Walsh

In the years before circuit racing was established in Britain, hillclimbing was a popular way of proving a car's abilities and attracted great commercial interest as a result. Its fortunes waned when Brooklands became available, but recovered after the First World War, albeit on a less commercial basis. Hillclimbing has remained a basically amateur sport ever since, despite another brief period in the limelight after the second world war when, with Donington and Brooklands lost and new circuits not yet established, it once again became a major focus of sporting activity.

Throughout all this the world's oldest motorsport venue in continuous use has remained practically unchanged. A driver with a time machine, projecting him and his car forward from the opening of Shelsley Walsh in 1905 to the present day, would notice that the top of the course had been lengthened (this was done not long after it was initiated) and that the unsurfaced road had acquired tarmac, rumble strips, drainage and fencing. He would also notice, if he had time amid the task of piloting his veteran steed up the hill, that facilities had vastly improved. But the track and its adjacent buildings would all look remarkably familiar. Even the briefest glimpse at archive photos proves the point.

Part of the reason for its survival is purely practical: when hillclimbing on public roads was banned in 1925, Shelsley was almost alone in being unaffected — then as now it was on private land. Instantly it became the hub of British hillclimbing and throughout the '30s attracted large crowds, top notch drivers and (in real terms) considerably more prize money than is offered today. Only when the Bugatti Owners Club began to popularise Prescott in the years immediately preceding hostilities was its pre-eminence even open to question.

But it owes its continuity to far more than a mere accident of ownership, for the nature of the hill itself also exercises a powerful and enduring fascination. Cars have become unrecognisably faster, both in a straight line and on corners, but somehow they have never outgrown Shelsley. For it is a power hill, with a very fast bottom section which brings you storming up to the sharp left-hander of Bottom S at a speed which your genes tell you is suicidal. Even seasoned campaigners hold the place in awe; after 33 years on the hills and hundreds of ascents, Roy Lane freely admits that Shelsley is the climb which he still finds daunting. 'It's balls flat out, a brave man at the end of the day. It's not a technical hill.'

For these reasons, and a lot more intangible ones besides, Shelsley has a unique aura. It is hallowed ground. Just as Monaco has a special place in the F1 calendar, so this Worcestershire venue is the place where drivers feel they are not just sensing history but in their own small way making it. To compete is to

Tim Barrington.

Alan Thompson.

63

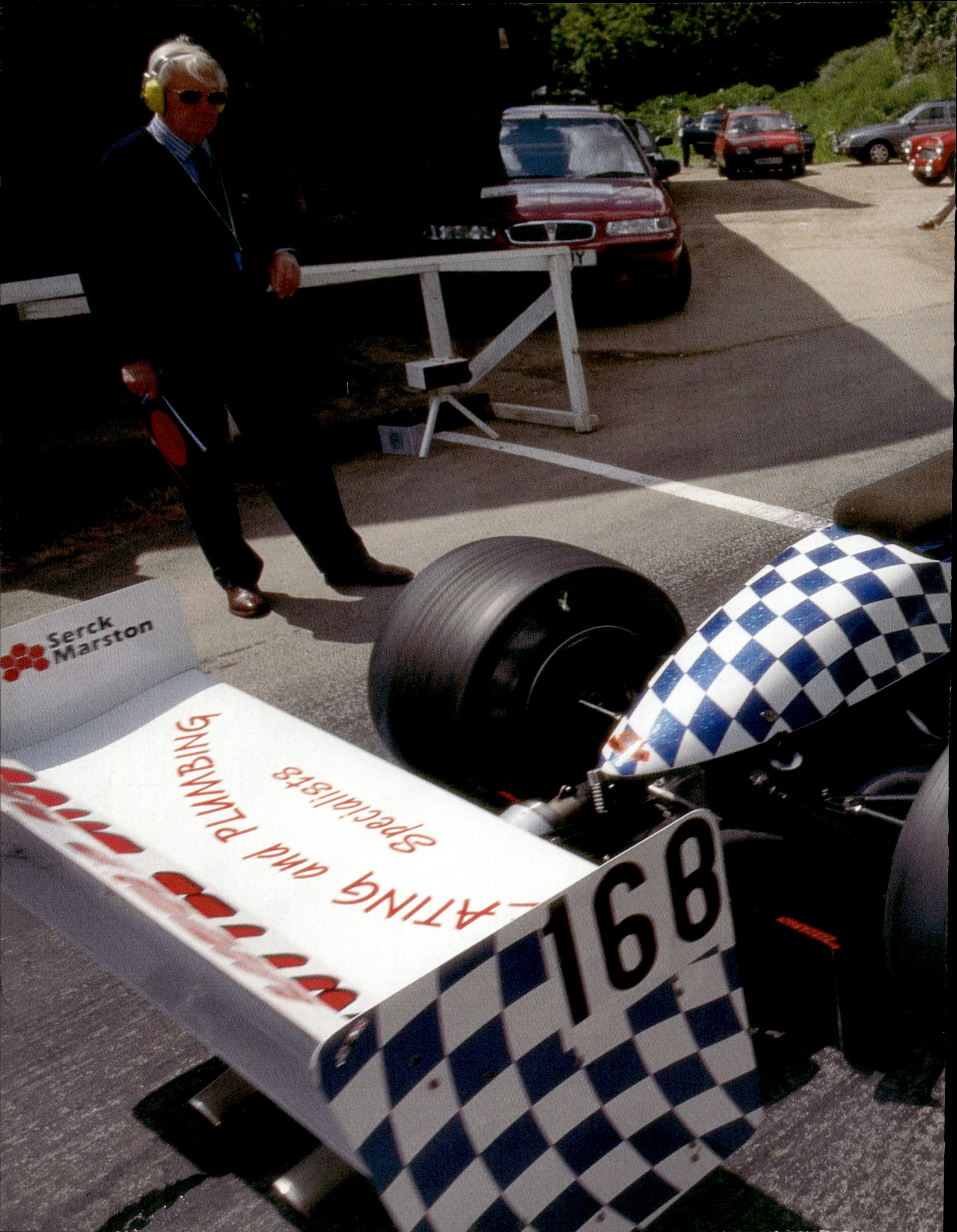
Serck Marston
ATING and PLUMBING
Specialists
168

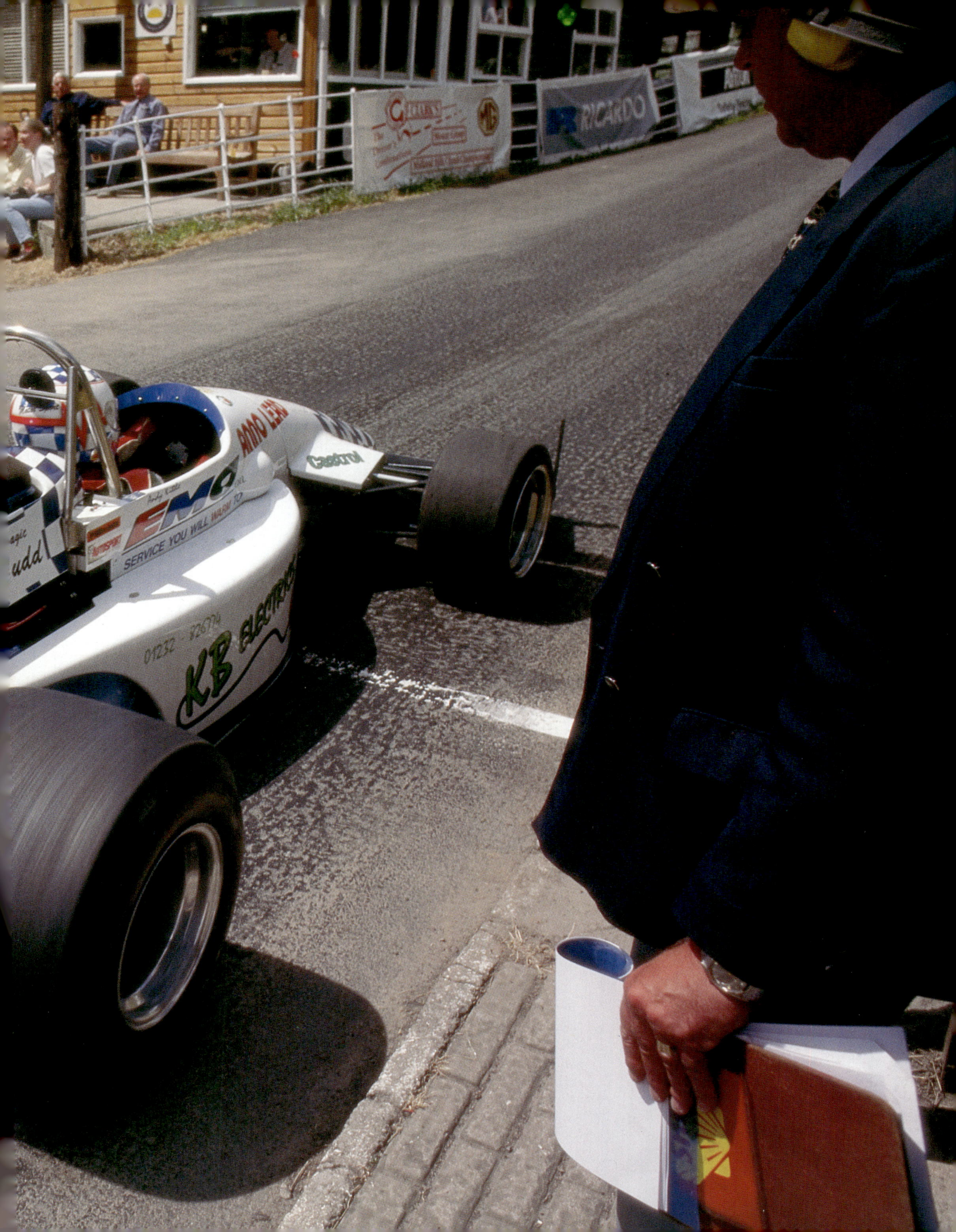

RICARDO
MG
Castrol
SERVICE YOU WILL WARM TO
KB

LIVING WITH SPEED

add your name to a list which stretches back to the dawn of motoring and includes hundreds of illustrious drivers, among them some of the finest the world has ever seen, men like Campbell, Stuck, Caracciola and Moss.

The heart of the place is the paddock, row after row of simple wooden pits, each with a nameplate recalling someone who has contributed to the hill's history in some way. They are barely wide enough now for the big cars to squeeze into, but it would take a brave man to suggest bulldozing them down in favour of something high tech. The Midland Automobile Club, which has run the place since its inception and itself dates back even further, to 1901, has too great a sense of history for that.

The site layout is distinctly haphazard, for just as in 1905 Shelsley lives cheek by jowl with a working farm, its barns and cottages intertwined with racing facilities. It's illogical, but it works. And like so many things which are unplanned, it has atmosphere. Roy for one is very happy with the place just as it is; he describes the paddock as simply 'the finest place in British hillclimbing. The atmosphere in this little area, this paddock, is the ultimate.'

The course is not just a straight blast from the start to Bottom S. There are two shallow left-handers en-route, at Kennel Bend near the start and Crossing about halfway to Bottom S. Both can be taken fast, both *must* be taken fast if a decent time is to be achieved, either can easily put an end to your day's sport. Despite these bends, the faster cars approach Bottom S at around 125mph.

From here it's a short climb to the tighter right-hander that constitutes Top S and then a straight blast to the finish, although there is a strategically placed drain on the inside of Top S which can catch out the unwary. When you're driving that fine line between a controlled drift and a lurid slide, it pays to avoid a rectangle of well-polished cast iron.

The topography does nothing to reassure the fainthearted. As you storm into Bottom S, a steep bank confronts you and another falls away to your left — no run-off areas here — while banks on either side of Top S ensure that there is no room for error if you are to avoid ricocheting off the vegetation.

As if that wasn't enough, Shelsley has another trick up its sleeve: red clay. When it rains it washes off the banks and on to the track, seeping into every crev-

---

Man on the Hill

Willem Toet

Shelsley, August meeting.

Hillclimbers are used to travelling around the country to pursue their sport, but no one travels further than Willem Toet. He flies from Italy to take part.

This sounds like enthusiasm gone mad, but it's all in a day's work as far as he is concerned. For this intensely motivated, vigorous individual is an aerodynamicist with the Ferrari F1 team and thinks nothing of flying from his present base in Italy to England for a day's work with Ferrari designer John Barnard, and then flying back again, getting home around midnight.

It's a lifestyle that would destroy many marriages, but it's the kind of dedication which F1 demands, and Willem's wife Susan appreciates that — she has to, because she also works at Ferrari. Motor racing has been an integral part of their lives since they day they met, at Le Mans, in Willem's first year as chief mechanic for Ray Mallock's team, running Group C cars and also Formula Atlantic machines. He was just under 30 at the time.

It was a fortunate meeting in more ways than one, for the marriage enabled the Dutch-born Australian to stay in the UK. A few years with various other formulae followed before the big time beckoned and he joined the Benetton Formula 1 team. From there Ferrari was the logical, and very exciting, next step.

He had his first taste of the hills around five years ago while at Benetton, pairing up with Richard Marshall to share a roadgoing Peugeot 205.

'Had an absolute *whale* of a time, I *really* enjoyed it, but in the end I wasn't able to come over and look after the car at all, and it's now been taken over full time by Richard.'

'I thought I'd really like to learn to drive an open wheeler — a small one. I watched Richard Marshall try a big car (Patrick Wood's MP58-DFZ/R) after the Peugeot — it's very difficult, such a big, big step. I had a one-off drive at Gurston Down in the works Pilbeam, which I adored, but it was a little bit expensive, so I've come to an arrangement with Ben and we share this car.'

'This car' is an MP52, originally designed as a Formula Ford 2000 and run in recent years as an 1100. It now boasts a Cosworth 1600 engine, in which form Willem shares it with Ben Boult.

'Hillclimbing is fantastic socially because it's very friendly. It gives us a good excuse to come over to England to catch up with friends and family.' It also forces him to unwind after the pressures of the working week. 'You *have* to clear the brain. When I'm sitting on the start line I can't be thinking about Reynolds numbers and vortex generators and various things about aerodynamics, I've *got* to think about driving.'

He plays down any suggestion that his Pilbeam might boast some clever Ferrari-esque aerodynamic tweaks. 'We've done a few small modifications but I don't think we've done anything dramatic or anything that's made a big difference.'

But that won't stop his rivals studying his wing profiles *very* carefully.

---

ice of the tarmac. Even after it dries, it stays there, filling and smoothing the surface and spoiling the grip. All tracks are at their best just after resurfacing, but Shelsley in particular deteriorates markedly with time and it is no coincidence that the fastest climb ever recorded, to

CHAPTER 8

Car on the Hill

Audi S1

Tom Hammonds, Sports Libre Cars Over 2000cc

Norman Burr

Prescott, May meeting.

On paper at least, Tom Hammonds' Audi S1 is the most powerful car in British hillclimbing today. A colossal 720bhp is claimed for the 2.1 litre turbocharged 4WD car, well in excess of anything a single-seater runner will admit to.

Tom himself is dubious about his superiority. 'The lads won't tell you too much, they keep it under their hat.' The 580 claimed for Roy Lane's Judd he 'takes with a very large pinch of salt. I suspect it's a hell of a lot more', but he admits that the Judd is tuned for torque rather than outright power, whereas his Audi is very peaky. 'You get a lot of power at the top end. I find it a bit of a handful, especially in the wet.'

Like the Metro 6R4s with which it frequently competes on the hills, it is a remnant of the fearsome Group B cars produced in the mid '80s for rallying but subsequently banned from that sport.

'I got it from Audi, from the factory. I'd got a roadgoing version of it, short wheelbase, and I was at Milton Keynes. This car was there and I said jokingly to the service manager "I wouldn't mind buying that." He laughed, because at that time they were still using them. When they banned them four or five years later he rang me up, he remembered me.'

'I modified it to Pike's Peak specification, got the correct engine, the gearbox, the transmission. Audi let me have the wing that fits on the back, and the front apron.'

One thing he definitely didn't get from Audi is the 'Rolls Royce designed by Pininfarina' badge on the back, a present from an ex-Crewe engineer who used to work for Tom and 'just happened to have it in his box'.

British hills are a bit short for a car of this nature: the 6R4s, while lacking the outright power, handle a lot better in Tom's opinion. A sortie to a Continental hill appeals, but cost is the barrier.

What Tom needs most, he admits, is more time behind the wheel. He's not a motorsport professional or even a motor trade professional (he's in the furnishing business) and doesn't use the car on the road.

So the only chance he gets to acclimatise himself to his 720bhp projectile is a few minutes at a time at hillclimbs, plus the occasional sortie to Curborough or MIRA.

It's an easy car to compete with in other respects, however. There's no temptation to tinker with the mechanicals because the management looks after everything, you couldn't alter it if you tried. And routine maintenance is 'ever so simple. You've got to remember it was designed for rallying and fettling at the side of the road. You don't need any special tools to take the gearbox to pieces, or the engine.'

Tom has looked into the possibility of buying a single seater but has no immediate plans to change the car.

So this monster-winged beast with its popping, whistling turbo should be pleasing the hillclimbing crowds for a while yet.

Richard Brown at 25.34 seconds in a Pilbeam MP58-Cosworth DFR, was set in 1992 on new tarmac.

There's a £1000 reward for the first person to break 25 seconds at Shelsley but no one is likely to win it today. Without a fresh surface, or at least a thoroughly cleaned one, the hill record is simply out of reach.

'It was absolutely magic for the first couple of meetings', comments Roy. 'But now the track is in a disgusting state. Every year we've gone slower and slower because more and more red clay gets ingrained into the track and it gets slippier and slippier. Just before they resurfaced it we were having a job to do 26-27 seconds. Then suddenly we were doing 25s and now we're back doing 27s. The surface has gone off the top of the tarmac again.'

The MAC committee responsible for the hill is aware of the problem but has other worries too. For the hill itself tends to move, as the clay swells and shrinks with the seasons. 'Each year another dip or another bump comes' Roy comments.

'Sometimes you find freak results here, like you do at Barbon,' he continues. Noticing that Richard Brown is well within earshot he adds mischievously: 'Like when Richard Brown paid thousands of pounds to David Grace for a drive once and screamed up on a nice day when the track had just been surfaced and got the record.'

'I've been an also-ran for years here' Richard protests, 'paid a lot of money to have a lot of oil put down too!'

The oil to which he is referring was laid in the starting area shortly before today's meeting started, ironically the result of an attempt by the MAC to wash the track clean of clay and dirt. The power wash equipment suffered a hydraulic failure and succeeded only in spraying a long streak of oil on the track, making things worse rather than better. That, added to the fact that changeable weather has put grip at a premium anyway and given the red clay a field day, has the drivers grumbling openly.

'I thought it was diabolical yesterday morning. It really was undriveable,' complains Patrick Wood. 'It's a shame. Here we are, the Mecca of British hillclimbing and the track's got clay impregnated into the surface. It needs to be jet-washed at least once a year.'

But he can't resist extracting a little humour from the situation, so he strolls up to Roy Lane.

'And who got dry runs yesterday then?', he asks with mock jealousy. Yesterday in practice everyone was holding back, hoping for the track to dry a little more. Eventually, with the start line empty and everyone watching the sky, the organisers appealed to drivers to

67

LIVING WITH SPEED

Richard Drewett and Lotus 30.

John Pascoe exercising his Volvo 122S.

take their practice runs. Roy, wily as ever, seems to have read the meteorological runes better than most and managed a run in the 27s just as it started to spot with rain. Or maybe he was just lucky.

Today, by contrast, the weather is dry and settled, albeit somewhat cloudy.

'Patrick, your problem is you need a few more years yet', he chortles.

'I know, I'm getting closer to the 60 mark but...'

'Just a little bit more experience... I reckon 20 years and you'll be quite good!'

'I've actually done a calculation that I'm going to catch up your all time record when I'm somewhere around 758!'

Their speculation about Patrick's route to stardom is interrupted by a man with a calendar. It is the first Shelsley calendar, showing heroes from past and present, and he wants to show Roy a picture he may recognise: of one R T Lane, on the hill in the '70s with an open-exhaust V8 — no competition silencers in those days, just ear muffs for the start-line marshals.

I wander past that same start line and climb up to Bottom S, past the memorial seat to A F P Fane, one of only three men to better 40 seconds on the hill before the Second World War.

Today John Bowman from Solihull is having no trouble doing the same in his MGB V8, negotiating Bottom S neatly but aggressively just as I settle down to spectate, on his way to 33.51. From this viewpoint, it looks as though many drivers tend to turn into the bend too quickly, getting too close to the apex. Is this fear of adverse camber on the outside, or is it sheer self-preservation, slowing a fraction earlier than is theoretically possible?

A dozen or so cars later my speculation is interrupted by the news from the startline that one car I particularly wanted to see driven in anger, Paul Parker's spectacular 6.2 litre Royale-Chevrolet, is being wheeled away from the start line, smoking. So I start back down, to investigate.

In the paddock I find Paul and his team stripping the transmission. The cause is soon revealed: a gearbox output shaft has snapped clean off despite being crack tested and shot peened. The only place the Royale is going today is back on its trailer, a disappointing end to an already frustrating weekend.

Queuing at the paddock exit.

'I'm not a good driver in the rain,' admits Paul. 'I see too many pound note signs. I just don't feel comfortable — probably ease off a good deal more than most.'

He's only been hillclimbing since the beginning of 1993, but has been following the sport since he was a small boy. 'I used to ride my bicycle over to Prescott when I lived in Gloucester at the age of 12 or 13 and I fell in love with hillclimbs then.'

'I came back to it in 1992 helping Tim Elmer, who has the Phantom which now has a BDG engine in it, he and I were at school together. I vowed at the end of 1992 that one way or another I would start in 1993. I'd got to the age of 40, a mid-life crisis.'

LIVING WITH SPEED

At first he shared a V8 Rover-powered Mallock with Rick Fielding but that sadly came to an end in a big way at Gurston last year. 'It gained a puncture in the paddock, came to the line, and the marshals noticed that the tyre was deflating too late to say "I wouldn't go if I were you". I got down into the dip, the thing finally lost its air and the car turned right into the trees. I was alright, all I had was a slight bruise on my left knee.'

Paul attributes his escape more to Rick Fielding's engineering than to luck — 'he strengthened the car far beyond what it was when it left the Mallock factory. Any engineering he does is always built with strength in mind because he has a drag racing background: if it needs two locations he'll put four in.'

Rick is now involved in developing the Royale, which on a dry day Paul reckons is more than a match for Metro 6R4s — 'and nine times out of ten I'll beat Tom Hammonds as well. Tom and I had some good battles last year, we went all over the country including the Channel Islands.'

Tom too has hit a snag today, his awe-inspiring Group B Audi S1 being briefly sidelined with a blown turbo hose — an easy problem to fix. Paul rates the Audi, along with Jim Robinson's Pilbeam MP43C and Christian Mineeff's SPA Judd, as 'probably the best three libre cars in the country now'. Jim he considers to be the top Libre driver.

Meanwhile Andy Priaulx is filing the front tyres smooth on the family Pilbeam, providing moral and practical support for his father's return to the hills after the big off at Wiscombe. Graham openly admits that the bang on the head affected him more than he at first realised and he is not yet back up to speed, either mentally or physically. FTD is not on the cards, but he needs a respectable result to rebuild his confidence.

It's particularly difficult for a Channel Islander to get race fit. You can't go even out for a fast blast in a road car because the roads are permanently busy and the speed limit is 20mph. 'You have a month of that, your brain goes to sleep,' complains Graham. The best he can manage to wake it up again is the occasional afternoon's testing at Curborough.

In the circumstances, he is well pleased with the steady downward progression of his times: 33, 32, 29.95, 28 dead. Will he be in the 27s by the end of the day? 'Probably.' But he is worried

Championship Top Tens after Round 7		
RAC		
1	Roger Moran	51
2	Patrick Wood	50
3	Roy Lane	47
4	Tim Mason	39
5	Bill Bristow	24
6	George Ritchie	24
7	Simon Durling	23
8	David Grace	15
9	Tim Barrington	14
10	Tom Brown	12
Leaders		
1	Phil Cooke	51
2	Justin Fletcher	49
3	Mark Waldron	48
4	Martin Groves	44
5	Tony Lambert	43
6	Tom New	41
7	Andrew Russell	34
=8	Mark Lawrence	33
=8	Jim Robinson	33
10	Alan Thompson	30

Sandra Tomlin blasts off.

CHAPTER 8

A helping hand.

that a bad second run could see him squeezed out of the Top 12.

Shortly after this conversation it becomes clear that Graham is not going to get a second run at all, as an oil pressure problem has developed. Will he make the run off?

The answer is yes, comfortably, as his 28.00 is good enough for sixth fastest. However, it is by no means certain that he can get the Pilbeam fixed in time to take advantage of it.

The crowd milling around the start line disperses as the racing cars complete their second runs and the classic cars come to the paddock exit. But I hang around, because I have a particularly soft spot for the Sports Racing & Racing Cars which are coming next, particularly for Richard Drewett's Lotus 30, which makes me go positively wobbly at the knees. One of Colin Chapman's less successful designs, it uses a mid-mounted V8 and was not well liked in its heyday. But with its low, low front, big bulbous wings and the most menacing idle I've ever heard, it looks and sounds magnificent. Moreover, this example is a former class record holder at Shelsley. If this is failure, I'll do without success.

A special class for Ferraris follows, after which it is time for the Top 12 run off.

Graham's problem turns out to be nothing more than an oil pipe routed too near the exhaust, so we have a full house for the climax of the day's proceedings.

As the run-offs proceed, times tumble and several drivers enter solid 27 second runs. Only two, however, get into the 26s; Roy Lane on 26.31 and Roger Moran on 26.97. Patrick Wood, who runs last by virtue of what had previously been the best run of the day (26.49) cannot repeat the trick when it matters and drops to fourth on 27.33 behind David Grace's 27.08. Graham is well in the hunt with 27.68.

Come the second runs, David Grace improves slightly to 27.03 but it's not enough to improve his placing. Roy still leads and Patrick, who has the privilege of taking the last Top 12 run of the day, is the only man who can beat him.

Fingers are firmly crossed in the Steel King camp as Patrick thrusts the Target Pilbeam up the hill. It's a quick one, an improvement — but it's not enough: 27.11 still leaves him fourth. The old master has notched up another win.

Just for once, however, the meeting does not end with the Top 12. Although there is not much crossover between British hillclimbing and its Continental counterpart, what little there has ever been has been centred on Shelsley, and so it is today. This meeting is a round of the FIA International Series, and Luxembourg and Belgium hillclimb champion Christian Hauser is here as a result.

Incorporated within the class runs, the FIA entrants have already taken their climbs, but the distinguished Shelsley visitor takes one final demonstration run in his nicely turned out Martini Mk69 which looks rather wider than a typical British hillclimb car. He's already shown why he became a champion by taking the reclassified 2500cc class, albeit not by much. His best was 28.51, just enough to beat the 28.63 of West Countryman Richard Fry.

Now it has to be said that the FIA International Series does not exactly set the British public alight. In fact most people, both inside and outside the paddock, were probably not even aware that the results counted towards the series — the commentators and programme did not exactly make a fuss about it.

However, sometimes the symbolism is as important as the substance. To see a talented foreign driver giving his best on Britain's most historic and internationally minded hill somehow seems an appropriate end to a fascinating day.

Top right: the site layout is distinctly haphazard, but it works. And like so many things which are unplanned, it has atmosphere.

Roy relaxes with John Chalmers in the pits. He calls Shelsley's paddock 'the finest place in British hillclimbing.'

71

LIVING WITH SPEED

'Takes no prisoners, this place'

Doune

Doune

Location
on the outskirts of the town of the same name on the A84 north west of Stirling.

Organising club
Lothian Car Club (Edinburgh) Ltd, c/o Miss S Fenwick, 16 Polton, Loanhead, Midlothian EH20 9BZ. Tel 0131 440 4061/0131 225 2532.

Length 1477 yards.

Outright hill record at start of 15.6.96 meeting
Overall: Andy Priaulx, 37.99sec.

KEY
Track shading indicates gear ratio...
- White striped is first gear
- Tints are intermediates (darker tone equals higher gear)
- Black is top gear

Because ratios and patterns in racing gearboxes can be altered at will, a particular shading on one map does not indicate the same ratio as on another: shading is relative only to that particular venue.

V indicates good viewing area

0 — 100yd

Track features: Meadow, Junction, East Brae, The Esses, Tunnel, The Gate, Oak Tree, FINISH, Top Paddock, START, Bottom Paddock

Roy's Run

'A very demanding hill where you have to keep your momentum flowing all the time. This year we worked hard on the car the week before Doune and the Pilbeam felt ever so good.

'Off the line, change up before the first corner (some drivers do it afterwards but I prefer to be set up beforehand), hold second (a 115mph gear) all the way to top of East Brae, at top of East Brae change across the box to 'third' (a 95mph gear). Charge through the Esses, hard and aggressively, hope you miss everything in between, get round the last corner carrying as much momentum as possible, and change up into 'fourth' (110mph gear) for the finishing line.'

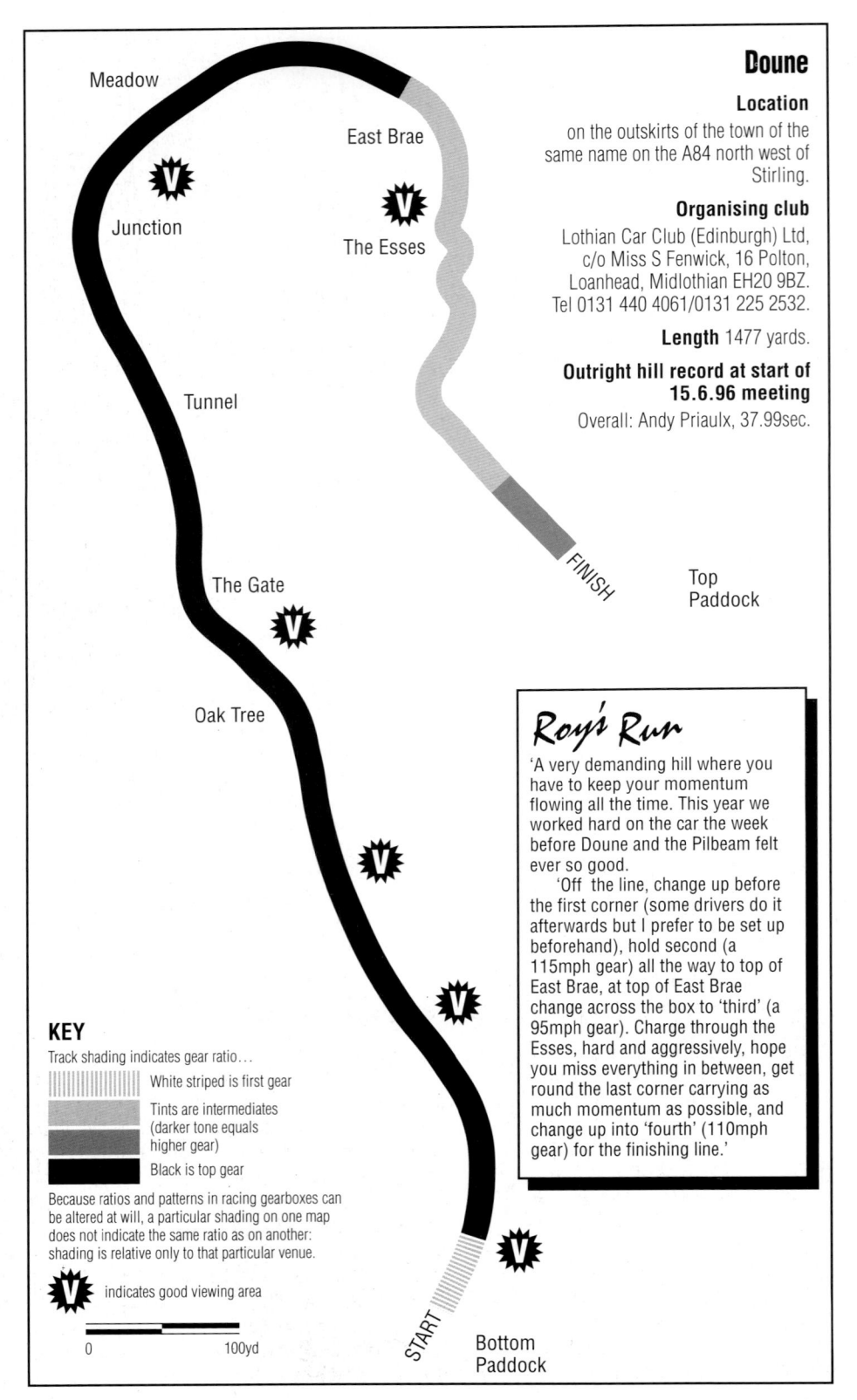

It may be a matter of debate whether Shelsley Walsh or Prescott is the spiritual home of English hillclimbing, but there is no such debate in Scotland. One hill stands head and shoulders above the others in prestige and facilities — Doune, near Stirling.

Its reputation is helped enormously by the fact that it was purpose-built specifically for the sport, and by the fact that a motor museum shares the same estate, making it economic to build a restaurant which must be the envy of every other climb in Britain.

Nowhere else in the country can you eat lunch surrounded on three sides by a racing car paddock and on the fourth by a splendid collection of motoring nostalgia (to which, incidentally, all competitors get free entrance). There's nothing wrong with the food, but if you like fine motor cars, and in particular *quick* motor cars, you'd patronise the place even if there were.

Back in 1967 none of this existed. There was just a small bungalow at the base of a hill, a cart track leading up from it and a landowner who loved cars and was worried about the state of Scottish hillclimbing. That landowner was Lord Doune, now the Earl of Moray.

Bo'ness hillclimb was about to be lost to housing development while Rest and Be Thankful, whose pedigree was very nearly as long as Shelsley's, was having increasing difficulty satisfying safety regulations — indeed, by the end of 1970 it had seen its last hillclimb, although it is still occasionally used as a rally stage.

Lord Doune invited the then secretary of the Lothian Car Club, Norman Thompson, to assess the feasibility of opening a new climb on the Doune estate.

Together they drove gingerly up the track, a track 'so narrow that the brambles were sweeping the doors of Lord Doune's Rover 2000', recalls current Clerk of the Course Frazer Madder. It was going to need a lot of work but yes, they decided, it did have potential.

Two things were essential apart from the obvious necessity of proper surfacing: widening, and a new extension to make a course of worthwhile length.

72

CHAPTER 9

Ken Snailham exits the Gate and accelerates into Tunnel.

Long time competitor Ray Fielding was called in to handle the design and he produced what is now acknowledged to be one of the most challenging courses anywhere in the British Isles.

The end of the old track was dubbed Junction and was extended through open meadow up the steep climb of East Brae which at one point has the steepest gradient of any British hillclimb (1 in 3). At the top of East Brae is a ninety right, followed by a series of Esses through woodland which lead to a finishing straight and the top paddock. Despite roughly doubling the length of the track, the extension involved relatively little disruption of the estate: three trees were felled in the Esses, and that was about it.

When Sir Nicholas Williamson, later to become a two-times British champion, took his Brabham BT21C to the win at the newly surfaced track's opening event in 1968, the venue was just that, a track. There were no buildings of any kind in bottom paddock. The museum came later, when someone suggested that it would be nice if his Lordship's collection of old cars were put on public display.

This is one course which you really have to walk to appreciate properly. The first corner, a left hander, comes up just a few metres from the start and takes drivers into an intimidatingly narrow straight lined with Armco both sides. Forget any talk of choosing a racing line; on the lower part of Doune, if you aren't scraping the barrier, you've got the right line. And this has been widened, remember.

Nevertheless, this is a flat out

73

LIVING WITH SPEED

Ford Fiesta
Jim King, Modified Saloon Cars 1400-2000cc

Car on the Hill

Saloon car classes have always been well supported in Scotland, partly because of the weather. At a wet meeting a saloon is the most comfortable place to be, and Scotland has more than its fair share of wet meetings.

If there is such a thing as a typical modest-budget hillclimb saloon, Jim King's Fiesta XR2 is probably it. A Mk1 model, with the crossflow rather than the CVH engine, it is in Jim's words 'quite well developed.' Power is now up to 155bhp courtesy of a different head and Weber 45s among other things, and transmission is through a four-speed straight-cut box. A five-speeder is no use on the hills: apart from first at the start, the whole of Doune (for instance) is tackled in second and third.

This 36 year-old garage proprietor from Inverurie has been competing 'on and off for about six years'. The Fiesta is totally unsponsored except for one local jeweller who has plastered the car with stickers. Does he pay a lot for the privilege?

'Nae very well, but he thinks he does!' The money helps with petrol and entry fees though, which are £60 here.

Jim is by no means new to the car but nevertheless he is feeling his way today because he's just uprated it from road saloon to modified saloon. All the trim's been stripped out, the glass has been replaced with perspex and everything possible has been lightened. 'Feels like a racer now' he says. 'Turns in a lot better.'

The biggest change of course has been the change to slicks. This is the car's first meeting on racing rubber and Jim's 'learning the car all the time. The car's good but there's a lot of differences from what it used to be. Had my fair share of problems today'. His aim is to compete in all five of the hills which make up the Scottish Championship: Forrestburn, Durris, Fintray, Rumster and Doune.

Does he have aspirations beyond saloons? Jim is noncommittal: 'I would like to one day, whether we manage to succeed in getting as far as that I don't know.'

'straight' (actually with a right-hand curve on it), on which the big cars touch 100mph before easing off for a left-hand bend round Oak Tree. Although the drivers don't have time to notice, a few trees in full blossom overhang the track, their beautiful white flowers scattered over the tarmac by the airflow over the cars. Another short armco 'tunnel' follows before the right hander at Garden Gate where the road, amazingly enough, gets even narrower.

Like the Gate at Wiscombe, Garden Gate is not as sharp as it looks and Roy reckons it is one of the most critical corners on the track. Take your instincts' advice and you will lose too much momentum and forfeit any chance of a good time. Overdo it and you'll end up going straight on through the gate — assuming one of the very substantial gateposts doesn't stop you first. If you're going to go off at Garden Gate, it's important to do it *accurately*, so that you slot neatly between the posts. If you get through but are still crossed up, more armco lurks further up, a stretch of barrier that bears multicoloured evidence of many a misjudgement.

The next section climbs steeply through dense woodland, so dense that it is actually known as Tunnel. With trees arching overhead and stone walls on either side, it is a pretty intimidating place to drive, made more so by the gentle left hander on the way in. This has a hump which elevates you just long enough to get you nicely out of shape in time for the stone walls. Patrick Wood has clocked 113mph towards the end of this section, at which point the stone walls have given way to trees. The ones on the left are well within hitting distance and although they have some tyres around them the provision looks rather an afterthought: the lie of the land is such that any car leaving the track would probably ride over them and hit the trunk higher up.

White countdown markers across the tarmac give drivers a reference point for braking distances, a huge help on a course as demanding as this.

At the end of Tunnel is Junction — 'another very tricky corner', says Roy, where various tyre marks bear witness to the expeditions of the last 36 hours. Junction is taken at 80-90mph by the fastest cars and marks the start of the 'new' section, as cars emerge into open fields, known simply as Meadow. Now there is no shortage of run off areas: the track sweeps across the grassland via a right hander and then another long right which contains several apexes.

Meadow is relatively flat except for a dip at the end, which is followed abruptly by East Brae, a short but extremely steep climb topped with what Roy calls 'a real severe right hander, people don't realise how severe it is'. To plunge into the dip on full throttle with such a steep climb looming up ahead is to launch yourself at the horizon, it must be the closest thing to riding a rollercoaster this side of Blackpool. Gouge marks at the bottom of the dip bear testament to the ferocity of the gradient change. And once you start the climb, the bend at the top becomes completely impossible to see.

From East Brae the track twists through another wooded area, known with startling originality as the Esses, before turning left on to the finishing straight. As you leave the Esses the trees open out, giving a fabulous view of the valley below — if you have time to look, which is unlikely as 120mph can be achieved over the finish line given the right machinery. Just as you are winding down from the drive, you come across a timing board, so you know your time even before you've turned into the holding paddock.

Roy has had his moments of glory at Doune, but not many — it is 19 years since he won here. He has never found it an easy course and is acutely aware that today could end the run of success which has given him four wins from six

CHAPTER 9

rounds entered this year. 'It's a hill that needs lots of concentration, where you've got to carry your momentum and you mustn't brake too hard,' he summarises. 'You've got to keep the car flowing all the time. It's very nerve-wracking.'

Patrick Wood is more forthright. 'It's terrifying. Every bend is blind. When you're driving the lower part, it feels as though there are hydraulic rams on each side of the track which are speed sensitive, so the faster you go, the more they push the armco out.'

The fear is that you'll end up bouncing back and forth between them, but in that respect Patrick reckons the barriers do a good job. 'It's actually safer than you think, because if you do hit the rear corner, say, on a barrier, you might lose that wheel — which I've done — and then the thing just bounces along between the barriers for quite a long way, whilst you try and stop it. But you don't actually hit something hard.' Later in the day we were to see the proof of that statement…

As for Tunnel, 'that is just scary'. He recommends it as a good place to spectate but has no intention of joining the crowd between runs. 'If I went and watched, I just wouldn't do it.'

A comment from longtime Scottish competitor Martin Pieraccini, currently Reynard mounted, sums up most drivers' opinions. 'It takes no prisoners, this place', he says succinctly, 'it really bites back'.

Today the competitors at least have the weather on their side. It's glorious: the few wisps of early morning mist in the valleys have long been burned away by a hot midsummer sun and with no prospect of any cloud to dampen the holiday atmosphere, it's shirtsleeves and watch out for sunburn.

The organisers, conscious that most drivers will have travelled a long way to compete, make a point of starting early to give everyone value for money. By the time I settle on the start line to watch, at 10am, two batches of cars have already climbed — quite an achievement in view of the fact that the previous night's ceilidh didn't end till 12:45am. 'They're mad people up here', smiles Roy.

There doesn't seem to be much grip off the line today, though no doubt that will improve as rubber is laid down during the day. Part of the problem is Doune's paddock, which unlike most others on the hillclimb circus is neither tarmac nor grass but gravel, dusty gravel at that. Though the top paddock has been surfaced recently, the bottom one has yet to receive the treatment.

The Steel King team, in common with other seasoned Doune competitors,

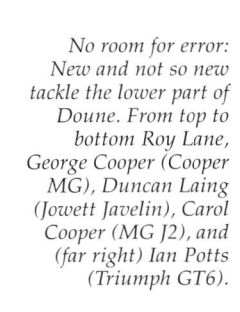

No room for error: New and not so new tackle the lower part of Doune. From top to bottom Roy Lane, George Cooper (Cooper MG), Duncan Laing (Jowett Javelin), Carol Cooper (MG J2), and (far right) Ian Potts (Triumph GT6).

75

LIVING WITH SPEED

come armed with cloths to clean down the front tyres on the length of track behind the warm up area, having learned the hard way that the horsehair glove-brushes they normally use are not enough to give you a good start at this venue. Of such attention to detail are FTDs posted and championships won.

Some competitors find traction however. Jedi-mounted Phil Cooke has obviously got the message, making a noticeably more effective attempt at warming up his tyres and getting the dust off them than most other competitors.

Paul Parker too, fairly rockets off the line in the big Royale with very little wheelspin. It all goes wrong higher up, however, leaving him with a 70.7 practice time and a lot still to do.

Graeme Wight Jnr makes no mistake, pouring on the power so ruthlessly that the whole car shimmies off the start line, taking him on to a 41.31 practice. If he keeps that up he'll be in the top 12 at the end of the day, a remarkable effort in a 1600-engined Pilbeam.

Richard Brown too makes a good start, tyres smoking nicely on the V8 Ralt he shares with David Grace. But there's trouble ahead for son Tom in the smaller Ralt RH430: a rear suspension component fails and the car ricochets back and forth off the armco, coming to rest with

What a difference the sun makes.

Above, Westfield driver Olly Ross chats in the paddock queue.

Left, in temperatures like these, it's better to watch other people do the work.

76

CHAPTER 9

Mind your back! Foreground, a preoccupied marshal, background, the Brown/Grace Ralt in action.

only one corner of the car intact, the front nearside. It's a sorry mess that is towed back down the hill to be trailered home, but Patrick Wood was right: the driver is completely unhurt.

Just a few metres from all this action is a bungalow, the same bungalow which was at the base of the cart track back in 1967. Now it is right on the start line, making for a truly bizarre contrast.

On one side of the wrought-iron front gate is a picture straight from a quiet suburb; a neat retirement home with a colourful garden, a pond, even a gnome or two. And to complete the picture of contentment, an old lady, sitting on a bench in her front garden, enjoying the summer sunshine while reading a book under a sun umbrella. There's a bird table next to her, though there's no chance of a bird coming within half a mile with all this row on the other side of the gate. It's so close that if she walked through she'd have to be careful not to disrupt the timing beam.

At one stage she puts her book down and leans nonchalantly over the gate to watch the Pilbeams burning rubber inches from her begonias, but otherwise she sits there practically all day, the hubbub and excitement passing her by, an island of tranquillity in an ocean of noise.

I wander up to the Meadow as Westfield-mounted Olly Ross breaks the Road Sports Over 1500 record with 48.06 on his first run. His joy lasts approximately one and a half minutes, about the time which elapses before the next runner, John Bruce, completes his climb. John, the record holder on 48.21 until a few seconds ago, is obviously displeased at losing it and is really fired up, driving right on the edge at Tunnel and storming through to a stunning 47.77. Class winner here in April, fastest at Fintray hillclimb near Aberdeen last weekend, he clearly remains the man to beat.

Equally committed but driving slightly *over* the edge is the next car up, a MkII Escort piloted by Alan Gunn in Road Saloon Cars over 1800. At Junction he bounces off the fencing on the left and then in the words of the commentator 'tries the grass on the outside, doesn't like it, tries the grass on the inside, doesn't like that much either, gets back on to the road. That's going to make a total porridge of that first climb'. Indeed it does: 92.24 seconds is not going to win anything, yet later in the day his second class run breaks the record on 50.52 (only to lose it within seconds to Gordon McIntyre's 2300 Chevette on 50.42).

What was the difference between Alan's runs? Maybe a flick of the wrist, a brake pedal touched a fraction of a second earlier or a tad harder, a gearchange rammed through quicker. In hillclimbing, the subtlest things can turn disaster into success — and vice versa.

The topography at Doune is such that off-road excursions often result in damaged fences, so a fencing contractor is as essential as an RAC Steward to the proper conduct of the meeting. As Torwood Fencing's Transit arrives and the hammering and levering begins, spectators at the Meadow look on lazily, all happy that the fencers are doing the work and they're not. The rescue van, the doctor with his trusty Subaru Legacy, the clerk of the course with his Honda Civic, all are redundant for a while. Children play, adults sunbathe, the snack bar does a roaring trade. One man judges he's in for a long wait and settles into the *Sunday Times*.

It isn't that long a wait, probably about 20 minutes, but it feels far lengthier, especially to the commentator. Sitting up at the Esses in what can only be described as a tree house, he struggles manfully to cope with the situation every commentator dreads — namely a total lack of action — and to put it bluntly, fails.

When the action recommences it proves worth the wait, for the records keep tumbling. On his first visit to the hill, Tim Coventry in the thunderous Westfield SEight breaks the Modified Production Over 2000 record in style, setting a 45.55 that neither Mark Waldron nor Tony Lambert can get near, though they continue to have their private duel, setting near identical times which as so often this season pan out in Mark's favour.

In the well supported Clubman's class, Alistair Naismith's diff seizes on the line and the Mallock Mk20/24B is towed back to the paddock. 'He's got a choice,' explains the commentator. 'He either gets his hands dirty or he goes home. But knowing how hillclimbing operates these days, by the time that car gets to its position in the paddock there will probably already be a bevy of people ready to offer help, support, bits… to get the car going again. That's the wonderful thing about hillclimbing. If something goes wrong, the other competitors are the first people to rally round to help you, even the people who will almost certainly come second to you if you manage to get the car going.'

I doubt if a single person in the pad-

77

LIVING WITH SPEED

Stuart Skeldon, Midas Gold.

dock would disagree with that sentiment.

Lunchtime comes and I admire the lovely metallic crimson and silver paint job on Ken Snailham's Pilbeam MP62, smile at the 'Kermit' insignia painted on John and Vaila McAllister's Westfield SPi (even though the green is too blueish to be regarded as a proper froggy hue), revel in the menacing idle of Alastair Crawford's V8 MGB.

I also track down George Tatham and ask him about his monster McLaren. It looks like an ex-Can Am car, and it is indeed a Can Am design, but this example has never been anywhere near Riverside Raceway. In fact it has spent practically its whole life in sprints and hillclimbs, having been built originally for Phil Scragg by the Trojan company, to whom McLaren subcontracted much of its construction at that time (and whose other claims to fame included the UK agency for Iso and construction of the German Heinkel bubblecar under licence).

Under the skin it's an M12C of basically Can Am specification, but with a smaller radiator as befits its short-distance role and with a skin from an earlier McLaren, an M6. 'The M12C had a much wider body,' explains George, 'but he didn't want the wide body because he was going to use it for sprints and hillclimbs, so he had the earlier M6 body put on, hence these things on the side.'

'These things' are riveted-on wheelarch extensions, made to legalise the M21C-width rubber.

It's typical of George's approach that he has never attempted to tidy up this somewhat Heath Robinson addition. Roy Lane, whom he has known for 'donkeys' years' and is incidentally exactly the same age, looks after the mechanics of the car but George has resisted every attempt by Roy and others to change its appearance, inside or out. The car is what it is, and it is what it has always been. Even a respray is *verboten*.

Certainly there's no pressing need to tune the engine. George reckons that the mighty 7.2 litre Chevvy puts out around 550bhp with a Holley carburettor. It's pretty hard to put that kind of power down on a technical course like Doune, which is one reason why the engine still has most of its original internals, even if the original aluminium block has long since been changed for a cast iron example.

It's unique in another respect, in that it's the only M21B with a left-hand gearchange. The model was normally built with a right-hand gearchange because the Hewland box comes out on that side. 'But Phil Scragg would not drive anything but a left-hand gearchange' and was prepared to live with a tortuous linkage to achieve it.

'Is it a bit of a handful?' I ask, bearing in mind that this must surely be the biggest engine in hillclimbing? George thinks for a moment and then simply says 'yes. Though I haven't driven it for four years,' he adds quickly. He did compete regularly for the previous 16, however, making this trout farmer from Malton only the second owner of the car.

Despite his sassenach origins, he is very much at home in Scotland and reckons he is the only current competitor who drove at Bo'ness. His competition career started with an Ace Bristol, after which he acquired the first Lister Jaguar ever built, from a most unlikely source — a trombone player in Mantovani's orchestra. He soon dropped in a works-tuned Jaguar D-Type engine which came certified as good for 283bhp, though the resulting package had its shortcomings.

'God it was quick in a straight line, but it was evil handling.'

From that day to this he has been in love with big engines and reckons 'it's 30 years since I've driven anything under 3.5 litres. Too many gearchanges! I make one here and two at Shelsley.'

That Lister was replaced by a much younger one, one of the last made. Coincidentally, this too was bought from Phil Scragg, after he had replaced the original Jaguar engine with a Chevrolet. It introduced George to competing in American V8s and he has remained faithful to the concept ever since, following it with a prototype Brabham BT17 sportsracing car before acquiring his present McLaren.

His reminiscences are interrupted by an announcement over the tannoy that Roy has just managed 38.98 on his first run, only 0.16 away from the class record. Will this one go too before the day is out? 'It's very fast today, that's why there's been so many offs' opines George. The atmosphere, the setting, the weather, have all gelled together so well that everyone feels inclined to have a go.

For all his affection for Scotland, this most engaging character does not count Doune as his favourite hill: that honour goes to Shelsley. With the Lister Chevrolet he held one of the classic records there for some seven years, an achievement with which he was 'thrilled to bits'.

CHAPTER 9

He also likes Bouley Bay very much, although it is many years since he made the trip to the Channel Islands — 'I got married instead' he explains apologetically. His wife Lou, an actress, is crewing for him today.

The first part of the afternoon's competition is devoted to saloons, and after the second runs, when the pressure is off, I seek out Chevette driver Gordon MacIntyre. I'd bumped into him in the car park earlier (metaphorically that is) and am curious to learn more about a car now little seen in any form of competition.

Gordon has got rather out of the habit of hillclimbing, preferring to sprint instead. His reasons have nothing to do with the sport itself and everything to do with the regulations: until this season, Scottish hillclimbing rules demanded that cars in the roadgoing class be driven to the event, a stipulation which did not apply in sprints.

'It was kind of ridiculous,' he observes. 'You're allowed to run a full-race engine and then they expect these guys from Wick to drive several hundred miles down here every weekend. It doesn't make a lot of sense — if you wrap it, what do you do?'

Gordon is a mechanical engineering lecturer at a college in Hamilton where one of the courses is — surprise, surprise — a degree in automotive engineering. Motorsport, he explains with a chuckle, has generated 'quite a few ideas for student projects!'

The Scottish Hillclimb Championship runs classes for road saloons 'which tend to be very well populated. On a nice sunny day like this you look at the single seaters or anything without a roof and you think "yeah, I'm fed up sweltering in this cockpit" but usually it rains. Also, I'm fairly substantial so I'm better running with something that's that much heavier.' Nevertheless he'd like to try a single-seater 'to see what they're like.'

His interest in motorsport started with marshalling on forest rallies and at races. Soon he thought 'Why couldn't I do that?' and started racing, sprinting and hillclimbing himself. However, he

Man on the Hill

Martin Pieraccini

Study the history of hillclimbing and you keep coming across examples of remarkable personal achievement, of people with disabilities which would make many people think twice about driving at all, let alone in competition.

Martin Pieraccini knows all about what it's like to readjust your life to a new and permanently changed physical reality. Several years ago he lost an eye in a shooting accident ('I used to shoot pheasants in the winter') and had to ask himself where that left his motorsport career.

He'd started off on the hills in Imps, but when he got back into a saloon he had trouble seeing out of the car; the pillars just kept getting in the way. Rather than give up, he decided that his future lay with an open car. He bought himself a small racing car, a Delta, and in his own words 'never looked back.'

'It was great for me because I could see my wheels, I could put the car virtually where I wanted. I had some really good results with that Delta.' He kept it for a couple of years, during which time he managed a record 44.52 here at Doune, and then decided to go 1600.

His choice of car was an unusual one at the time, an ex-F3 Ralt RT30. It was one of the first stiffly suspended F3 cars on the hills 'and a lot of people said it wouldn't work, but we persevered and we got some results. Then I had a bad accident in that, sold the wreck to Kenny, he built the car up and won the Scottish Championship with it.'

'Kenny' is longtime Scottish hillclimber Kenny Allen, with whom Martin now double drives. Currently the pair are campaigning another F3 car, a Reynard 873H, bought as a rolling chassis some four years ago and extensively reworked since. A John Beattie-prepared 1600 BDA has gone in, the pods have come off, the wings have been changed and there are bigger wheels on the back. Now Martin reckons the car is 'getting better all the time. I like it fine.'

But in view of its circuit origins, has it got enough suspension movement? 'It's got *no* movement!' He acknowledges that it's not an easy car to drive.

The Reynard proudly displays an Italian flag, in recognition of Martin's Italian descent, although there's nothing remotely Latin about his sandy hair or Inverness accent.

He makes light of his disability but admits he has had to adjust his driving style. 'You can't accurately judge a corner, you've got to drive it as you're in it. They used to call me the last of the late brakers, but… you're asking a guy with one eye where he brakes? The answer is — too late!'

Does he think the loss of an eye has driven him on, made him faster now than before the accident? 'I don't know, I'd probably frighten myself if I had two eyes!'

Martin in action at the June Doune meeting — easy to spot, as his helmet is painted in Italian national colours.

found racing very expensive, particularly as 'they keep changing the rules and it makes my car illegal.' This year, for instance, he can't race because his adjustable pedal box has been outlawed.

Speed events — hillclimbs and sprints — he finds much more flexible. Gearboxes and axles do not have to be original and 'you can pretty well do anything you like with suspension. The engine's got to remain more or less the same capacity, you're allowed an overbore but you're not allowed to stroke it.' The interior trim is also supposed to remain in the car, though judging by some of the distinctly non-luxurious interiors in the paddock, this particular regulation is fairly liberally interpreted. 'The modifications allowed here are pretty lax really.'

Despite this liberality, he reckons money is less critical in the road-car classes than with more exotic machinery. 'My car's probably not the most expensive in the road car classes but it is one of the quickest.' He could change the gearbox and axle, but finds the car competitive with the originals, albeit aided by different final drive ratio and a limited slip diff. And today he has proved his point by winning his class in a new record time of 50.42.

Up in the 1600cc racing class, things have gone exactly as Martin Pieraccini predicted that morning. 'I reckon Kenny and young Graham will be chasing the record today', the Reynard driver had commented after he'd found himself third behind co-driver Kenny Allen and Graeme Wight Jnr's Pilbeam MP62. And that's how they finished, both the first two beating the old 40.98 record comfortably, with bests of 40.52 and 40.44 respectively.

In fact Kenny's and Graeme's times in 1600 cars are both good enough for Top 12 places, a remarkable demonstration of the difficulty which the big cars have in getting the power down at Doune. It's also a demonstration of the skill and determination of Graeme Jnr, who has to drive in a brace as a result of breaking his back in an Imp several years ago. (Graeme Snr, incidentally, co-drives the Pilbeam.)

Geoff Kershaw's 4WD Sierra joined a big selection of saloons on Scotland's premier hill.

Kenny's delight is short-lived, an oil leak preventing him taking his place in the Top 12, but Graeme is in scintillating form, posting the fastest ever 1600 climb at 40.08 seconds, good enough for eighth overall. One place ahead is Simon Frost who notches up best 2 litre performance on 39.74, leaving the top six to the big guns. The other fancied 2 litre runner, Justin Fletcher, is unable to match Simon, brushing a barrier on the first run and producing a steady 40.61 on his second.

Also keeping the fencers busy is Tim Barrington, who grazes the armco on the first bend in an unsuccessful attempt to get into the top ten and earn championship points. At this rate the Transit will get more runs up Doune than any of the competitors.

Championship Top Tens after Round 8

	RAC			Leaders	
1	Roger Moran	59	1	Phil Cooke	57
2	Roy Lane	57	2	Justin Fletcher	55
3	Patrick Wood	55	3	Mark Waldron	54
4	Tim Mason	45	4	Tom New	50
5	George Ritchie	33	5	Tony Lambert	47
6	Bill Bristow	24	6	Martin Groves	44
7	Simon Durling	23	7	Andrew Russell	38
8	David Grace	22	8	Mark Lawrence	37
9	Tim Barrington	14	9	Jim Robinson	33
10	Richard Brown	13	10	Alan Thompson	30

But two men, the only two under 39 seconds, are rising above the drama, intent instead on playing out their own bit of theatre. Those two are Roy Lane, whose times have been the ones to beat all weekend, and former Scottish Champion George Ritchie, a local man who knows the hill well.

Roy has the luxury of running last and manages a fine 38.58 on his first run, giving the rest of the competitors everything to do. George gives his all to thrust the orange MP72 up in 38.61 but it is not enough. Everyone else is around half a second behind, best of the rest being George's co-driver Roger Moran on 39.04.

So by the time Roy takes his second run it's all over. Nevertheless he starts in a businesslike manner, intent on using this 'free' run to try out some softer compound tyres, but half way up he backs off and produces a time around a second down, anxious not to let some last minute error ruin a memorable day. And after nearly two decades without a win at Doune, who can blame him?

As Roy rolls back into the paddock there is more unalloyed happiness on his face than I have ever seen before. Any good driver can go well at his favourite venues; the mark of a champion is to chalk up victories at the others, and today Roy has looked like a champion. Doune has elevated him from a driver who is having a good season to the title favourite. He still trails Roger Moran by a couple of points, but Roger has one more score in his tally and this will count against him later in the season when drivers start discarding scores under the 'ten best to count' system.

The Steel King team get packed up, ready to go their separate ways: Roy and Bett in the motorhome for a few days holiday in the Highlands, the rest of the crew back to Warwick.

Within an hour the awards ceremony brings to an end a brilliant day's sport, in which no less than eight records have fallen. Not long afterwards the Lane motorhome is rolling north, its driver no doubt reflecting on what must surely be one of the most satisfying wins of his long career.

CHAPTER 10

'A big rain cloud is clearly visible from the paddock'

Harewood

Harewood is a topsy turvy sort of place. At most hills you assemble at the bottom, make your climb and then wait in a top paddock to come back down, but at this Yorkshire venue the waiting arrangements are completely reversed. The main paddock is at the top of the hill with the cars being taken down in batches to a small starting area.

At least that's how it was until 1992. For that year the course was considerably lengthened to what is now at 1584 yards the longest mainland hill in the British championship. At the same time, a completely new road was built from the paddock to the new start area, creating what on any other hill would be called a return road and solving completely the difficulty which the old arrangements posed for double drivers. The result is a compact course of which a high proportion can be seen from the paddock. When you're sitting on high at Harewood, you've got the best view of any hillclimb course in Britain.

Slap bang in the middle of it all is a working farm — *really* in the middle, with the track running right between the

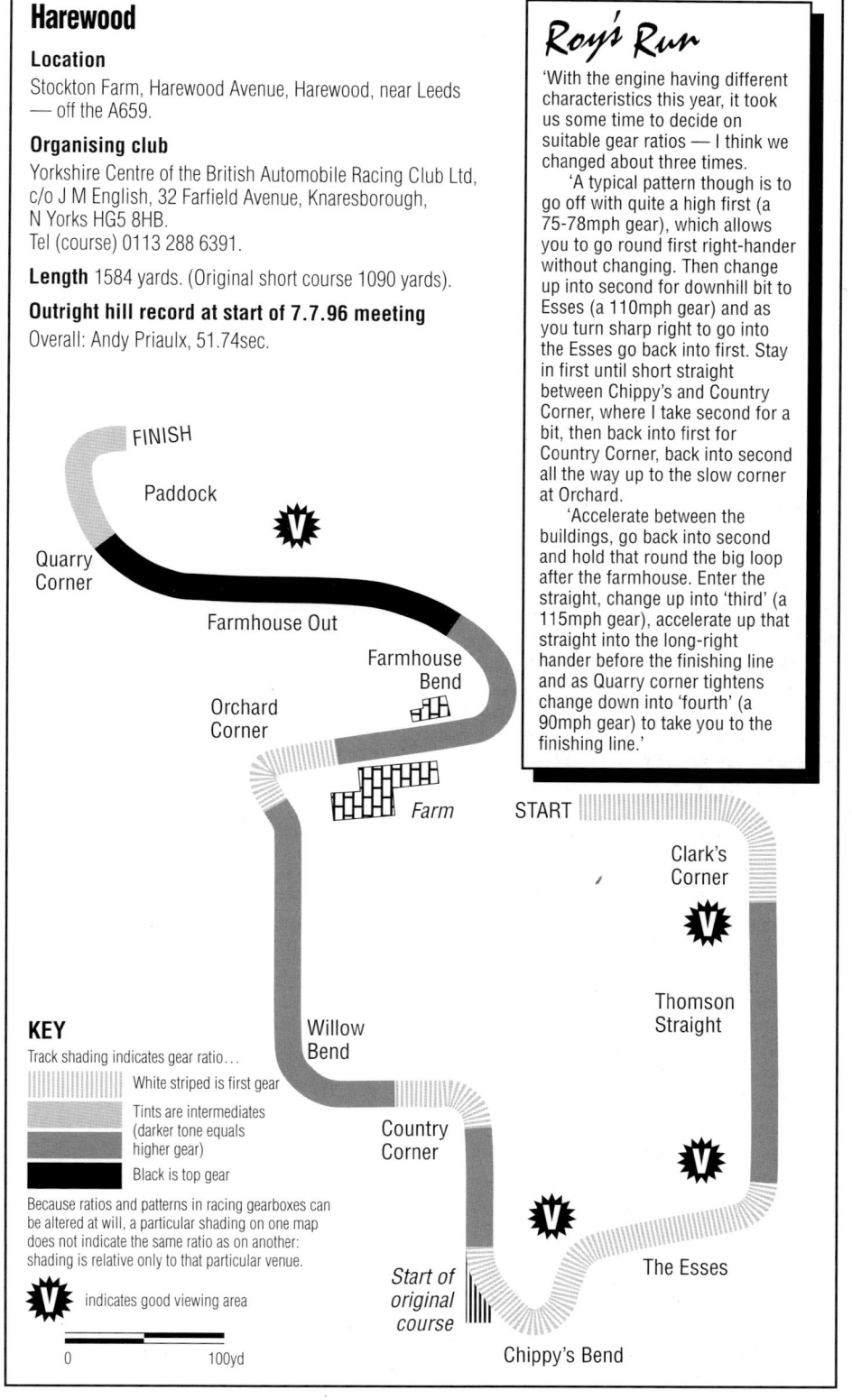

No crowds around the Harewood startline, it's well away from the paddock.

Harewood

Location
Stockton Farm, Harewood Avenue, Harewood, near Leeds — off the A659.

Organising club
Yorkshire Centre of the British Automobile Racing Club Ltd, c/o J M English, 32 Farfield Avenue, Knaresborough, N Yorks HG5 8HB.
Tel (course) 0113 288 6391.

Length 1584 yards. (Original short course 1090 yards).

Outright hill record at start of 7.7.96 meeting
Overall: Andy Priaulx, 51.74sec.

KEY
Track shading indicates gear ratio...
- White striped is first gear
- Tints are intermediates (darker tone equals higher gear)
- Black is top gear

Because ratios and patterns in racing gearboxes can be altered at will, a particular shading on one map does not indicate the same ratio as on another: shading is relative only to that particular venue.

V indicates good viewing area

0 — 100yd

Roy's Run

'With the engine having different characteristics this year, it took us some time to decide on suitable gear ratios — I think we changed about three times.

'A typical pattern though is to go off with quite a high first (a 75-78mph gear), which allows you to go round first right-hander without changing. Then change up into second for downhill bit to Esses (a 110mph gear) and as you turn sharp right to go into the Esses go back into first. Stay in first until short straight between Chippy's and Country Corner, where I take second for a bit, then back into first for Country Corner, back into second all the way up to the slow corner at Orchard.

'Accelerate between the buildings, go back into second and hold that round the big loop after the farmhouse. Enter the straight, change up into 'third' (a 115mph gear), accelerate up that straight into the long-right hander before the finishing line and as Quarry corner tightens change down into 'fourth' (a 90mph gear) to take you to the finishing line.'

FINISH
Paddock
Quarry Corner
Farmhouse Out
Farmhouse Bend
Orchard Corner
Farm
START
Clark's Corner
Thomson Straight
Willow Bend
Country Corner
The Esses
Start of original course
Chippy's Bend

81

buildings. Drivers simply aim for the gap in the stonework and hope that they're on target, which is easier than it sounds as it's halfway along a straight. Overall, Harewood is a pretty safe course, with mainly right-angle or 180° bends and relatively few trees or solid obstacles, plus useful run-off areas at many of the bends, so much so that parts of it feel more like a sprint course than a hillclimb. By far the trickiest hazard is Quarry Corner, a long, tightening right-hander with the finish line right on the exit, after which competitors slow before swinging into the paddock.

The hill dates back to the early '60s, since when it has become a favourite with many drivers, not least Roy Lane, who has won here more times than anybody else.

Its setting in the Yorkshire hills is spectacular but today we will not see it at its best for the weather is distinctly unsummery, with rain clouds scudding overhead and a chilly wind which is keeping temperatures well down — as I know to my cost because I've driven straight from home in a friend's Morgan, *sans* hood. Walking the hill, I tell myself, will put me in just the mood to be warmed up by a bacon butty.

Mentally fortified, I stride off down the 'return road' to the start. In its present form Harewood begins with a short blast into Clark's Corner, named after Simon Clark, the chairman of the British Automobile Racing Club's Yorkshire Centre. This 90° right-hander leads into Thomson Straight, also named after a hillclimbing stalwart, or rather a whole family of them: father Jim and sons Tim and James.

The straight has a little dip in the middle, sharp enough to acquire a fine collection of gouge marks at the bottom, and takes drivers into the inevitable Esses and thence to Chippy's Bend, a 180° right hander. Chippy's, named af-

Sandra, Phil and Oliver. The badge on Sandra's overalls reads 'Best mum in the world', presumably Oliver's way of asking to borrow the Brabham.

Phil Chapman, Sandra Tomlin & Oliver Tomlin

Son and father combinations are quite common in hillclimbing, son and mother less so. To have son, mother and grandfather competing in the same event — which is precisely what is happening today — must surely be unique. But then the Chapmans and Tomlins are a remarkable bunch.

It's grandad who set the pattern. Phil Chapman built a series of four Mercury V8-engined specials — Mercury I, II, III and IV — in the late '40s and early '50s and competed in them in all kinds of motor sport.

Daughter Sandra recalls: 'My father was circuit racing till '54, but he did the odd hillclimb before that.' And when he gave up the circuits 'I just spent my whole life every weekend from March to October going to hillclimbs, which was good fun'.

At that time there were few other kids in the paddock, unlike today, so young Sandra would have had every right to become bored. But she didn't; her interest in the sport was deep rooted even then. 'I can sit and watch every run at a meeting from 9am to 5pm and not go down the hill and not have lunch. I always had my goal — when I'm 17 I'm going to be hillclimbing.'

But just as she was readying herself to climb into the driver's seat, dad upset her carefully laid plans. 'When I was 16 my father gave up hillclimbing, much to my annoyance, sold his car and bought a glider, so I had to go and learn to glide.'

Fortunately for Sandra's racing aspirations, aviation proved to be merely an interlude, albeit one which was to last 10 years. 'My father eventually found that gliding didn't give him the buzz that hillclimbing did. That's why in about 1975 he went and bought a McLaren M10B which he campaigned for about three years.

While Phil was busy substituting gearsticks for joysticks, Sandra was busy getting married ('I met Bill because I drove a Morgan and he couldn't afford one, so someone engineered a blind date for us'). When dad piled up the McLaren at Shelsley and decided to sell, Sandra wanted to buy. 'What are you going to do with it?' Bill gently enquired, wisely pointing out that a McLaren was

82

CHAPTER 10

Tim Thomson trying a little too hard at Country Corner but collecting it neatly. The Thomson family are longtime supporters of hillclimbing through their Guyson company, so much so that a corner at Harewood bears their name.

something of a tall order for someone with no racing experience whatsoever. 'I'll just sit and look at it, OK?'

Bill's counsel prevailed and the car was sold elsewhere in 1979, for just £3500. 'It would be nice to own a really historic racing car', she muses, and to this day she regrets not buying it.

'But anyway I didn't. And then I twiddled my thumbs...'

Four years went by. By this time Phil had bought back the third of his specials and was busily getting reacquainted with his creation on the hills. This gave Sandra, then 33, the chance she'd been looking for ever since her teens: she asked to borrow the Mercury. 'I decided that I was fed up with sitting on the sidelines watching and I was going to do it. So I got a competition licence and did

Family on the Hill

Prescott. It was pretty pathetic but I slowly got better.'

After a couple of years, however, 'I found that my parents were vetoing certain events. It was very good of my dad to let me compete but if they thought that something like Shelsley was a bit too much for me to cope with, he would think of some reason why I couldn't have the car or why something was wrong with it.

'I thought "I'm not having this" so I went out and bought the TVR, so I could go the meetings I wanted to compete at.' But it was a road car, and a rare model at that, a Turbo SE. 'They only made 63 Turbos and only eight of them were Special Equipment with Compomotive Wheels, flared arches, walnut dash and leather interior.

'It really was jolly good of my husband and very indulgent of him to buy it for me but after a bit I realised I wasn't pushing it because I didn't want to bump it. With a track car you can buy a new wishbone and cobble the bodywork together and off you go again, whereas if you pile up a road car it's *very* expensive to put right.'

Initially she only did about four meetings a year, but as the children became older and more independent she gave her passion its head. Soon the lack of a track car became really inhibiting.

'I went up to London and bought a Sports 2000 Tiga, brought it home and my dad vaguely fettled it. I set off on the hills with that and so enjoyed competing in a racing car *on slicks* that I was absolutely bitten and had to go down that avenue.'

Inevitably, she started thinking about more power, but the Tiga wasn't the answer. 'It wasn't worth developing that to take a large engine because you needed to uprate everything, so it was better to sell it. Derek Young had the ex-Malcolm Dungworth Brabham BT38/MP22 for sale so I went to that. In original spec it had a DFV in the back but I bought it with a 2.5 Hart. I was having *very* good fun with it when I bumped it at Shelsley.'

Bump is something of an understatement. 'A rear suspension bolt broke as I went through the speed trap at about 94 mph so I entered Bottom S with no steering and no braking... It was quite funny actually, the front wheel came up to greet me and I thought 'Gosh, it's just like it is on the television'. I thundered into the Bottom S and declutched and thought "Oh bother", and suddenly the marshals came rushing at me, took the steering wheel off and said "Can you get out?". I said 'well, I think I'd better switch off first.'

'Until I got out I didn't realise that I'd taken off the rear corner as well as the front. It really was a hell of a thump but the tub wasn't damaged, I wasn't damaged, I didn't have a bruise or anything. If I could have got in it the next day I would have done. That's what I thought was brilliant about these cars — and we're talking about one built in 1976.

'That concentrated the mind even more and I thought 'if I'm going to do anything now I want an even better racing car, something that's been purpose built for the hills rather than altered. That's when I bought Jackie Harris' MP58 which had won both the Northern Ireland Hillclimb Championship and the British Sprint Championship.'

She acknowledges that none of this expense and commitment would have been possible without the support of her family. Bill has no roots in hillclimbing ('I dragged him into it') but has always been a car nut and owns two Lagondas. 'He's had to learn how to run a Hart engine and build a Hewland gearbox.' If he isn't spannering on the hills for Sandra, she's supporting him at a vintage rally. And if Bill can't get there, 'my son or my father will push the battery trolley and help. It still is very much a family sport.'

Daughter Amy's idea of horsepower has four legs and competes in one-day eventing, but she too can often be found crewing for her mother. 'There's more social life for younger people now,' Sandra comments. 'When I was young there were very few kids around, but my children are friendly with the Harratt children and with Tim Barrington's and Robin Boucher's. I think it's more fun for them than it was for me.'

Son Oliver is quite clear about his aims. At 20 he's just cutting his hillclimbing teeth on Bill's roadgoing Morgan Plus 8, but he fancies a Jedi and has been eyeing up mum's BT38 enviously. The Brabham was repaired after its Shelsley mishap, is still in the family, and at the time of writing was scheduled to appear at Curborough in October with Oliver behind the wheel.

'That will be very much in at the deep end with a 2.5 Hart', observes Sandra. 'But I'm happy to put my son back in the Brabham even though he might not be able to handle it. At least if he has a knock he's going to be fairly safe. I like larger cars; if you have an accident there's a bit more there to look after you.'

Nevertheless she still finds herself holding back a little.

'I'm convinced it's deeply genetic, that men are the warriors and women are not, that men will go to the edge and go over, a woman won't. That's why there's never been a really brilliant woman racing driver.' On a strictly practical level, she's also conscious of the financial burden on the family if she heads for the trees. 'Probably I'd be better off with a Formula Ford which cost a couple of grand. I might be a bit more cavalier and drive it a bit harder. But I like the *power*...'

At 46, with 13 years competition behind her, Sandra would by now surely be dubbed the First Lady of Hillclimbing if Maggie Blankstone hadn't got there first. Her hair may be grey but the freshness of her complexion and the sparkle in her eyes are the best possible advertisement for a life of fresh air, adrenaline — and a 2.8 Hart.

LIVING WITH SPEED

ter longtime Harewood competitor Chippy Stross, boasts an escape road which is actually the old start area; as you pull out of the corner you cross the old start line and join the original track.

The course starts to climb in earnest at this point but flattens out just before the 90° left-hander at Country Corner, ensuring that you are driving completely blind on the approach. Country Corner, I decide, is like a little piece of Doune.

Willow, a 90° right hander, follows in short order and opens into a brief straight with a little left-hand kink at the end, a kink immediately followed by the very sharp Orchard Corner, a right-hander.

Then it's foot flat to the floor and accelerate through the farm, Stockton Farm to be precise, with its stone wall on one side and stone building on the other and dauntingly narrow gap in between. Flashing through here at 100mph must feel very fast indeed.

Farmhouse Bend follows, a long one-eighty with a slight bump on the exit which tends to lift the inside wheel just as you're trying to settle the car for the uphill blast that is Quarry Straight. Finally comes Quarry Corner, the long 180° sweep which tightens up on you and frequently sees cars running out of road only a few metres from the paddock entrance.

Quarry is the venomous sting in Harewood's tail and witnesses far more incidents than any other part of the course.

Arriving back at the cafe for the sustenance I promised myself, I notice that I'm actually at a very good vantage point. The organisers run up to three cars on the hill at once here and from this spot all three can be seen for most of their run. Only the start, which is hidden by farm buildings, and the finish at Quarry Corner are out of sight.

Despite the ominous clouds, the view is splendid: rolling hills leading to a distant escarpment, with fields of vivid yellow rape in the valley. A few trees dot the landscape and the occasional farm building shows as a grey dot, but all in all it must be as unspoiled a piece of England as it is possible to find without going on to the moors or inside a military no-go area.

Colin Stewart: potentially successful day zeroed by gear selection problems.

Tim Coventry storms up in the mighty V8 Westfield.

Over at the Steel King trailer Roy is readying himself for his first practice of the day. Roger Moran is quickest so far with Roy a few tenths behind, but it has been an unpredictable sort of weekend. After his good run yesterday, Roger found himself going slower and slower in subsequent ascents and cannot work out why. The unpredictable weather isn't helping: 'You wouldn't think it was July would you?', says Roy, more by way of a statement than a question.

He has had his own frustrations recently, for his development of the Ralt has become rather expensive of late. The car has broken two crown wheel and pinions this year, the second of which only managed three runs up Prescott before crying 'enough'. It was promptly sent back to Hewland for metallurgical analysis.

I leave the team to its preparations and settle down near the 'return road' to watch final practices, observing how the two-seater drivers take a passenger down to brush the tyres off at the start.

Sandra Tomlin spoils her last practice by missing a gear on Farmhouse Out. Roger Moran is trying very hard to rediscover yesterday's form; he snakes out of Farmhouse Bend determined to get the power down as early as possible and is rewarded with 55.60, by no means the fastest of the weekend but good nonetheless.

Bill Bristow is well in the hunt on 55.67, Graham Priaulx hangs the tail out round Willow Bend on his way to 54.88, Patrick Wood logs a tidy 55 dead. Roy doesn't look like a winner on 56.20 but it's early days yet and the guv'nor is known to like to keep something in reserve.

Most impressive of all, however, is a name which has not appeared on many hillclimb entries this year: Roger Kilty. He's a local man from Boroughbridge in North Yorkshire, a Harewood champion from his days with a Formula Ford 1600

CHAPTER 10

Scrutineering Mike Anthony's Bardon-Turner.

Les Proctor contemplates the hill as dark clouds gather overhead. Car is a Westfield XI.

car (for which, incidentally, there is a special pre-1992 class here today). He knows his way up Harewood blindfold.

Now he is putting that knowledge to good use in the big class, driving the Pilbeam MP47 which took Charles Wardle to the hillclimb championship back in 1988. I notice that Roger's car, now powered by a F1 Cosworth DFR engine, is geared *exactly* right for the course, allowing it to tackle the whole of Quarry Straight in the same gear without either running out of revs at the top or bogging down at the bottom. This forethought is rewarded with a 55.79 practice and a lot of respectful paddock gossip.

It keeps threatening to rain but nothing much comes of it and all the first runs pass off dry. Indeed, conditions are good enough for a few records to tumble, starting with Dennis Crompton in 2 Litre Touring Cars, who takes his BMW 2002 Touring up in 65.26, later bettered to 65.06, nearly half a second improvement on the previous record.

Then in the Unlimited Modified Production Class, Tim Coventry storms up in the mighty V8 Westfield to clock 59.36, eclipsing the previous best of 59.91 by Mike Kerr in a similar car. Behind him there's a dead heat for second, between Porsche-mounted Richard Jones and Ferrari pilot Tony Lambert, both on 61.37, a tie resolved in Tony's favour on the second runs, though neither can catch Tim who goes even faster to record 59.34.

Drivers definitely not having a good day include Colin Stewart, who looks fast and clean in his Elan until he ruins his first run with gearchange problems on Farmhouse Out, and Metro-mounted Matthew Pinder, who is red-flagged on no less than three successive runs through no fault of his own. This is the downside of running several cars simultaneously: the chances of your run being stopped by trouble ahead are that much higher.

Tim Elmer is happy enough though, continuing what is becoming a very impressive season with a new 2-litre Libre record of 59.88 in his Phantom, the first sub-60 time ever recorded in that category. Behind him is another tie, between Vision-mounted Bob Prest and Mallock exponent Roger Thomas on 61.33, this one eventually going Roger's way.

Almost certainly the youngest driver on the hill is 20 year-old Oliver Tomlin, out in his father's roadgoing Morgan Plus 8 for only the third time. Insurance difficulties prevent him familiarising himself with it off the track, so not surprisingly his times are unremarkable. However he's probably setting a record of a different kind just by being here, for his mother Sandra is competing in Unlimited Racing Cars and his grandfather Phil Chapman in Unlimited Sports Libre. How many motorsport events can boast three generations of the same family competing at the same meeting?

Sandra is not the only woman in the big class, for today she is joined by Amanda Furby in the Atol Judd, devel-

85

oped from a Lola F3000 car by Keith Walker. Though having a good year in sprints — she qualified for the run off at the British Sprint Championship at Aintree the previous weekend — her 63.16 puts her out of contention for top honours here, graphic evidence of how different the disciplines of sprinting and hillclimbing are.

Much closer to the honours is Tom Brown, who after comprehensively crunching his Ralt at Doune is having his first championship drive of father Richard's big V8 example. He logs 56.77, good enough for the Top 12 until, ironically, he is pushed out by David Grace in the same car.

Another good effort comes from John Moulds, currently the outright course holder for the two-lap Curborough sprint. Commentator Robin Boucher assures us he is still sorting the bugs out of his new 2.8 Hart-powered MP62 but nevertheless he manages an impressive 55.94.

Barbon winner Tim Mason posts a respectable 56.19, bettering co-driver Ian Stringer's 57.77 but only after twice stalling on the line. He manages to salvage the run both times because the rules state that if the car stops before the back wheels cross the line the run is deemed not to have started. In other words, if you're quick on the brakes when the engine dies, you get another crack. Roy reckons Tim's problems are due to overgearing, but Ian seems to cope well enough in the same car.

Roy himself improves to 55.39, but it's not up to the standard we have come to expect from Steel King this season and there's surprise in Boucher's voice as he reads out the relatively poor time of the man he describes as 'the most prolific winner ever at Harewood'. By way of explanation he adds 'He's just warming up for the run-off one suspects, not giving too much away.'

The drive of the afternoon comes from that man Kilty, as Boucher enthuses: 'He took a brilliant outright win at Three Sisters sprint last weekend, in only his fourth outing in the car. And look at that, he really has got used to the 600hp very quickly, the fastest time of the day so far by a long way, to Roger Kilty, 53.91.'

The second runs start, with the sky looking darker than ever and the wind getting stronger. And sure enough, the first spots of rain are felt just as the single-seater classes get under way. The 500s escape, and a few of the 1100s, but in the larger classes the drivers know they have already produced their best. Some don't even bother to take the start line.

By the time the Top 12 is ready to run the rain has stopped and the track is drying. Boucher warms up the crowd — metaphorically that is, for it will take more than words to increase the crowd's temperature on a day like this — and discusses the form of the runners. Seventh place in the running order, he explains, goes 'to the man who you just watch later on, Roy Lane.'

With the weather so uncertain tyre choice is going to be critical, but in one respect there is no choice at all, because practically all the tyres used on the hills are Avons, for the very good reason that no one else makes crossply racing tyres — at least not seriously. Dunlop, Yokohama and M&H have dabbled in the market, but none has a serious presence now.

The fact that crossplies are almost universally used will come as a surprise to those schooled in the prevailing wisdom of tyre technology, namely that crossply construction has been consigned to history and that radials are now universal, both on road and track.

In fact the wisdom is very nearly right. Radials have a number of advantages, among them the fact that they run cooler as their sidewalls are more flexible. However, cool running is the last thing you want on the hills, where you only have a few seconds to get the specially developed soft compound hillclimb tyres up to working temperature.

Some drivers tried in the past to get the best of both worlds by combining

Haydn Spedding's much modified E-Type has become a familiar sight on the hills.

86

radials with tyre warmers, GP style, but the warmers were banned on safety grounds a few years ago amid fears that running 240V cables across open and often wet paddocks where there are plenty of flammable liquids around, not to mention curious small boys, was not a safe practice.

The ban had two effects. Firstly it reduced costs, since no one could gain a tyre advantage by finding the cash to buy tyre warmers. Secondly, it turned attention back to crossplies, leaving Avon, the only tyre maker producing racing crossplies in any quantity, in a virtual monopoly position.

Having found itself a tidy niche, Avon makes the most of it, ensuring that its products are the natural choice for the hillclimber by making them accessible. At every RAC round the Avon van is there courtesy of its agent BMTR, and doing good business — checking, replacing, balancing and grooving.

To anyone used to road tyres, the idea of regrooving must sound like something they thought had been outlawed by the introduction of the MoT test decades ago.

But on racing tyres, providing the wear limiter built into the tread has not been reached, it is perfectly acceptable. Even the top competitors give tired slicks a new lease of life by rolling them over to Paul Smith in the Avon van and getting him to turn them into wets.

Watching him turn a slick into a wet with a hot-tipped rubber cutter is fascinating — and curiously therapeutic. As there's no way to undo a mistake, you'd think that sometimes, just sometimes, you'd see a wet with a groove which was out of position, but you never do. Every cut seems to be in exactly the right place, every time.

As the climax of the meeting approaches and the Top 12 runs start, the drivers are very glad of Paul's skills for all of them choose wets. True, the track is drying, but it is not yet good enough for slicks.

Patrick Wood and Roger Moran have the best of the first runs, being the only two to get under 60 seconds. Roy is still off the pace, languishing in seventh. His

Barbon, June meeting.

Car on the Hill

Subaru Impreza
Richard Hargreaves, Touring Cars Over 2000cc

Although they have well and truly made their mark in the rallying world, Subarus — and indeed any Japanese cars — are still a rarity on the hills. Anyone who studied Richard Hargreaves' four-wheel drive Impreza Turbo, however, could well conclude that this situation owes more to sentiment than engineering.

Richard is no stranger to the hills, having started competing in 1965. 'I started off with Minis, progressed to an Escort, through to a supercharged 3 litre Capri, mainly in club events, then I had a little single-seater called a Motus.'

This kart-derived design was his only venture outside saloons and it cost him dear; the car was banned for safety reasons 'after I crashed mine at Oulton Park. I broke three ribs and bruised my spleen so I gave up for about six years. I came back in with a Cosworth Sierra, as a road car, which I developed over the years. 'He developed it well enough to take several class records and win the Harewood Championship in 1991. 'Then thought I'd progress a bit and do the RAC Leaders, which I had no success in whatsoever!'

He's a big man, 6ft plus, with short blond hair, greying at the temples, and what in a younger person would be called designer stubble. The sort of man who has enough physical presence not to need to speak loudly. Swap the pipe for a cheroot, the racing overalls for Levis and you'd have a perfect riding partner for Clint Eastwood.

You have to tease facts out of him as he tends to speak in understatements. 'It's just a road car really, I just put slicks on it for today. I drive a Land Rover all week. It's my wife's shopping and business car.'

What made him buy a Subaru? 'I tried one as a road car. I thought "this is a bit different". I just liked the shape of the thing, the aesthetics of it, the way it went.' And when he's not amalgamated with other classes, he finds it a competitive package. 'I'm leading the Longton & District Sprint & Hillclimb Championship with it at the moment.' (He went on to finish the year with a maximum 1000 point score.) 'I took it to Three Sisters last weekend and I won the class there. I've got maximum points in the Longton Championship and I got maximum points in the Sprint Leaders Championship. It's the first round I've done of the Leaders and I'd like to chase that next year.'

All this in a shopping car? 'Well… It isn't *just* slicks. I mean… the suspension's slightly uprated, I've Prodrive suspension on it. Not a lot, it'd take me half an hour to put it back to standard.'

No different chips on the engine management, no subtleties like that? 'Well if I come clean, yes I have! I have to have that bit of an extra edge. It's producing about 280bhp from a flat-four quad cam 16 valve turbo — a fairly advanced engine really.'

Open the bonnet, with its big scoop to ram air into the turbo, and you're confronted with an unfamiliar sight. He admits that when it comes to serious maintenance on such a high-tech unit 'I just wouldn't know where the hell to start really. If it was dead serious and I had to strip the engine down I don't think I could approach it.'

Unlike some turbos, there's no fan to cool the puffer after you switch off, but Richard warns that 'like any turbo engine, you should leave it running for about half a minute after you've been caning it.'

There's a brace across the suspension turrets, obviously an absolute essential for coping with the Tesco car park. That's 'something and nothing', he protests with a grin. 'I haven't done a *lot* to it have I? Haven't gone berserk with the suspension or anything like that.'

I peek inside; to give him his due, it looks pretty standard — but he just couldn't resist a set of drilled metal pedals.

He didn't buy the car locally — it was imported from Northern Ireland — so how did he get Lancashire Subaru dealer Gibsons to sponsor him?

'I just took them out for a run in it. That convinced them they should be backing me.'

Richard Hargreaves is clearly one mighty persuasive *hombre*.

87

LIVING WITH SPEED

only chance is that conditions continue to improve so that everything ends up being decided on the second runs. Will the weather gods allow him another chance?

As the second runs approach, the track is in that awkward nether region between dry and wet and drivers are in a quandary: if they fit slicks and the track is still damp by the time it's their turn, they could be desperately short of grip. But if they stay with wets, they could find themselves at a disadvantage on a drying track, maybe even chew up an expensive set of tyres.

To complicate things, a big cumulo-nimbus is clearly visible from the paddock, accompanied by a huge veil of grey rain and proceeding remorselessly up the valley. It is only a matter of time before everything is very wet indeed — the question in every driver's mind is:

Aim at the gap in the buildings and floor it: Roy Lane in the farmyard.

Championship Top Tens after Round 9

RAC			Leaders		
1	Roy Lane	66	1	Phil Cooke	61
2	Roger Moran	64	2	Tom New	59
3	Patrick Wood	57	3	Justin Fletcher	55
4	Tim Mason	51	4	Mark Waldron	54
5	George Ritchie	33	=5	Martin Groves	53
=6	Bill Bristow	32	=5	Tony Lambert	53
=6	David Grace	32	7	Mark Lawrence	46
8	Simon Durling	24	=8	Mark Coley	38
9	Tim Barrington	14	=8	Andrew Russell	38
10	Richard Brown	13	10	Peter Hannam	35

Roger Kilty was in superb form but was robbed of Top 12 points by the unpredictable weather.

88

CHAPTER 10

Alan Newton earned himself four RAC championship points.

will it bucket down before or after I get to the start?

In the middle of these deliberations, Clerk of the Course Richard Hardcastle makes a controversial decision. In order to give everyone the same chance, he will not start the runs until everyone who wants to change tyres has done so. He reasons that it is not unknown in changeable situations for drivers to hang back in the paddock in the hope of gaining an advantage on a drying track.

Down at the start Tim Thomson, twelfth fastest, is already on the line but he is told to switch off and wait. An ever lengthening queue builds up behind him. Most are on wets, but as the clock ticks by and the track continues to dry, those nearest the start want more and more to change to dries, while those further back are hoping against hope that the track isn't totally awash by the time it's their turn.

Roy, who will be seventh to run, takes a chance and changes to dries — easier said than done at the Harewood start because it involves your pit crew humping tyres right down the hill. But Antony and John struggle down with a wheel under each arm and the job is done.

Up in the paddock things are moving more slowly than the Clerk would like and in frustration he threatens drivers with the two minute rule. This rule is designed to stop deliberate dithering and states that any car failing to come to the start line within two minutes of being called can be excluded. It is debatable whether it could legally be applied to a car which cannot get to the start line anyway on account of there being eight or nine cars waiting in front of it, but the point is made and eventually everybody is ready.

In the second runs times come down dramatically. Tim Thomson starts a trend which driver after driver follows, chopping nearly six seconds off his time, from 65.25 to 59.59. Three cars later John Moulds posts an even bigger improvement, over ten seconds, from 68.68 to 58.50.

Roy's time tumbles too, from 63.88 to 56.15, not FTD but faster than any other Top 12 run so far. But although the rain clouds have been kind to him, victory is not to be his today, for the next run is David Grace's and he takes the Ralt Gould up in 55.93.

All the while the sky is getting darker and the sheet of rain is sweeping higher and higher up the valley. It's touch and go now whether the remaining four cars — Graham Priaulx, Patrick Wood, Roger Moran and Roger Kilty — will get meaningful second runs at all.

In the event it is Graham Priaulx who seals the fate of the other three. He tries just a little too hard at Quarry and falls off into the waiting gravel bank, requiring several minutes' effort from the marshals to clear the track.

By the time they've done so, the rain is pouring down and the last three runners have no chance, regardless of what tyres they are on. The very inequality which the Clerk had tried to avoid has blown the chances of the three drivers who looked like having the best chance of winning. Ironically, if he had not made everyone wait, all 12 would probably have had dry, or at least dryish, runs.

As bedraggled drivers and spectators huddle in the beer tent afterwards for the presentation, a rather surprised David Grace is presented with the award for winning the Top 12, the first blood which his new Ralt has drawn from the Pilbeam fraternity.

'I'd like to thank the rain gods — and Graham Priaulx' he says in his acceptance speech. It has been a lucky win, but he is not complaining.

Roy is not complaining either. Today's winner is a man who currently offers no threat in the championship on account of his late start to the season, and Roy has come second.

Seeing your main rivals drowned out is a less than satisfying way of earning nine points, but after his misfortune at Barbon he is not about to feel guilty over being on the receiving end of a bit of good luck.

John Moulds had one of his best results of the season, fourth in the Top 12.

89

LIVING WITH SPEED

'I think I'll leave it to the experts'

Radio Hairpin at 101%: the run that gave Roger Moran his first RAC victory.

Roy's Run

'Bouley Bay is basically a two-gear course. Off the start line I use a relatively low first (70mph) to cope with the tight hairpin at Radio Corner higher up. I take first all the way round the first left-hander, then round the right-hander, then on to max revs and into second (a 90mph gear).

'Next comes the right-hand kink at Sleemens, which is a brave man's corner. That leads into the long left-hander at Les Platon. Sometimes I take this in second, especially if I have a torquey car, but this year I decided that to keep control of the car I'd go back into first. Change up into second out of the corner, through the zig-zag bits, back into first for Radio Corner. Round Radio, accelerate like mad, change up into second, up to the last corner, back into first, round that corner, accelerate like mad, change up before the finishing line.

'I could miss an awful lot of meetings at home just to go to Bouley Bay. I love the place, I love the people. It hasn't got the grip, but then you're not going the speed of Shelsley. It's all within an old man's pace!'

Bouley Bay

Location
On public roads on the north east coast of Jersey.

Organising club
Jersey Motorcycle & Light Car Club, c/o Mrs E Le Cornu, Midway, Croix De Bois, Five Oaks, Jersey JE2 7TU. Tel 01534 35853.

Length 1011 yards.

Outright hill records at start of 18.7.96 meeting
Overall: Andy Priaulx, 38.65sec.

KEY

Track shading indicates gear ratio...

White striped is first gear

Black is top gear

Because ratios and patterns in racing gearboxes can be altered at will, a particular shading on one map does not indicate the same ratio as on another: shading is relative only to that particular venue.

V indicates good viewing area

Arnie Corbet

CHAPTER 11

Bouley Bay

Mid-July is traditionally the time of year when RAC Hillclimb contenders cross the English Channel to Jersey and Guernsey. It's the nearest the 'circus' gets to a Continental event — from the upper reaches of Jersey's famous championship ascent, the northern coast of France is visible across the water, sparkling through the midsummer haze.

The Jersey Motorcycle & Light Car Club is now in its 76th year of organising a varied programme of motorsport, and this year's visit to Le Charrieres du Boulay, the wide but tortuous public access road that snakes up from the Bay, is particularly significant.

Apart from Prescott and Shelsley, Bouley Bay is the only climb to have hosted an RAC round every year since the series' inception in 1947, when just five hills made up the championship trail. Each of the Midland hills has occupied two places on the National calendar since 1958, and the current season is the first that Ulster's Craigantlet climb was not a round of the championship. So with the remaining inaugural venue at Bo'ness long gone, submerged beneath an Edinburgh housing development, 1996 will hold a unique place in the history of the JM&LCC as it marks the 50th consecutive running of Bouley Bay's annual RAC counter.

It also, incidentally, establishes a remarkable record for club stalwart Ernie Bouchet, JM&LCC's Secretary and Honorary Vice President, who has officiated at every one of those 50 events since he first marshalled on the hill in 1947.

For RAC contenders it's the second time this year that they have the opportunity to unleash their steeds on public roads. But while the Isle of Man's ultrafast Lerghy Frissel had received disappointing support back in May, most of the championship front runners have made the Channel crossing.

Like any event which involves a ferry trip with a competition car it's not a cheap exercise but the two events, Bouley on Thursday followed by a Friday boat trip to nearby Guernsey for Saturday's sortie at Le Val des Terres, are in many cases seen as a summer holiday break for mainland competitors. Sea crossings are always fully booked and most competitors of necessity leave the previous weekend to make a week of it.

The Waters' Edge Hotel is the place to stay. Right next to the centre of the action, it's alongside the Bay's picturesque — though somewhat cramped — seafront paddock.

With the startline just outside the hotel's back door, the sight and sound of an F1 V8-engined single seater launching out of the busy harbourfront into the blind left-hander at Cafe, before blasting past beautifully manicured gardens and on up the hairpin-punctuated thousand yards of wooded slopes, is to experience just one way in which hillclimbing stands unique among motorsport disciplines.

But it's quite on the cards that the top mainland V8 contenders will encounter serious local opposition today. Not least from Peter Le Gallais, whose famous surname is something of a legend in Jersey motorsport. The Jaguar powered LGS of his late father Frank guaranteed spectacle during the '50s. Peter will pose a major threat today, and on Guernsey's 'rival' hill in two days' time, aboard his Pilbeam MP62. 'Motorsport is something of a family tradition in Jersey. My own son, Tim, is also competing here in his Caterham, powered, like the Pilbeam, with a 2-litre 16V Vauxhall.'

In fact Tim would concede the GT Sports class win by less than a second to the similar machine of Frank Le Jehan.

Like all the 'overseas' rounds, Jersey's event does not count for Leaders points, so local classes rule and divisions are broadly drawn between saloons and sports, motorcycles, sidecars and even karts. RACMSA regulations may not permit karts in mainland speed events, but on the Channel Islands they're welcome and the drivers of these diminutive machines frequently produce staggering form.

This year it's the turn of Nigel Davis to set the kart pace in his Anderson Rotax. Had he been eligible for the British championship Nigel's spectacular shot, deep into the 41s, would have qualified in third place for the run-off — ahead of Roy Lane and the Steel King Pilbeam...

As is often the case on the mainland, the more outrageous machines can be found within the sports libre category,

With one of the biggest engines in British hillclimbing, Peter le Druillenec's Miller Exocet is aptly named.

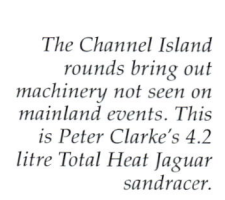

The Channel Island rounds bring out machinery not seen on mainland events. This is Peter Clarke's 4.2 litre Total Heat Jaguar sandracer.

91

LIVING WITH SPEED

Roger Moran talking to Jerry Sturman at the end of the August Shelsley meeting.

where David Render and Paul Parker have crossed the water to take on the locals.

For the remarkable Render, now in his 70s and a stalwart of the British motorsport scene — he raced in a Morgan at the first ever Goodwood meeting in 1948 — this is only his second competitive event since major heart surgery over a year ago.

His first was here in Jersey a fortnight ago, driving his Pilbeam Hart sportscar in the Five-Mile-Road sprint. And a very satisfactory comeback he made, since he won the event! He will also go on to win Bouley's 13-strong sports libre class and qualify in a remarkable seventh place for the run-off…

Much in demand as an after-dinner speaker, David is asked to address a large evening gathering at the Club's Golden Jubilee Bouley Bay dinner after the hillclimb. It's a sumptuous affair, held in a marquee in the grounds of St Helier's prestigious Le Haule Manor Hotel and providing, among other

Roger Moran

Like thousands of others, Roger Moran owes his motorsport career to the Mk1 Escort, in which he started rallying in the late '70s. By the early '80s he was making 'a concerted effort' at the *Motoring News* rally championship in an RS2000 before progressing to tarmac stage rallying. 'I did one or two forest rallies but found them too damaging'.

Having decided that tarmac was his metier, he found that rallying was getting increasingly impractical. For tarmac events, 'you needed to go to Ireland and I found the expense too great.' Travelling time was another factor, for like most people in this amateur sport, he has a living to earn, in his case at the Moran motorhomes business. The result was that he abandoned rallying completely in 1989.

'A friend of mine had been trying to get me into hillclimbs for years', but he'd always resisted. 'Having been used to a saloon car with all sorts of steel roll-over hoops and cages, I didn't think that driving a single-seater racing car up a narrow hill where there's trees and all sorts of obstacles was the safest thing to do.'

Contenders from other motorsport disciplines agree. 'During this trip to the Channel Islands I've talked to Derek Warwick and he thinks we're absolutely, completely and totally insane. It is dangerous, but as long as you're aware that it's relatively dangerous, then you can keep on a level. Serious accidents are rare, but they do happen.'

Man on the Hill

Eventually the lure of tarmac competition at an accessible distance and price became irresistible and 1990 saw him enter the sport with 1100 Imp-powered Delta 'just getting used to the Midland hills really. At the end of that season Patrick Wood offered me his Delta with an 1100 BDJ which had been a regular class-winning car, and I thought buying a proven package was the way to go.'

He was right, for the ex-Wood machine proved an instant class winner. 'I won my class in the Midland Hillclimb Championship two years in succession against fairly strong opposition — people like Simon Durling, Chris Johnson, Ben Boult, John Corbyn, Phil Jefferies — all hard people to beat.'

After two years I wanted to move up into the 1600 class and ended up buying a new Pilbeam, an MP62, for 1993. I was fortunate enough to get help from Swindon Racing Engines who supplied us with an engine for a very reasonable maintenance cost and in my second year with the car I won the Leaders Championship. As a result they gave me a 2 litre Vauxhall engine to the latest Touring Car spec for 1995 and I managed to win the Leaders again, and finish seventh overall in the RAC Championship.

That seventh place is the highest anyone's finished with a 2 litre in recent years but Roger is characteristically downbeat about his contribution to the achievement. 'In my opinion an MP62 with a good 2 litre Vauxhall is as quick as a good 2.8 Hart, if somebody can pedal it — it's light and nimble.'

He seems genuinely surprised to be in contention for top honours in his first year with a V8. 'I certainly didn't expect to be in this position. Everybody said "don't be surprised if you go slower" but it wasn't in my nature to go backwards really.' Despite his modest demeanour, there's a strong streak of determination inside this quietly spoken competitor.

When the car first appeared at Loton Park at the start of the season, Roger and co-driver George Ritchie's entire experience of the car was just four test runs at the same venue. Feeling at a disadvantage, 'I made a fairly determined effort from the start'. He qualified well, which gave him confidence in the car, and although 'I messed up both of the run-offs at the top of the hill' simply by overdriving the car, his second place overall was good enough to set him up for the season.

Rapidly emerging as a champion in waiting, Roger will be disappointed if he fails to beat Roy to the title this year but will certainly not begrudge the man he calls 'Mr Hillclimbing' a fourth national championship. 'I don't think anybody can deny that he's done brilliantly to still be driving like he is at his age. As for me, I've got plenty of time to win it.'

Roy has been talking about competing less next year but Roger is cautious. 'That would be quite good for the rest of us I guess! But we don't take too much notice of what Roy tells us. He's always trying to lull us into a false sense of security'.

92

CHAPTER 11

Car on the Hill

Royale RP42 Chevrolet
Paul Parker, Sports Libre Cars Over 2000cc

While it may be outgunned for ultimate power by the big single-seaters, for spectacle and raw excitement there is nothing to beat Paul Parker's Royale.

It's big, wide, heavy and very fast, courtesy of a Tom Laffey developed 6.2 litre Chevrolet V8. Apart from local man Peter le Druillenec's Miller Exocet, it's the biggest engine on the hill. Power is no less than 470bhp, and there's 490 lb ft of torque to back it up.

Torque like that puts a fair strain on the transmission as Paul discovered at Shelsley earlier this year when a shaft failure ended his day's sport. In this and other respects Paul is still developing the Royale, although it is already one of the fastest Libre cars in the sport.

To look at it now you'd think it was a sports racer in the Le Mans tradition, but the car was actually developed for hillclimbing, specifically for the old Special Saloon Class which preceded Libre. The rules there stipulated that cars had to have at least the shape of a production saloon, so a fibreglass shell resembling (of all things) a rear-engined Skoda sat atop the Royale Chassis, in which form the car won the 1990 Leaders Championship.

Despite this successful history, when Paul bought the car in 1995 he found the chassis 'undriveable'. Stiffer spring rates courtesy of Peter Needham improved things, but the geometry is still not right and Paul's highest priority for 1996 is to remedy this with the help of Adrian Hopkins.

Weight is the major enemy, for at 710kg this must surely be the heaviest car on the hill, fully 150kg heavier than a single-seater with an F1-derived V8. Around half this deficiency is down to the humbler origins of the Royale's power unit, a production Chevrolet block, but Paul hopes that much of the rest can be steadily pared away.

'Over next winter hopefully we'll get some lighter bodywork made.'

He's already made a start, with a new Rick Fielding designed wing. Fully triangulated and substantially built (Paul is full of praise for the robustness of Rick's engineering), it is nevertheless 'a significant saving compared with what was already on the car, which you'd almost need a forklift truck to move — incredibly heavy.'

Despite this weight penalty, its contribution to downforce was questionable — except through sheer weight! 'We did some measurements and discovered that it was 6cm lower than it need have been. So it wasn't in the airstream anyway.'

'We're going in the right direction with the car', he asserts confidently, although he makes no claims to driving stardom. 'I would not confess to being a top notch driver but... good enough. I'm a sports car lover, that's why I'm in Libre and I'll never drive a single seater. Well...' he qualifies himself, 'I may drive one but I'll never own one.'

Wiscombe Park, April meeting.

Grunt department of the mighty Royale.

things, a unique chance to see hillclimb drivers swap racing overalls for evening wear as early as midway through the season. Some wear lounge suits, some black tie — and in George Ritchie's case, full regalia as befits a patriotic Scot. But Render's typically risque address, eagerly anticipated by those who've heard him before, soon dispels any pretensions of formality — even with a speech toned down several notches below David's usual level.

Back in that cosmopolitan sports libre class, another contender anxious to qualify for the run-off is Guernseyman Geoff Guille. A frequent Gurston and Shelsley habitué with his Mallock, Geoff is well aware of the extent of the mainland challenge, but has to give best to Render in the class runs.

Together with engine builder Ken Snailham — sharing the QED MP62 with fellow '80s Leaders champion Simon Frost — Guille just fails to make the cut for the Top 12 in a three-way Vauxhall-powered battle for the final place.

It's Nick Fletcher who finally emerges triumphant, the Shrewsbury housing developer delighted not only to qualify the Pilbeam for his first ever British championship run-off, but also with son Justin's efforts, whose brilliant qualifying shot takes the 2-litre Pilbeam clear of all but Roger Moran's V8 MP72.

But it's the fearsome Chevron-based Miller Exocet of Peter Le Druillenec that tops Bouley's sports libre charisma list. With a 680bhp 6.3 Chevy built by American drag racing ace Ron Shaver, this de-

93

LIVING WITH SPEED

Championship Top Tens

RAC after 10 rounds
1. Roy Lane 74
2. Roger Moran 74
3. Patrick Wood 57
4. Tim Mason 54
5. Bill Bristow 41
6. George Ritchie 33
7. David Grace 32
8. Simon Durling 24
9. Graham Priaulx 18
10. Justin Fletcher 16

Leaders after 9 rounds
Unchanged since Harewood (Channel Island events do not count towards this championship).

The atmosphere in Jersey brings competitors back year after year, despite the travel costs. This shot was taken in 1994.

vice surpasses even Parker's Royale for sheer cubic capacity. The massed crowds at Radio Hairpin, the hill's most popular vantage point, step back a pace as the red monster thunders into view. But despite the sound and fury Guille's nimble Mallock has the edge through the never-ending hairpin bends to nab second in class.

Beaten only once at Bouley Bay since 1991, five times Jersey winner Roy Lane arrives in the Channel Islands with the further psychological advantage of the championship lead — albeit by just two points — over Roger Moran, who has yet to score his first championship win. As Roy relentlessly piles on the pressure, his sixth win of the year now in his sights, Roger knows that this must be the turning point of his championship challenge. Sure enough, a determined assault in the MP72 sets the pace, topping the qualifying sheets as the main protagonists prepare for the run-off.

Roy is content to bide his time in fourth place, just a tenth behind Isle of Man hero Bill Bristow. Bill's new Beattie engine, installed in the Ralt for Harewood a fortnight earlier, is clearly producing the goods — though during the class runs neither could match Davis's incredible pace in the Anderson Rotax kart. Simon Frost lines up the QED Pilbeam a strong fifth, his best championship showing so far, leading Graham Priaulx's V8 Pilbeam into the run-off by just five hundredths.

Once championship points are at stake, Bristow is the first to raise his game. His determined opening shot is the first of the day to break the 40 second barrier, shading out Moran by 15 hundredths. Roy keeps in touch, a similar margin behind his arch rival but a second ahead of Fletcher's MP62.

But it all goes wrong for Lane second time up; a fraction early on the power out of Radio Hairpin and a gasp from the gallery signals trouble — the Steel King Pilbeam has snapped sideways and stops, wedged between the high banks. The run is blown and Roy could yet end up fourth. It would be his worst Bouley finish for 10 years.

As Graham Priaulx struggles to make up for a first run fail — he was adjudged to have launched the Pilbeam DFL on a red light — the Guernseyman slips ahead of a recovering Fletcher. Le Gallais restores local honour by demoting Frost, but none can better Roy's opener so the championship leader is at least safe in third place.

Scenting a second British Hillclimb victory, Bristow is on a charge as the Ralt storms into Cafe.

But the low sun is his undoing. Momentarily dazzled, the squeal of tyres can be heard right up at Radio as he misses his braking point and the Ralt skates straight on.

With no harm done, except to his pride, Bill tours up to face his most nerve-wracking wait of the year — can Moran pull one out of the bag on the final run of the day and deny him the win?

With a maiden victory in his sights, Roger makes no mistakes. Powersliding the orange MP72-Judd confidently out of Radio, he surges up to the final hairpin and rockets over the line to pip Bristow's opener by a tenth of a second and level with Roy at the top of the championship table.

His delight, and those of his fellow competitors, is clear. 'What a fantastic place to take my first win!' he exclaims after collecting his trophy from local Honda dealer Derek Warwick.

We ask the former Grand Prix driver and 1991 World Sportscar Champion if he'd ever considered competing in hillclimbing at this level. His reply is short and to the point.

'No. I think I'll leave it to the experts.'

CHAPTER 12

'Local knowledge can be a distinct advantage'

Le Val des Terres

'The Monaco of hillclimbing' — one way, perhaps, to describe the paddock ambience at Le Val des Terres. The bustling St Peter Port harbour is a focal point for Guernsey tourists during the summer, and when the RAC hillclimbers arrive on the Saturday, hotfoot from Thursday's round in neighbouring Jersey, it's converted into a Channel Islands equivalent of the Monegasque Principality as race cars line both sides of the long, wide promenade. The significant difference is that it's a free show, and spectators mingle with competitors in the sum-

The locals know precisely which kerbs they can ride over with impunity. Here Colin le Maitre straightens the racing line in his 2 litre Pilbeam Hart.

Le Val des Terres

Location
On public roads, climbing out of St Peter Port harbour.

Organising club
Guernsey Motor Cycle & Car Club, c/o Mrs M Rumens, Glenesk, Sandy Hook, St Sampson, Guernsey GY2 4ER. Tel 01481 46099.

Length 850 yards.

Outright hill records at start of 20.7.96 meeting
Overall: Andy Priaulx, 30.46sec.

Roy's Run

'Val des Terres is a strange place, each year the surface gets worse and worse. It's got no grip, so an engine in the front with the driver sat on the back wheel is the way to go. This year proved it once again: a lot of the local boys who know the place so well like to show up these idiots who are doing the British Championship.

'First off the line — it's very slippery, has lost all its grip and is uphill straight away — change up as you go up what they call the Ramp. Try and use the kerbs, up and around the Wall, into the long, long left-hander, then a quick burst in between the two into the right-hander. On top straight, change up to third and hold third all the way to the finishing line.'

Arnie Corbet

KEY

Track shading indicates gear ratio...

White striped is first gear

Tint is intermediate

Black is top gear

Because ratios and patterns in racing gearboxes can be altered at will, a particular shading on one map does not indicate the same ratio as on another: shading is relative only to that particular venue.

indicates good viewing area

0   100yd

Top Paddock
FINISH
Top Straight
S Bend
The Ramp
START
Bottom Paddock

95

LIVING WITH SPEED

A little piece of Monaco: this 1994 shot sums up the Guernsey atmosphere.

mer sun, fully equipped with the obligatory sun hats and ice creams, to soak up the race-day atmosphere.

At the southern end of the prom lies the start line, situated — conveniently some say — alongside the Guernsey Brewery. Others may be less enthusiastic, as herein lies the next clue as to why Le Val des Terres is a venue apart. The constant passage of brewery vehicles over the years means that the road surface has acquired a heavy patina of diesel and consequently, both here and on the rest of the hill, grip is at a premium.

Setting off up the course, we leave the sunbaked start area and suddenly the steep climb out of the harbourfront becomes almost claustrophobic as the pavement-bordered road winds between sheer rockfaces on one side and imposing wooded estates on the other. Those pavements with their low kerbs can double the width of the road and are utilised to the full by the quick men. Some kerbs, however, are lower than others and here, more than at most of the championship hills, local knowledge can be a distinct advantage.

The almost total tree cover, particularly when punctuated by intermittent dazzling sunshine where the sun breaks through, makes visibility a problem, particularly at the vicious, swooping double S-bend halfway up.

But when the light finally bursts through for good you know you're nearing the end of this steep, concentrated 850 yard dash. Now in view of massed ranks of enthusiastic spectators at the top, the road threads between grassy banks, a fast, 100mph straight and a left-hand kink being the precursors of the hill's sting in the tail — the tight right-hander before the finish which has caught out almost as many competitors over the years as Harewood's notorious Quarry Bend.

The enthusiastic Guernsey Motorcycle & Car Club run several meetings a year on Le Val des Terres, so when the British Championship circus makes its annual visit the regular locals pose a significant threat. The Mallocks in particular have tended to humble the big racers with surprising regularity over the years, none more so than the Mk20B of 'adopted local' Martin Groves.

While not actually a Guernsey resident, Martin's business connections bring him here frequently and if they should happen to coincide with a club hillclimb, well… More than once has the Oxfordshire driver been known to ruffle a few feathers during the run-off and he's on top form again today, a successful record breaking bid for sports libre class honours suppressing the Mallocks of 'genuine' locals Jason Carre and Paul Brehaut.

Brehaut's fuel-injected machine, arguably the most immaculately turned out Mallock in the history of the Roade marque, sports an on-board video camera today. But if the former record-holder needed a further reminder of which way the road went, Groves has no such doubts as that class-winning run has qualified his Ford pushrod powered, front-engined car an amazing second fastest overall for the run-off.

And to reinforce the point, all three Mallocks, plus the Vauxhall powered version of fourth-placed Ian Le Messurier, make the cut too.

Another Guernseyman delighted to qualify is Adrian Duport, who held off the rest of the 1100cc single-seater opposition — which included Tony Tewson's MP62-BDA — with his 'budget' racer. This is an ageing Rostron powered by a Transit van engine and driving through a Volkswagen gearbox. 'For the last two years we've run 13th with the car, so it's great that we finally made the championship run-off, whatever the outcome.' Sadly gearshift problems stemmed his progress and eventually dropped him out of the points, but even that failed to dampen Adrian's enthusiasm.

To be fair to Tewson, it was the first time that he had visited the Channel Islands. Somewhat surprisingly, bearing in mind his long hillclimbing career, Tony Lambert was another mainlander making a maiden trip to Guernsey. The former Leaders champion brought a week's touring holiday to an end in style, getting his Ferrari right in amongst a local battle spearheaded by class record-holder Bob Olliver's thundering Westfield-Rover. After Olliver twice reset his modified sports mark, Lambert all but caught Chris Martel for second place as the SEight spun out.

Unique to the Channel Islands, the Jaguar-powered sand racers never fail to thrill the crowds. These leviathans of the single-seater world run conventional transmission without transaxles, despite a rear-engined layout which leaves the driver perched, apparently somewhat vulnerably, up front. Peter Clarke's Total Heat backed machine had been their sole representative in Jersey, but had failed to make the pace for the run-off.

He's shooting for a place in the elite 12 here in Guernsey too, but it's local class record holder Roger King who tops the class in his thundering Rocksand machine. He pips Clark by half a second, though mechanical bothers thwart a last-ditch attempt to reset his record.

96

CHAPTER 12

Wiscombe Park, spring meeting.

Car on the Hill

Ferrari 308 GT4

Tony Lambert, Modified Production Cars Over 2000cc

Although he has been competing in hillclimbs on and off ever since the '60s — 'when even Roy Lane was relatively young' — Tony Lambert has been faithful to Ferraris since 1989 and is now so strongly identified with the Italian marque that he has acquired the nickname Antonio Lambrusco.

The Ferrari link came about 'more by accident than design — I like competing in things that are a bit different.' He's stuck with the car because he enjoys driving it so much, and because it has brought him a lot of success. 'I call it the four seater Fiat because the GT4 is a 2+2 — a cracking chassis with a nice long wheelbase which makes it very user friendly.'

This ferocious 1977 308GT4 started life as a well used 80,000 mile road car and even today is taxed and insured for the road, though Tony finds the 3 litre unit noisy and intractable in that role. On the track, however, this 400+hp twin-turbocharged V8 comes into its own and has a string of class records to its credit.

'They last quite well,' says Tony, when asked whether running a competition Ferrari needs a huge bank balance. When he got the car 'the engine was in superb condition. Even the box I've got has done over 50,000. The bodies don't though, they get rusty'.

The turbos were fitted by Janspeed in readiness for the 1991 season, helping Tony raise the stakes in the Leaders Championship, which he finally won two seasons later. The car's season-long tussle with the TVR Tuscan now driven by Mark Waldron has actually gone on for several seasons, ever since Barrie Lines owned the Blackpool growler. The TVR had the edge in '92 but in '93 and '94 the position was reversed. 1995 was 'about level pegging, but Mark's had me this year.'

Tony is convinced the Ferrari is capable of further development, but the gearbox has been troublesome this season and seems to have reached the limit of what it is willing to transmit. Since the car left the factory with a mere 255bhp, its reluctance to cooperate is as understandable as it is frustrating, especially as other transmission parts like driveshafts still work reliably at the original spec. In seven years Tony has only suffered one driveshaft failure.

'We thought of turning the engine through 90° and putting a Hewland on the back. I thought it would be the cheaper answer, but it didn't turn out to be, so we're back to square one.' Nor, apparently, is there a gearbox from a more powerful Ferrari which can easily be substituted.

The latest plan is to use the existing five-speed casing and fit into it four specially made larger gears. 'It should take the extra power then, with a bit of luck.'

Another distinctly nonstandard feature is the rather dubious logo which appeared on the car at Loton Park in March, courtesy of Robin Boucher. Styled after the famous Ferrari motif, the 'prancing sheep' alludes to the inflatable sheep given to Tony as a joke at Doune in 1995. It so amused Tony that he has adopted it as his personal motif, even threatening to have matching T-shirts made.

It's enough to make Il Commendatore revolve rapidly in his grave. But if he saw the way the car storms up Val des Terres, he'd soon rest in peace.

As the July sun moves across to leave the arid start area bathed in the welcome shadow of the Brewery, the top contenders begin to jostle for position in the qualifying order. It's now not only the Mallocks who are causing a degree of head scratching amongst the V8 'establishment' after another inspired shot by Justin Fletcher. Ousting fellow 2-litre runners Peter Le Gallais and Guernseyman Colin Le Maitre's superbly presented Autocare Refinishers MP58-Hart, the Fletcher Homes MP62 will remain firmly at the head of the RAC line-up, with a run just three hundredths inside Groves's amazing qualifier with the Clubmans Mallock.

Despite course record holder Andy Priaulx's circuit racing contract precluding his participation, family honour is still very much at stake on home ground and he's naturally on hand to help father Graham defend it. Indeed the Bank of Bermuda Pilbeam-DFL is the quickest V8 in qualifying, lining up just five hundredths behind Groves. Roger Moran is next up but Roy Lane is only fifth fastest. So far for Roy, this year's Channel Islands trip is fast becoming one to forget, and it's not over yet...

Spectators at the top of the hill get the best view of the unfolding drama of the championship run-off, lining the bank opposite the finish to watch the cars burst out of the gloom of the lower slopes and into the final straight before their all-out attack on the last bend. Buoyed by his performance in Jersey two days earlier, Moran's opener leads the way after the first runs. But Priaulx is on top form in front of his home crowd and trails by three tenths with another local, Le Maitre, charging his French hillclimb spec Pilbeam through to third place ahead of Le Gallais. And the flamboyant Fletcher? The early pacemaker's challenge fades with a spin on the lower slopes. A cautious follow-up will get him in the points, but only just.

Aside from Moran, it's Groves who leads the mainland contingent in fifth place, the Mallock barrelling out of the S-bend with all four wheels on the pavement before switching across the road at the last minute to take the right-hander. But his time fails to match that record-breaking qualifier and with a second run a hundredth slower still, Martin has to be content with the six points.

Bill Bristow is a mere nine hundredths behind the Mallock at the break, but a missed gearchange off the startline scuppers his chances of improvement and the Ralt rounds off the top half-dozen.

A bout of understeer through the tricky S-bend stems Le Maitre's last-run charge too. Together with Le Gallais, who also fails to better his opener, he holds station. At third and fourth respectively, however, they have both demonstrated the value of that local knowledge.

But it's the battle up front that holds the crowd's attention. Moran is on a charge, determined to back up his maiden win in Jersey with another on Guernsey and become one of the select

Home territory: Graham on the final bend at Le Val des Terres.

Graham Priaulx

It's impossible to talk about Graham Priaulx without mentioning his high-flying son Andy, and Graham wouldn't have it any other way, since he never misses a chance to promote his talented offspring. Indeed, so serious is he about this task that he plans to soft-pedal his own motorsport in 1997 in order to manage his son's circuit-racing career — that same career which for most of this year has denied hillclimbers the spectacle of seeing the current champion defend his title.

But descriptions like 'absolutely the most devastating display of raw talent the sport has witnessed in 20 years', which is what *Autosport* called Andy in 1995, are only half the story. For Andy wouldn't be where he is if he did not come from a line of redoubtable competitors.

The Priaulx family stretches back over 1000 years in Guernsey but Graham is only thinking back one generation when he asserts that 'driving must be something I've got in my veins.' For it was Graham's father, a motor trader who built up his own business from nothing, who started it all.

'In later years he was very interested in racing — he didn't have the money to do it early on. I probably get my enthusiasm from him. He started hillclimbing when I was only a boy in short trousers. He introduced me to it in saloon cars because we couldn't afford anything else and I progressed from there.'

Graham followed his father into the motor trade and started racing almost as soon as he got his driving licence at 17. At 18 he took the 1000cc saloon record in Guernsey, which he held for four years until he gave up the class. That was with a Fiat Abarth 1000, with which Graham was initially told he would never achieve anything. 'After I broke the record the pits went rather silent because we'd actually beaten the beloved British Mini Cooper with a Fiat', he recalls with evident amusement.

A Fiat X1/9 Abarth came next, its engine enlarged from 1300 to 1600cc. 'I did some hillclimbing in that and also raced at Castle Donington in the Six Hours Sports Car race run by the 750 MC. I ran under the Radbourne name in the same team as Stephen Soper... That would have been about 1978-9.'

'In 1980 I commissioned Tiga to build me a sports racing car. This was a proper racing car, a monocoque chassis with a 2 Litre BDX which I later improved to a 2150 alloy block, but still Cosworth. I ran it on methanol injection above and below the trumpets, though in those days you could also use nitro.'

With the Tiga Graham started to make his mark on the UK hills. In 1983 he won 11 of the 14 events he entered. However, he rates his best season as 1984 'when I didn't enter the championship, I decided that I would just pick and choose. I improved my times and I took the outright record at Guernsey in 1984, at 31.46 seconds. That was the overall Channel Islands record, I believe at the time it was a national record also.'

But another attraction was to tempt him away from motorsport: powerboat racing. For three years Graham raced in Class 3 offshore, ending up Channel Islands powerboat champion.

Safety is not usually given as a reason for entering motorsport, but ironically, it was concern for Andy's welfare that was to bring Graham back to motorsport and to the hills. 'My son was doing motocross and I could see that there were a great many injuries. I decided to pull him off the motor-bikes, for fear of him breaking his legs and collarbones like his classmates, and I put him into a Mallock.

'He then tempted me back to drive. I initially resisted because I didn't really want the pressure back again but he wooed me into the car and together we developed it.'

Man on the Hill

Another Mallock followed, this time with a twin-cam engine, after which a Pilbeam MP57 introduced them to open wheelers. 'We started an attack on the UK hills together, three years ago'.

After one year they obtained a three-year sponsorship deal worth £10,000pa from the Bank of Bermuda. And by the end of the first year Andy was showing his ability, notching up some third and fourth place finishes. As Graham put it: 'The writing was on the wall that he was a very capable driver.' The temptation to buy a top class car and go for the title was irresistible; an MP58 was acquired from Ken Ayers.

'We stripped it right down and redeveloped the whole car; new wishbones and ground effect underneath, coke bottle sidepods, Haggis wings — and then in '95 Andy and I made an assault on the championship. He won ten consecutive events and took eight national records.'

This unique achievement — even Roy Lane in 1975 didn't break as many records — brought Andy to the attention of the professionals. Andy's promotional literature talks of him driving in F1 by 2000, an ambitious but not unrealistic target. For unlike most F1 hopefuls who come up through karting and F3, Andy already knows what it is like to drive a big racer, and in a very demanding environment where there is far less room for error than on a circuit. If he succeeds in the big time, no one will be prouder than the folk on the hills.

Except perhaps his dad.

group of only half a dozen drivers who have achieved the Channel Island double. Up on the kerb and a shade too fast into the final bend, the Pilbeam snaps broadside across the line. Roger holds the slide, but his earlier 31.32 was quicker by far.

Now Priaulx bounds into sight, his 101mph through the speed trap the best of the day as the vocal partisan crowd wills him on. The MP58 bellows over the line and the clock stops — at 31.33. Graham has missed a home win by just one hundredth of a second...

For Roger, it has been the most momentous two days of his hillclimb career. To take your first ever championship win and follow it up with another two days later is quite something, and with the Lane camp not having enjoyed the best of fortune during this year's Channel Islands foray it's enough to extend his championship lead over Roy by seven points.

Jason Carre's eight hundredths advantage over the Steel King Pilbeam — yes, in a Mallock — came after an all-out bank-clobbering final effort and leaves Lane's Guernsey tally at an eminently discardable three points. Eighth place is not what he came here for.

But when the series returns to Shelsley Walsh in three weeks time, Roger will be the first to drop scores as the title chase enters its closing stages (only the best 10 scores from the 16 rounds count). He will desperately need to back up his two wins with a few more, as with five maximum scores already in the bag, Roy will have a round in hand.

The battle off the coast of Northern France may have been conclusively won, but the war in England is far from over.

Championship Top Tens

RAC after 11 rounds

1	Roy Lane	84
2	Roger Moran	77
3	Patrick Wood	57
4	Tim Mason	54
5	Bill Bristow	46
6	George Ritchie	33
7	David Grace	32
8	Graham Priaulx	27
8	Simon Durling	24
10	Justin Fletcher	18

Leaders after 9 rounds

Unchanged since Harewood (Channel Island events do not count towards this championship).

CHAPTER 13

'I tried there, I really did'

Return to Shelsley Walsh

Left: Body language says it all. Roy Lane and Sean Gould at the end of a long and slightly frustrating day.

Main picture: Top S at Shelsley leads on to the fastest part of the course.

Shelsley in the rain. The red clay is having a field day. We squelch down the grassy slope out of the car park, trying to avoid the red-brown tramlines worn into the meadow by the incoming spectators in case our backsides end up a similar colour. Right now the weather looks miserable, but the forecast is hopeful and all the drivers are going about their business regardless.

Practice yesterday owed as much to meteorology as to driving and for once it was the wily master himself, Roy Lane, who got caught out. Like other competitors he waited and waited for the track to dry in the hope of setting a halfway decent practice time, but unlike some he waited too long. The rains came down again and suddenly he was worse off than if he'd gone an hour before.

By 11:10 the rain has pretty well stopped but the track is still very wet as I work my way up the footpath to watch the bikes at Kennel. Today competitors are tackling the world's oldest motorsport venue on two, three and four wheels and I reach Kennel just as the bikers begin feeling their way up on their first runs.

Although elapsed time is the criterion for hillclimb success, like most venues Shelsley adds spectator interest by measuring speed as well, with a trap between Crossing and Bottom S and another check at the finish line. It is surprising how frequently the highest speeds do not equate to the fastest times — overdo the right foot on the straight and any gain is more than countered by a ragged attack on the next corner.

The riders are showing understandable caution in the slowly drying conditions, exhibiting very different styles in these difficult circumstances. There is always less room for error on two wheels than four, and half-dry conditions are a particularly unknown quantity. I remember Graham Priaulx remarking that although the times don't reflect it, driving in half dry conditions is far more dangerous and far more difficult than in the streaming wet, when you at least know where you stand.

Less cautious than most is KTM rider Paul Jeffery, who runs too wide coming out of the Kennel, drops it, and ends up unhurt on the grass. 'What we call horizontal parking' observes the commentator. But 'these boys are quite used to a few little agricultural excursions' he reassures the crowd. 'Paul is improving immensely this year — although of course to finish you've first got to get to the top of the hill', he adds with stunning perspicacity.

On a power hill like this, however, the winning rider is likely to be riding a 500, not a 350. And of the 500 riders, Yamaha-mounted Jamie Mitchell is a strong candidate. In a stirring and highly effective ride which nearly has him on the tarmac both at Kennel and higher up he hangs on — or is if off? — for dear life as the bike slides around underneath him. He sets the fastest two-wheel time for the first runs at 36.91 and crosses the finish line at 87mph. In the second runs he will improve again to 34.89 as the track dries, the only biker in the 34s on the day.

It could scarcely be in sharper contrast to the next bike, the BSA JAP of Paul

LIVING WITH SPEED

Alan Thompson, Mallock Mk 21/24.

Lumley which thunders up in 44.50 and assails the crowd with British bark in place of Japanese yelp. He crosses the line at 67mph after a careful run, keeping a high gear through both Esses and then changing down to accelerate away to the finish, but he does it in style, riding in the traditional leg-trailing fashion beloved of prewar speedway riders. No steadying feet here, that's for wimps.

The BSA is a fine sight, proof that history is never far away when you spend a day at Shelsley. Hundreds of JAP-powered vehicles on two, three and four wheels have competed at Shelsley throughout a period spanning well over half a century and still the fascination with Mr J A Prestwich's engines remains.

Then it's back to modernity with David Wills on a Honda and a different style again. He puts the power on early at Bottom S in a low gear, the back end drops away, he catches it and then leans across the tank up through the gears, over the line, all to quite good effect; 39.10, and 89mph through the trap.

Peter Short, also on a Honda, looks a class act, quick and undramatic. He keeps both feet on the pegs at Bottom S but decides discretion is the better part of a valiant time and has a quick dab at Top S, all very neat and good enough for 37.32, 81mph through the trap and 91 mph over the line. The latter is the quickest of the day so far but he's still down on Jamie Mitchell, a situation which is destined to continue all day.

A 500 seems the right size bike for Shelsley. Terry Alderslade takes the big 1100 Suzuki to a storming 104mph over the line but manages only 76 through the trap and 37.47 seconds. Feeding that amount of power and torque through one little patch of damp rubber is not easy.

There are two three-wheelers here, each utterly different in concept. First up is Filth 1, the fearsome homebuilt Suzuki-powered trike piloted by Bill Chaplin and Livvy Klimpke. The pair have been shattering records at hill after hill all year and their time of 36.75 seconds (91 mph across the line) is altogether too much for the conventional Kawasaki-powered sidecar of Stu Stobbard and Mark Perry. The best they can manage on their first run is 41.55 and 82 respectively.

Although the track is drying by the time we move into the racing car classes, Top S is still very slippery under the trees and most top runners opt for slicks on the back and wets on the front. But the car which particularly catches my eye is not a top runner, just a very pretty one: the lovely Brabham BT21B of Simon & Jane Harratt. I keep seeing it at meeting after meeting: high time, I decide, to take a closer look. I saunter back to the paddock to wait for its return.

It's warm and sunny now and the drivers' body language is getting more upbeat, the spectators' more laid back. Little snippets from the commentators, and disconnected observations of my own, lodge in my memory as I walk. I learn that Barry Whitehead is a retired vicar from Wigan, drives a supercharged RBS 4F in the 1100 Racing Class — and runs it on Castrol R judging by the whiff as he streaks past. Two cars later it's the turn of the Crumpet Special, a 1968 car driven by a local policeman Phil Nuthall. Despite its age it ends well up in its class.

Back in the paddock I collar the Harratts and their immaculate blue and gold Brabham BT21B. Immaculate is an overused word but sometimes no other adjective will do; it is certainly appropriate for this 1969 Formula 2 Brabham. From its highly polished wishbones to its pristine gold nose, it is utterly spotless.

It is also extremely pretty, a wonderfully neat and restrained shape from the era when the high-headrests of the front-engined '50s 'roadsters' had gone and the wings of the '70s had yet to make their mark, an era when everyone had read the gospel on neatness and structural efficiency according to Colin Chapman and no one had yet written the Book of Revelation, on ground effect and downforce.

For the best part of a decade the custodians of the BT21 have been Jane and Simon Harratt, who freely admit to the car being the 'family pet'. Believed to have been originally campaigned on the circuits by Alan Rollinson, in whose hands it came second in the British F2 championship, the car then took to the hills, where it has stayed ever since. This probably explains why it has survived so long.

The Harratts are the third hill-climbing owners. They say 'believed' in connection with its circuit history because like most teams Brabham swapped engines, gearboxes and other parts around to the point where by the end of the season even the mechanics had trouble working out who drove what and when. Ask them 25 years later and you've no chance.

Chassis plates are not much help either. 'I know a man whose got a box of those, and he hasn't been working for

100

CHAPTER 13

Farley Special Mk2
Tim Cameron,
Racing Cars 1100-1600cc

The Farley Special Mk2 looks like no other car in the Shelsley paddock. To be frank, it looks distinctly bizarre. When it was first unveiled at Shelsley last year there was much scratching of heads, a few gasps, and no doubt one or two suppressed giggles. But when you talk to its creator, retired psychiatrist Dr John Farley, you find yourself struggling to fault the logic that lies behind it.

'I suppose what I wanted to do was build the sort of car that Godfrey Nash might have built if they'd carried on making cars,' John begins. He has studied racing history and noticed that the fortunes of chain and shaft drive have waxed and waned with the decades. Shelsley records show periods of considerable success for chain driven cars — the Nash era, then the Cooper era, and now the Jedi/OMS era — interspersed with times where shaft drive was the prevailing wisdom. John has no regard for engineering fashion: he built a JAP-engined special back in 1955 using chain drive and has stayed faithful to the concept ever since. This logic behind the new car is to exploit the advantages of chain drive to the full.

'I think a chain driven car is best with a beam axle, because a beam axle properly located keeps the wheel very nicely on the road and also allows one to use twin wheels, which you can't with a wishbone. The best wishbone suspension in the world can't keep the wheels flat on the road under all conditions unless you've got no suspension movement.'

The twin rear wheels allow you to put more rubber onto the road but, to keep down unsprung weight, they are very small — kart wheels in fact. They are matched by similar pairings at the front, making the Farley the only eight-wheeled car in motorsport. 'The advantage of this layout with wee wheels is that you can very simply get a low roll centre because your Panhard rod's very near the ground — you can't really avoid it!'

'Basically what you need to locate an axle properly is long radius rods — horizontal to the ground if you're going to have a reasonable travel and keep the axle geometrically right — very low unsprung weight and a 3 inch above ground roll centre.' And that's just what the Farley's got: 'pretty optimum location of the axle' in John's opinion.

To keep unsprung weight low there are no brakes on the back axle apart from a small hand-operated one, only added to keep the scrutineers happy. Their concern arose from the fact that rear braking is normally through a brake on the countershaft at the other end of the drive chain, and would thus disappear if the chain broke.

'I've got this very sophisticated set up on the suspension which differentiates between bump movement and roll. The advantage of it is that you can have the dampers set independently and you can control tramp, this is the theory.'

Currently, practice is not following theory, John admits. 'I think I've got the valving wrong in the damper, so there's a lot of development work to come, but at the moment it's running on fairly soft settings. It has to be valved so that bump and rebound are identical otherwise you get all sorts of peculiar effects, and that's a slight compromise, but I think it's going to work.'

Unmistakable rear end of the most original design in British hillclimbing.

Front brakes and suspension are relatively straightforward — a simple wishbone layout with inboard units.

The chassis looks Heath Robinson at first sight because the bodywork, such as it is, consists mainly of flat panels. But beneath the unlovely skin is a fully triangulated space steel frame which in John's words is 'very, very stiff indeed. You can't do any development on the handling of a car unless you've got a really stiff platform to work from.'

The power unit is again unique, a supercharged V-twin built specially for the car by speedway and grasstrack specialist Godden. John chose it for reliability reasons: 'This is pretty beefy, not as powerful as a four cylinder but a good practical banger.'

Japanese bike engines he rejected because he feels they aren't strong enough to take a blower. 'I'm supercharging at very high boost. I looked at the Japanese engines, they're very frail, if you try and do much with them they go pop.'

Output is currently 'about 200bhp I think', from 1139cc supercharged, which equates to 1595cc normally aspirated under the 1.4 ratio used in hillclimbing. 'It's enough, because it's a light car, and I think once we get it right it'll be quite competitive.'

Transmission follows the lines of his earlier car, again with a heavy emphasis on chains. 'The drive goes forward to the gearbox and then to a countershaft which has the brakes on it and then a traditional long side chain back as per Edwardian cars.'

Though designed in 1990 the car was not finished until 1995 so it has had very little running time. First time out, at Shelsley last year, 'we had a problem with the self-aligning bearing on the countershaft which had a plastic cage; unfortunately it broke, so we had a big redesign there. The second time we came we had trouble with the tyres lifting on the beads, losing air, so I've had to fit tubes all round.' Third time out, however, the car started to produce respectable times.

The last word should come from a fellow builder, Steve Owen of OMS: 'You've got to be a bit careful that you don't snigger. It's dead easy to knock somebody's ideas — and then they go quick. I don't discard it and I think one day it could surprise us all.

'But I couldn't market it, because it does look strange.'

Conventional racer and Farley Special: Leslie Stone's Delta T79 provides a sharp contrast at the Shelsley June meeting.

LIVING WITH SPEED

Brabhams for about 30 years!', Simon laughs.

Whatever its history, the car is a credit to its owners and still gives a good account of itself. The Harratts are not fanatical about originality, but they do insist on all changes being reversible, so that originality can be restored if desired. Welding on a bracket is taboo: better to mate a new fabrication to an existing mounting, and take a photograph of how it was before.

This year, for instance, they have added engine management, but ar-

Top: Old friend — Peter Voight in Roy Lane's Tech-Craft Buick. Compare the Brabham-like nose with the BT21B opposite.

Immediately above: Beautiful Tasman Ferrari of Dudley and Sally Mason Styrron.

Right: Bill Chaplin and Livvy Klimpke stirring the blood.

Bikers, clockwise from top left: Peter Short, Terry Alderslade, Jamie Mitchell, Dave Wills.

Below: Julian Ghosh and Jaguar C-Type.

ranged so that only eight bolts stand between it and refitting the carburettors. At the same time pump petrol has been substituted for methanol, 'so that we don't have to have engine rebuilds every year. Methanol is terribly corrosive on metal', Simon explains. The net result is 'less power and less torque, but it is as easy to drive, and a lot less hassle'.

Rivalling the Brabham in the concours stakes is Roger Thomas' Vision V91 which has been rebuilt to a very high standard indeed. I wonder if its condition inhibits Roger from achieving quick times, but it seems not: he ends the day third fastest on 33.40. Moreover, so close is the competition in this class that a mere seven hundredths separate

this spotless Vauxhall-powered car from a class win.

'It looks a darn sight smarter than this', observes the owner of the other red Vision in the paddock. The words come from Andy Smith, and he is referring his pride and joy, a hill-scarred ex-circuit racing ex-Clubmans machine on which he and car owner Tom Hughes expend disproportionate amounts of energy.

Andy's a bit like his car, less than immaculate but purposeful. He looks young for his age — maybe it's the beard — and can trace his hillclimbing back some 20 years. 'I started around '76', he recalls, 'in conjunction with another guy, Rob Oldaker, in a car called the March Austin Turbo — March 722 with a turbocharged A Series. It went quite well.'

In fact it went well enough to take the record for the fastest forced-aspiration

102

Shelsley Special in the 1600 Racing Class, a record which amazingly it still holds at 29.27. Anyone who has read that definitive history of British hillclimbing, *Uphill Racers*, will know that there is a long tradition of Shelsley Specials starting in the prewar years, weird and wonderful machines constructed with the express object of emerging from Top S as quickly as possible and preferably in a straight line. In its own way, the March Austin Turbo had quite a pedigree.

'Unfortunately it needed a transmission rebuild after every meeting and when I got married it wasn't practical. Neither was hillclimbing by the time the third child came along so I retired for the best part of 10 years, then I got back into it with my pal here and this Vision.'

Clearly the blower concept has got a powerful grip on the Smith psyche be-

Main picture and inset: the Harratt Brabham watched by an appreciative crowd.

cause the Vision is also force fed. Initially Andy and Tom went the whole hog and bolted on both a turbocharger and a supercharger 'with the aim of getting about 450hp out of it.'

The machine ran in that form at Barbon and Gurston in 1995 but it didn't work very well. 'The wastegate wasn't big enough', Andy explains. 'We only wanted a small amount from the turbocharger and the matching of the turbine and the compressor was such that we had an awful lot of exhaust bypass. Then we ran into fuelling problems so we thought we'd better go back to something we half knew about.' The turbo was removed. 'We'll get back to it sometime' he threatens.

With only a mere supercharger to help it along, the Vision's Cosworth YB puts out a paltry 320bhp, but it's still enough to produce some respectable re-

LIVING WITH SPEED

Doune, June meeting.

Paul Shipp
Man on the Hill

Play back a tape of a Paul Shipp interview and you find sections of normal speech interspersed with groups of words spoken so fast that they take a bit of deciphering, as though his mind has started to run ahead of his lips and his mouth has turned up the boost in an attempt to catch up. And this is what Paul Shipp is all about: intense, committed, sharp, always moving on, planning the next stage.

This young engineer from Ford's Dunton facility in Essex will tell you he has no particular ambitions to move on from the 1100 and 1600 classes where he divides his entries depending on what size engine is fitted to his OMS at the time, but that's a strictly practical decision, based on the costs of going bigger against the likely results. It certainly doesn't mean that he intends to give less than 100%.

Anyone doubting that need only look at his competition record. It contains a lot of victories but also enough accidents to prove that for Paul, finding the limit has sometimes only been achieved by exceeding it.

'We started about seven or eight years ago,' he recounts. 'A friend of mine at work was building a Westfield to go sprinting with so I built one as well. We ran that for two or three years just doing clubman's stuff. It started off as a roadgoing thing but progressed to slicks and rose joints and dry-sumped engines and all the rest of it. We started winning the class everywhere we went.'

In practice 'everywhere' was still relatively local to his Chelmsford base and consisted mainly of club sprints in the South East and South West. 'For some reason we never thought of going national.' Hillclimbs hadn't entered the equation at this stage.

'Then we made a bad mistake and sold the Westfield for a Davrian,' he explains. It was an ex circuit car, a 'very fragile' full-race device. 'I never really got to grips with it' he admits. Part of the problem was that he couldn't feel at one with a car he'd had no hand in constructing: 'When you build a car, nothing's a mystery, because you put it on in the first place, but these things… I didn't want to touch it even.'

Within six months or so he'd given up with the Imp-powered car and sold it. It was time for a rethink anyway because his sprinting partner was moving to a new job in the States. A Mk1 Fiesta followed. 'We did a little bit of work on that, ran that for about six months and started racing. I rolled that at Goodwood, built another one, raced that for two years in the works saloons.'

Marital problems then intervened. 'I left home and ran out of money. So I sold that and did nothing for a while.'

He couldn't leave motorsport for long though. Eventually he acquired a Renault 5 Turbo road car, entered five sprints in it and won the class every time.

'Then I had a motorbike. I fell off that and broke my collarbone, so I sold that and bought an OMS.'

It was not the first time he'd considered a single-seater. 'When I sold the Westfield I'd almost bought a Jedi.' But in the interim he'd seen some articles on Steve Owen's cars and arranged to meet him at Shelsley. The result was a sale for OMS and a competitive package which Paul ran for two and a half years.

The car was not a winner 'straight from the box', however. He suffered engine problems at first and solved them by installing an 1127cc Suzuki unit, which placed him just outside the 1100 class. 'It didn't matter initially when we were only doing local events but when we started doing nationals I got put in the 1600cc class.'

He was never going to win much by giving away nearly half a litre, so over the winter he commissioned TTS to build a 1200 engine for 1995. Even that didn't prove fast enough to win any events, but everywhere he went Paul came a solid second, for which consistency he was rewarded with the 1600 class in the Leaders Championship.

Buoyed up by success, he was in a receptive frame of mind when Steve Owen suggested building a new car for 1996. The class-winning machine was sold to fund the project and the result is a much narrower, neater car with inboard suspension and, in the early part of the season at least, a 1371cc engine. He could have had the new car built in carbonfibre but opted instead for a spaceframe as the weight penalty was only 10-15kg.

To help fund the operation Paul is again double driving, this time with his girlfriend Angela Hewitt, who also works at Dunton. Paul is at pains to point out that she is not merely a casual driver but half-owns the car. However, she prefers not to compete at every meeting, which gives Paul's brother Andrew an occasional outing. 'He may even buy a pair of wheels and tyres for it, that's his price for driving it this year.'

It's been a mixed season, with some class wins but also some mishaps. At Gurston he spun off on the last run and at Shelsley earlier in the season he hit the bank, damaging an upright and a chassis tube. Andrew too has not always managed to stay on the tarmac.

Paul finds this rather fraught. 'I don't mind sharing with Angela because I'm convinced she's not going to go off. But when you're sharing with somebody who you know is going to try hard, it's a bit of a nerve-wracking experience. You see them off the start line, then you watch and hope they get a time — or the red light comes on.'

Trying hard clearly runs in the family.

---

sults in the Over 2000 Sports Libre Class and worry the likes of Tom Hammonds and Jim Robinson. Their finest hour came in 1993, when Tom and Andy took the Vision to fifth and seventh respectively in the September Doune run-off.

'It runs on methanol' he continues, 'which is very difficult to find a filter for, as it's hygroscopic and the water blocks the filter up.' Paper filters are actually too effective — when you get a bit of water in them they clog. The only solution, Andy has concluded, is to filter the fuel very carefully before it goes in.

Andy works for Rover, looking after ride and handling. So the Vision should handle well 'if ever we get a chance not to be meddling with the engine all the while'. He's worked for the company, and for BL before that, for many years and as a young engineer received a lot of practical help and encouragement with the March Austin Turbo. Now he is returning the complement and just across the paddock is the beneficiary: Andy Kitson and his Rover 114. 'Basically that project was started to try and encourage engineers. I thought it was good to try and support the next generation.'

I'm struck by the historical continuity of this. The Midland Automobile Club has always been the natural focus for the engineers and enthusiasts of Britain's motor industry which even in the early 1900s was tending to concentrate

The March 782 of Phil Price and Paul Smith.

in and around the Birmingham/Coventry area. Initially Shelsley was where the engineers came to prove their wares; later, when alternative motorsports reduced hillclimbing's commercial importance, they kept on coming simply for sport and for fun. And, as the two Andys demonstrate, they're still coming.

Further proof of Shelsley's attraction as the professionals' playground is not far away, just across the paddock in fact, in the form of a Ralt RT3 and its driver John Wood. John is managing director of MIRA and it is no accident that the Nuneaton motor industry test facility is now more open for motorsport events than it has ever been.

As big racing cars start their second runs the first to go is a car which has no chance of winning but which everybody wants to see and hear; the ex Jackie Ickx, ex Chris Amon Ferrari Tasman of Dudley Mason-Styrron. It looks and sounds gorgeous, and even if it isn't driven with quite the abandon of some others in the class, it's great to see it being put to use rather than stuck in a museum.

I watch the climax of the meeting, the Top 12, from Bottom S. On the first runs Patrick Wood is *much* faster through this corner than all the others — is this traction control or just good driving? — yet his time is not the best. Is his car below par, or did he lose out somewhere else?

Patrick, Roy Lane and David Grace are occupying third, second and first places respectively after the class runs. No one is under 28 seconds, David's best being 28.20. As the Top 12 progresses, times tumble into the 27s and it becomes clear that one of these three is going to go home with FTD and the Raymond Mays Shelsley Cup. Come the second runs, Roy improves on Patrick's best of 27.62 to log 27.22, so only the last run of the day, by David, can rob him of victory.

And rob him he does, with the only sub-27 of the day: 26.95. The carbonfibre Ralt has won in its own right, not through a freak of the weather. 'I count this as a proper win' a delighted David Grace is to comment later at the presentation ceremony. The victory at Harewood, welcome as it was, could hardly have been described as satisfying. Today, however, he has beaten the Pilbeams fair and square.

A look of genuine disappointment spreads over Roy's face as he reads 26.95 on the timing board. 'I tried there, I really did', he sighs. He reckons understeer on the first bend cost him the win; he tried playing with the tyre pressures to get rid of it, but couldn't quite get round the problem all day.

He looks more down now, with nine points under his belt, than he did at Barbon with zero — understandably, as his situation has changed greatly since then. Back in Cumbria the season was young and there was no particular reason to think this would turn out to be an exceptional year for the Steel King team. Now, with his championship challenge in full swing, he can smell his fourth title and he is driving himself very hard. Even small disappointments loom large.

But it is not in his nature for his body language to be negative for long. A second championship win at his all-time favourite venue would have been wonderful, but even second place takes him away from the meeting equal on points with Roger Moran, having joined it seven points behind.

All season he has been lurking behind Roger, content to build up good results while leaving the pressure of championship leadership on somebody else's shoulders. Now he is level. Indeed in real terms he is ahead, for the season is drawing to a close and drivers are starting to drop points (only the best 10 results from the 16 rounds count).

Roger, the only top contender to have entered every round so far, has reached this point at this meeting and in consequence the seven points from his fourth place add only two to his overall tally, as he has to drop five from his worst result.

Today has been a turning point in the championship chase. The initiative, which seemed to have shifted towards Roger following his two fine wins on the Islands, has now moved firmly back to the man from Warwick and looks like staying there. From now on Steel King will be the team to beat.

Championship Top Tens

RAC after 12 rounds			Leaders after 10 rounds		
=1	Roy Lane	86	1	Tom New	65
=1	Roger Moran	86	2	Justin Fletcher	64
3	Patrick Wood	65	3	Martin Groves	62
4	Tim Mason	59	4	Phil Cooke	61
5	Bill Bristow	49	5	Mark Waldron	57
6	David Grace	42	6	Mark Lawrence	55
7	George Ritchie	33	7	Tony Lambert	53
8	Graham Priaulx	31	8	Andrew Russell	44
9	Simon Durling	26	=9	Pete Hannam	39
10	Richard Brown	19	=9	Jim Robinson	39

A day out with dad.

'You bastard, you're going to fly now'

After the downpour which greeted our last arrival at Gurston, it's a pleasure to look up at 8.30 on a Sunday morning and see clear blue skies. Only a few wisps of high cirrus spoil an otherwise perfectly azure August sky.

Mind you, it has been very wet quite recently, yesterday to be precise, and despite the warm sun the ground is still very damp underfoot and the track still wet. Despite the earliness of the hour, the renowned Gurston efficiency has the paddock buzzing with life and cars already ascending the hill. You don't manage four or five practice runs by having a Sunday lay in.

The weather turned yesterday's practice into a lottery. The morning was dry and Roy didn't try particularly hard, treating the first run as a warm up for the afternoon. However, the weather had other ideas and come the afternoon it was wet. Despite the rain, Roy gave it some stick on his second practice, not because he had any hope of beating his first but in order to learn the limits of grip on the wet track. If it stayed wet for the timed runs, he needed to know how far he could push the car in anger.

Later in the afternoon, however, the track started to dry again, after which practice times became thoroughly bewildering. Some got dry runs, some wet, some ran on slicks, some on wets, some on a mixture. At the end of the day the results were pretty meaningless as a guide to form and it would have been a brave man who would have predicted an FTD candidate on the basis of them.

Despite the promising start, it is soon clear that today too the sport will be dominated by the weather. Within only half an hour it starts to cloud over and before too long the Steel King team has erected what can only be described as a portable carport over the Pilbeam, a kind of tent without sides. It's large enough to cover the car, but the gear will have to take its chances. And there's plenty of gear to get wet: a typical Steel King 'pit' includes a bottle trolley for the air starter, a spare gas bottle, four sets of tyres (one of wets and three of dries in various stages of wear), a jerrycan, an engine warmer and associated gas bottle, jacks, chairs, a bucket, umbrellas and an unbelievably heavy toolbox.

Gurston is a particularly difficult track to predict when the weather is changeable, as it can be wet in the paddock and rapidly drying up on the exposed top section. 'It's such a lottery, this hill, in 10 minutes it can be dry up the top' observes John Chalmers.

One driver has already found this out the hard way. Mark Allen's Jedi is now sitting forlornly in the paddock looking rather the worse for wear, having made an unscheduled departure from the track at the Ashes. 'Be warned, Woody' shouts Jedi designer John Corbyn, pointing out the damage to Patrick Wood in the adjacent paddock slot.

John has not been much in evidence this season as a competitor, although his cars certainly have. Now, it seems, his back-seat role is about to change, because John has acquired a demon new engine and has built himself a brand new Jedi to put it in. He intends to contest the rest of the season to shake the new car down.

His rivals in the 500 Racing Car Class are probably glad he's entered the season so late. After practice he's the man to beat in the class, and though he finishes the day over a second adrift of class winner Adam Steel, he has signalled business.

Another man having a less than happy weekend is Mark Waldron. Yesterday the differential locked up on the Tuscan — fortunately on the straight so it wasn't too hard to hold. Mark promptly drove to Exeter and fitted a new diff overnight only to discover today that the gearbox has gone as well, presumably the result of shock loading from the diff failure.

'That's motorsport' observes the 36 year-old Midlander, philosophically. A consulting civil engineer whose work

Chris Merrick sets about his business.

CHAPTER 14

Return to Gurston Down

Man on the Hill

John with the 50th Jedi, a chassis number he reserved for himself.

John Corbyn

John Corbyn is an upfront sort of guy. What you see is what you get.

And what you see is a man with a very focused engineering approach, a very clear vision of what his cars should be and how they should develop.

He's not someone who veers off at engineering tangents. The Jedi practically created the 500 Class as we know it today, when John realised in the mid '80s that it was time to produce a modern equivalent to the 30 year-old Coopers which still made up the backbone of the class.

Twelve years on, the Jedi has developed enormously but a Jedi is still recognisably a Jedi, whether it be an early car or the latest off the line (he has now finished chassis 56).

Although an able driver himself, it is as a constructor that John is now best known. It wasn't always so, for at first his garage business took most of his time and the cars were merely a sideline. 'It's only in the last few years where it's reversed.'

Even so, making Jedis is not exactly a mass production operation. The whole job is done in house, even the paint, and 'there's only two of us working full time on them, so it does take time.

'The only things we have made out are the rack and the shock absorbers. It's the only way to keep a quality control.

'But that's the way I want it. I've got no aspiration to be a rich man.'

Like many middle-aged competitors, he started his competition career with road rallying in the very early '60s. He came across hillclimbing purely by accident.

'I went on holiday down to Penzance and had a problem with a road car, so it took me all night to get there. I fell asleep on the beach next morning and got sunburned. I couldn't stand the sun any more and I'd seen this sticker on the roadside — 'Trengwainton hillclimb' — so I went and had a look at it.'

He liked what he saw, so much so that 'three or four weeks later I was at Loton Park for my first hillclimb'. This was 1963, the same year that Roy Lane started. John has been on the hills ever since — 'on and off; do a bit of circuit racing in between'.

Cars are not his only passion however. 'My life's been divided between these and building model aeroplanes, which I'm very fond of. But unfortunately life doesn't allow you to do both does it?'

The two are not as unrelated as you might think, for 'a lot of the stuff in that car comes from model aircraft techniques, particularly the triangulation. Rubber-powered model fuselages have a very, very light geodetic construction, they stand an enormous amount of twist.

'Imagine a fuselage made of eighth-square balsa four feet long, that's got say 60 or 70 foot of rubber in it with enough energy to pick a man off the ground, that fuselage probably only weighs three ounces. You've got to make it right.'

The small matter of where to put the driver ensures that structural purity is not of course possible in a car, 'because you've got a big hole through the middle, but you make the best of it, don't you?'

He's been doing that for 12 years now and there's a whole generation of drivers out there who are glad he started.

LIVING WITH SPEED

The Gurston paddock can be a busy place.

has included among other things supervising the recent resurfacing of Curborough, he's seen plenty of ups and downs in a sporting career that started with Mk1 Escorts in the early '80s, when he competed in road rallying and single-venue stage rallying.

'We built the Escort up from a 1300, through the 1300GT and Mexico phases, eventually putting a Lotus Twincam in. Then, striving for more power, we used a BDA block with a Lotus Twincam head which was enormous fun to drive but unfortunately we were up against BDA Group 4 Escorts in those days in our class, so we didn't win anything. Then unfortunately — or fortunately — the opposite sex came along and distracted me for a while.'

Mark didn't get involved again until 1993, when he was foolish enough to tell Martin Silcox of Hagley & District Light Car Club that his roadgoing TVR was quite a good car. 'Martin asked me to put my money where my mouth was. He persuaded me to go to a club meeting in a standard road car and we had enormous fun. I competed for one season in the Association of West Midlands Motor Clubs Championship, which is now the Midland Speed Championship — and for my sins, I am now on the committee which runs it. Then in 1994 Barrie Lines asked me to share this Tuscan with him on the hills.'

Since then there have been few championship meetings where the rumble of the Tuscan has not been heard, though today is now certain to be one of them.

By 10 o'clock the clouds are much in evidence but the rain is holding off. Indeed, the track is now mostly dry, though still damp off-line. Times are starting to fall; Simon Durling, who often goes well at Gurston, logs 29.46 — the best time so far this weekend — only to have it beaten, seconds later, by David Grace's 29.09. The yellow Ralt was the sensation of the meeting when it debuted at this venue back in May. Will today produce the second victory in succession for last year's championship runner-up?

This and other questions are the type of remarks which Robin Boucher uses to keep his commentary alive during quiet moments on the track. As with the May meeting, Robin is back in the box today. It's not just commentator's chit-chat, however, for behind the words lies a serious commitment to the sport, not just in a vocal sense but also in an organisational one. An energetic and opinionated man who is not afraid to voice his views in committee, Robin has recently taken on a leading organisational role in the British Sprint Championship, a role which he will gladly enlarge upon in private moments with the mike switched off.

'Sprinting has suddenly become a lot lot more competitive. The time I did at Curborough in '88 would have earned sixth place in one of last year's run-offs there; this year I wouldn't have even qualified with it, by quite a long distance.

'The biggest bugbear in our sport is weather. We've discussed Hillclimb Leaders-type scoring systems for years to try and determine a method that's fair to all. Now we've got something totally different in Sprint Leaders this year. I think it's better than the Hillclimb Leaders scoring system but it's still not perfect if, for instance, it rains halfway through a class. You can't legislate for that.'

You certainly can't legislate for what is happening in the sky today, as Phil Cooke finds out at 11.30. A sudden shower sees Phil on the line on slicks and the track glistening with water. The hybrid Jedi has no chance, Phil forced down to 37.25 by the conditions. He has no hope of catching Mark Lawrence on the first runs now — his weekend's results will all hinge on the second runs.

It's not just one meeting's results that are at stake here, for with the season drawing to a close the Leaders Championship is reaching its climax and Phil is one of four drivers seriously in the hunt. He's in fourth place, but only four points behind Tom New, with Justin Fletcher and Martin Groves sandwiched in between. At this stage of the year an off-day is something he cannot afford.

The start is dry again by the time the big cars emerge. Local man Chris Cannell becomes embroiled in a private battle with co-driver Sue Hayes in their distinctive green Ralt RT1, the car noticeably more angular, and some would argue prettier, than most big single seaters. He manages 32.85, Sue shades him on 32.19, and later Chris will take his revenge by a couple of seconds in the second run — good enough, in fact to get him into the top 12. The Rover V8 sounds great initially, but a slight rough-

CHAPTER 14

At Barbon the RH430 was pressed into service for Tom and Richard, as the big car was not ready. This is Tom driving.

Ralt Gould RH430

Tom Brown, Racing Cars 1600-2000cc

Amateur motorsport is all about creating effective packages on limited budgets and there's no one more experienced at that than the Brown family. Richard has been hillclimbing since the '60s — he holds the outright record at Shelsley — and in the past couple of seasons son Tom has established himself as one of the fastest young drivers around.

This season the farming family from the Newbury area has run two cars, a Ralt RH430 in two-litre class for Tom and a half share in the David Grace Ralt Gould RT37 for Richard in the big class. If you wonder how one family can afford that, the following tale of how components have been juggled between the two may give you an insight...

The smaller car is built around a Ralt RT4 tub, basically the Atlantic car, although much altered by previous owner Adrian Hopkins. 'The front end is all the original RT4, the back end was some stuff that Adrian designed and made himself, which was good, but I had a prang...'

The prang was his expedition into the armco at Doune, which comprehensively demolished the back end of the car. 'A rose joint on the outside end of the top wishbone pulled out and the wheel just fell over. 'It was just one of those things', he observes philosophically.

At this point the big car enters the equation. The Ralt RT37 which caused such a stir when it first appeared at Gurston is actually an amalgam of the V8 from David Grace's Pilbeam of last year allied to the tub of Richard Brown's car, which last year ran with a Hart. However, creating this amalgam had entailed a lot of re-engineering, especially at the back. 'From the front end to

Car on the Hill

the back of the tub is identical (to last year), nothing's changed there at all apart from the front wing', explains Tom. 'From the back of the tub backwards it's all completely new, David Gould did all that design and built it himself.'

The rear-end rethink was forced on the Browns by the fact that the existing rear suspension simply wasn't strong enough to cope with a V8. The Hart engine was sold to Sweden but nobody wanted the old rear suspension, 'that was just left in the garage.'

And what did Tom need after his mishap in Scotland? A rear suspension suitable for a 2 Litre engine! The answer was already sitting on the workshop floor. Another phone call to the Goulds ensued and Tom set about stripping down the wreckage of the 'small' Ralt ready for David and son Sean to rebuild it around the rear end of last year's big one.

What Tom did not expect was that the car would improve as a result. 'It's gone on well actually, improved its traction a lot.'

However, Tom's troubles are clearly not yet over for today his engine has developed an untraceable misfire. (He will subsequently have a head gasket go as well, a fault which he thinks is unconnected). It's a complicated engine built by Jennett; a Cosworth Sierra YBM head, an ally Pinto block and 'all sorts of odd internals.' This is the first problem he's had with what he otherwise regards as 'a very good engine'. With around 275bhp on tap, it's as pokey as a typical Vauxhall though not quite up with the best. 'Ken Snailham's and Justin Fletcher's, I think they're around the 300 mark.'

As the season's end approaches, Tom can look back on a mixed year for the RH430. It started well: he worried the Pilbeam crews at Barbon, where he took the class record, then notched up a couple of second places, and then came Doune... Since then it's been 'a case of getting it all back together and going properly again.'

He is unsure whether to stick with the car for next season — 'it's actually my mother's car' — or to move into the big class courtesy of his father and David Grace.

But whether he drives the big carbon-tub car or not, he is convinced carbonfibre is the future. 'You can make the suspension work if it's a stiffer tub. In torsional rigidity tests, carbonfibre's just in a different league to even a good aluminium tub. There's nothing wrong with a good ally tub, you can still make them work very well, but I think the future isn't there.'

LIVING WITH SPEED

breaks the beam on the start line and an additional red light illuminates.

With the car correctly positioned between the beams (in other words, with a permissible 'run-in' of up to ten centimetres before crossing the start line) and a single orange showing, a marshal places what is best described as a small wedge on the end of a handle under a convenient (non-driving) wheel to prevent the car rolling, skilfully whipping it away as the car begins the run.

If a driver starts his run before his green 'traffic-light' comes on (a few yards ahead of him, at the roadside), the red indicator will light and the run will be disallowed, but in practice this is uncommon because there is no pressure to jump the start. Once getting the green light a driver may start in his or her own time, within reason. The clock only starts when the second beam is broken.

All timing gear is designed to log two and sometimes three runs simultaneously, to keep the meeting flowing, though more cars on the move means more chance of being stopped by someone else's red flag. A red flag, incidentally, is raised whenever a competitor's car would present a hazard — if, say, forward motion has ceased — not just when an accident has occurred.

Tim Mason comes to the line, gets the green — and stalls, just as at Harewood. But as at Harewood, he stops the car before the rear wheels have crossed the line, so he is allowed to restart. And on the restart he does it again, just as at Harewood. But when he finally gets under way he puts in a fine 29.72, so maybe stalling is all part of his psyching-up process.

Unbeknown to us in the paddock, a sudden shower at the top of the course has just laid a line of water across the finish. Tim, however, was later to report that he didn't even see it, so great was the veil of red mist which had descended.

Everyone else does, though some notice it rather too late. Chris Cannell takes to the grass, Bill Bristow and Simon Durling have heart-stopping moments.

David Grace, discussing the hazard later with Roy, exclaimed 'When I saw the dry line I thought "that dry line's getting narrower" — and suddenly there wasn't any dry line. That's why we all backed off. That's why Chris Cannell went in the field — he didn't back off!'

Roy concurs. 'It was so dry until suddenly you saw that patch and I thought "Christ, I don't believe this!" I reckon your eyesight's better than mine, David. You saw it before I did!'

Graham Priaulx, meanwhile, has other preoccupations. For today a stranger has appeared in the driving seat of the family Pilbeam. Not Graham, not Andy, but an inflatable rubber lady. Tomorrow is the Guernseyman's 50th birthday and hillclimbers, who grab any excuse they can find for a party, made the most of the opportunity in time-honoured fashion on Saturday night. The lady is a memento of the occasion, a present from his wife Judy and a few of the drivers, a gesture to ward off (or should it be exorcise?) any incipient mid-life crisis.

His first run time shows no sign of a hangover, however, coming in at 29.44,

ness has developed by the end of day which has Chris removing rocker covers to investigate. But even at its best the RT1 is not going to worry the class leaders, who now have their eyes fixed firmly on 29 territory.

I stand at the start, watching the marshals at work. A car leaves the line, the green light turns to red and the next competitor trundles up. Protruding from the front of the car is a vertical metal or carbonfibre strut, known as the Burt strut after its inventor, legendary hillclimber Patsy Burt (who was, incidentally, the first British Sprint Champion back in 1970). Its job is to break the timing beam in a uniform and predictable way, thus avoiding timing glitches due to irregular bodywork profiles.

Two parallel timing beams are in operation, one on the start line and one exactly 10cm before it. As the car is lined up at the start and the strut breaks the first beam an orange indicator light, in view of the startline marshals, comes on. If the car is too far forward, the strut

110

CHAPTER 14

Facing page, upper: Graham Priaulx with new girlfriend.

Facing page, lower: It could only be Gurston —Phil Price surrounded by farm machinery.

the fastest so far. But his birthday present lasts all of 60 seconds, about the time elapsed before Roy has completed an ascent on 29.26.

Towards the end of lunchtime the clouds get thicker and the rain, which hitherto has been unable to decide whether to fall or stay put, decides that the ground looks much more attractive than the clouds after all. By 2pm it is falling steadily. The meeting is beginning to look as though it will all be decided on the first run times.

This is bad news for Phil Cooke. He drew the short straw this morning with a wet first run, now his whole class is in the same boat. He opts not to take his second run, as do several of his competitors. It's a bitter blow to his Leaders hopes, the more so because it has all been totally beyond his control.

But the meteorological surprises are not over yet. Come 2.40 the sun is out again. It's too late to help Phil, but maybe the track will dry in time for the fast boys to have a dry second run...

Sure enough, it does. 'Slicks all round now' says Andy Priaulx, as he helps his father ready the Pilbeam for its second timed ascent. But there's an ominous black cloud over the far side of the track and some drivers are thinking of putting wets on the front as an insurance. Everything depends on timing now, your luck with the running order and the weather. The big cars have so much traction off the line that a couple of minutes drying time between one run and the next can make a real difference to times, maybe 0.2 or 0.3.

The biggest improvements on the second runs come from Simon Durling and Roger Moran, the latter obviously benefiting from the revised gear ratios fitted over lunch. Tim Mason clocks a mighty 132mph in the Hollow, one of the fastest speeds of the day, but David Grace blows it, missing a gear after the Ashes to record a dismal 36.67. But his first run is enough to ensure the top place in the Top 12, running last, with Roger Moran second and Roy third. Jus-

'I'm going for it this time!' Bruce White makes his point. The car is the Flash Special.

111

LIVING WITH SPEED

Racers in the mirror: Startline queue after the rain.

Championship Top Tens

RAC after 13 rounds			Leaders after 11 rounds		
1	Roy Lane	92	1	Justin Fletcher	73
2	Roger Moran	86	2	Tom New	72
3	Patrick Wood	71	3	Martin Groves	71
4	Tim Mason	63	4	Mark Lawrence	64
5	David Grace	52	5	Phil Cooke	61
6	Bill Bristow	50	6	Tony Lambert	58
=7	Simon Durling	34	7	Mark Waldron	57
=7	Graham Priaulx	34	=8	Pete Hannam	48
9	George Ritchie	33	=8	Jim Robinson	48
10	Richard Brown	23	=8	Andrew Russell	48

tin Fletcher is flying again, setting another new class record and once again mixing it with the Championship runners.

With the day reaching its climax, times tumble into the 28s as the pressure mounts. As Roger lines up at the start his eyes meet mine momentarily through the visor and I catch a glimpse of gritty determination. For sure, this will be a very fast time.

So much for my intuition. Roger posts a useful improvement, but not enough to prevent him slipping down the order, to sixth place. After the first runs it's Roy in the lead on 28.19 but David Grace is threatening on 28.47 and there's a whole gaggle of drivers in the high 28s. This is a very tight meeting, any one of half a dozen could still win.

Justin Fletcher, meanwhile, knowing that he cannot be one of them with only Vauxhall power to work with, is intent on beating the class record he has just set. He too looks really determined as he draws up to the line, a charging look on his face, eyes cast down, glaring up the tarmac in intense concentration. No chance of catching this man's eye. The result? — 29.98 and another new record.

As Roy takes the line for his second run his first-run time is still the fastest of the day, so he is assured of at least second place. Psychologically, however, a win is important, for he last took the laurels back at Doune, five meetings ago. Nine points is very nice, enough to put him in the lead in the championship for the first time, but a win will tell the sport that this is Roy Lane's season and they'd better believe it. A lot is hanging on this run.

We can hardly believe our ears as Roy storms off the line and then misses a gear as he accelerates down the incline. What a time to make a mistake! But then when we see the timing board, we can hardly believe our eyes: an improvement to 28.03! How on earth did he manage that?

Only one man can catch him, David Grace. It is the last run of the day and he will have to find around half a second to do it — a pretty tall order. But do it he does, with 27.79, the only driver under 28 all day. Not content with being the talk of the hill in May, he sets the crowd buzzing in August too.

Roy is furious with himself about the missed gear. 'I was so bad tempered after that,' he reveals to anybody in the paddock within earshot, 'that I thought "you bastard, you're going to fly now"'.

He drove the car so hard, he hit the rev limiter coming out of Ashes.

Hillclimbing is such a precise sport that it is extremely uncommon for a driver to make a mistake and still improve his time, but in this case Roy Lane, that most controlled and disciplined of drivers, has made up for an error with a rare display of raw aggression. As I drive home I find myself wondering: 'What on earth would his times be if he drove like that when he *hadn't* made a mistake?'

Daddy, can I have some? Please! Shush!, I'm watching this man warm up his tyres.

CHAPTER 15

'Fighting back the tears'

Return to Prescott

In some ways our second trip to Prescott starts in much the same manner as the first, with Roy and I watching the paddock go by over a mug of tea. But the backdrop to our conversation is very different. Then we had hopes, but only a modest measure of confidence; this time round we have plenty of both commodities. For the significance of Gurston's result has now sunk in; even though there are two rounds to go after this one, a first or second place today will be enough to clinch the championship and write Roy into the history books as a four-time winner of the RAC Hillclimb Championship.

Moreover, we are at a venue which he knows like the back of his hand, where he not only competes regularly but also teaches, and where he must surely be favourite to win.

Roy is very relaxed, and it shows in his conversation.

We are sitting on a couple of canvas fold-up chairs in the back of his trailer, talking about tyres. Specifically, about how long they last. 'We've got basically three sets of dry tyres,' he explains, 'and they work down a scale.' His best ones are kept for the championship runs, his second best set he uses for class runs, and then there are those which are only good enough for practice. Of wets he has just the one set.

'The slicks we've just taken off did practice yesterday, three runs. Now we'll put on the tyres which were our best ones back in June-July but are now only good enough for the classes. Behind us...' (he points to the rack in the back of the trailer) '...are our best tyres waiting for the championship run-off. When those best tyres have done say 25-30 runs they go down a scale and a new set comes in to be best. They're all numbered so we know exactly where we are.'

'I'm trying to be economical this year and basically do the season on two to three sets of tyres'. In other words, a set which is brand new at the start of a season will be no good even for practice by the end. Typically, although a set is demoted after 25-30 runs, their performance starts to dull well before this at about 15, but with tyres costing £700 a set for the big single-seaters, no one in hillclimbing can afford to replace tyres that often.

'Our best tyres have now done two runs at each of the last four championship rounds — Jersey, Guernsey, Shelsley, and Gurston — eight runs in all. They might just see the season out.'

He is also thinking ahead to the winter, and what to do with the car. 'That engine's done a lot of work now, with two seasons and two big test days on the test bed. I think by the end of the season it might need stripping down.'

Although he is not sensing any deterioration in performance at the moment — 'I think with the speed shown last week up and down Gurston, it's still as strong' — he acknowledges that hillclimbing, while gentle on engines in one way, in that they are only stressed for a few seconds at a time, is hard on them in another. 'What wears 'em out is starting them up all the time from cold, even though we warm them first.' Heating the sump with a space heater may seem like an indulgence, but a few bottles of propane are much cheaper than a set of pistons and liners.

Whether he will run this engine next year, however, is a moot point, for the paddock is alive with rumours — some admitted by Roy himself, some probably started by him — that Roy has been

Champion again! Roy Lane takes a victory run.

The BMTR Avon van: an indispensable part of the Prescott paddock, or any other hillclimb paddock for that matter.

113

LIVING WITH SPEED

How racing cars used to look: one colour and no stickers. David Grace in action in the Brown/Grace Ralt.

tempted by a good offer for the Pilbeam from one of his major rivals and might decide to sell, leaving him to concentrate on the Ralt for 1997.

As an ersatz team member, it might be expected that I would have an inside line to this speculation, but in truth I am almost as much in the dark as everyone else. Roy enjoys keeping people guessing, partly out of gamesmanship (remember what Roger Moran said about him liking to lull people into a false sense of security?), partly out of sheer mischievousness.

We spot Tom Clapham with his unique Lotus Seven and wander across. Although Tom is some six years older than Roy the two of them go back a very long way, having started hillclimbing at about the same time. Roy can't resist poking fun. 'Is this class for vintage cars or vintage drivers?' he asks Tom.

'Vintage' to Tom is taken purely in the oenological sense, as he explains to me after his run, for Tom firmly believes that in hillclimbing, age is not a barrier.

'I don't think you can really compare it with circuit racing because there you have a lot of factors which you have no control over at all.' He's referring mainly to the presence of other drivers, which he reckons makes people progressively more cautious as they see more and more examples of one person's mistake becoming another's accident. On the hills, there are no other drivers to sow doubts.

'The concentration level is higher than on a circuit, the performance has got to come within that short period of time. There's no missing a gear, losing a place and making up for it on the next lap. It's got to be right every second of the way. If you make a mistake the thing's blown. That's what I like about hillclimbing.' He has raced too, but prefers the hills. His message is that if you can maintain your concentration level with age you can maintain your times.

'Hillclimbing is vastly more professional than it used to be', he recalls, 'it's taken more seriously now. If you think back to circuit racing in the '30s, '40s and '50s, it was a case of going racing after getting together in the ale tent and everybody socialised and mixed and worked together. If somebody was stuck for a part they borrowed it. On the circuits that's all gone now, but the hills haven't gone that far even though they've gone a lot more professional. People will still borrow parts and still help each other out. Mind you, it doesn't make any difference to me — nobody's got any Climax bits anyway!'

Tom built the Lotus Seven himself, but today he is not the only long-standing competitor in a homebuilt car, for Phil Chapman is here. I resolve to track down the Chapman Mercury which I first saw at Harewood.

I find it next to a small energetic man with a moustache, who is only too happy to show me the innards of his creation.

'I built four specials, this is Mercury III', he explains proudly. 'Mercury I had a Triumph Southern Cross chassis. I put a sidevalve Mercury in it — used to run away from XK120s at circuit racing if the straight wasn't too fast. If it was they could gobble me up because it only did about 100, I think. It was very successful in trials, driving tests, rallies, circuit racing, you could do anything with the one car.

'Then in 1954 I built Mercury II, with the sidevalve Mercury converted to overhead valve, then Mercury III. This is it.'

Phil has always had a fascination with American V8s, which he took to its logical conclusion with the Mercury III, fitting a 7 litre Cadillac engine graced with 8 Amal carburettors which stuck out of the top of the bonnet. Not content with that, he went on to construct Mercury IV, which appropriately enough had four-wheel drive (and this, remember, over 30 years ago in a home-designed car). It used an Oldsmobile Rocket engine and was very successful in the wet — 'I wanted it to rain everywhere I went' — but was an unknown quantity in the dry. High point of this creation was a television event where it beat the BRM four-wheel drive car on four runs out of five.

He parted with Mercury III for many years but bought it back when he heard it was about to be sold to America. Now he is determined that it should stay in the family for ever.

There's a distinct look of C-Type Jaguar about the styling, but structurally it is utterly different, for it uses a separate steel chassis clothed in what was then a novel medium, glassfibre, the moulds having been made from chickenwire coated with plaster of Paris. The whole front tilts *á la* E-Type, as does the back once you have removed the petrol cap. In those days no one in the car body trade stocked fibreglass materials, you had to shop around for glassfibre in one place, resin from another, accelerator from a third. Having found the sources, Phil made this knowledge work for him and built up a successful business marketing glassfibre materials.

The Cadillac has gone now, in favour of a small block 5 litre Chevy with a single Holley. 'It had four twin-choke Webers but I found it was all or nothing. It would either cough, spit, or set the wheels on fire.' Components were drawn from the production and sporting cars of the day; front uprights are MG TD (though the rest of the front suspension is all his own), while the rear suspension is a home-brewed de Dion tube based on two Ford V8 Pilot propshaft torque tubes.

114

CHAPTER 15

Front brakes are HWM with Alfin drums on the front, a specification originally used on the back as well. However, the Alfins were ditched when the original diff destroyed itself and was replaced by a Jaguar unit with inboard discs.

Original items he definitely doesn't want to keep are the tyres. 'I've got to get rid of these Avon Turbospeeds' he complains. 'My daughter's just bought some new tyres for the Pilbeam because hers are more than six months old. I'm running on these, which I think were on before she was born!'

Although they are a rarity today, in the '50s and '60s there were lots of home-built cars on the hills. In that sense the Mercury is not unusual. What *is* remarkable though is its effectiveness, and its longevity.

Today is in danger of becoming a nostalgia trip so I decide it's high time to watch some competition. I park myself on the bank at Orchard Corner and relax in the sunshine. The forecast is to cloud over from the north but there is no likelihood of rain and right now it is lie-on-the-grass weather.

The single-seaters are starting their first runs and I arrive just in time to see Mark Coley continue a successful season with his Jedi Suzuki 021. The engine is an ex Grand Prix bike unit and it certainly gives Mark the edge, taking him to a first run time of 44.82 which turns out to be enough to win the class, even though he is destined to improve to 44.52 on the second run. The only other driver in the 44s is John Watts in a Jedi Suzuki Mk2/38, who manages 44.91 but fails on his second run.

One class up, Phil Cooke bounces back from his Gurston woes with a storming 41.88, well ahead of Martin Flamank's Hi-Tech Yamaha on 42.58. No one else is under 43 at this point and although Martin goes on to 42.05 on his second run, no one can touch Phil who rubs salt into his rivals' wounds with a second-run time of 41.22. Third is Steve Owen, by virtue of a 42.36 on his second run in the OMS CF/1 Kawasaki. Mark Lawrence, usually a threat in his OMS Kawasaki, is not on form today. On

Even in quiet moments, there's always something to do, or talk about, in the Prescott paddock.

his first run he spins through 180° on the approach to Ettore's and has to suffer the ignominy of being pushed back to the bottom of the hill. He recovers his composure to post a tidy 42.61 second time up, but it's not enough for a podium place.

Up in the 2 litre class, Justin Fletcher is again on scintillating form, posting the first ever sub-40 second time for the class with 39.25 on his first run. Tim Thomson, who has been having quite a good season with the ex-Roger Moran Pilbeam MP62 after several years off, can do nothing about it, his best of 40.39 being only good enough for third. Simon Frost makes the trip from Brechin worthwhile by nabbing second thanks to a fine 40.18 on his first run.

Of the big car drivers, it is Tim Barrington who impresses me most on the first runs. Although he has been bested at most meetings by co-driver Simon Durling, for my money he makes easily the most impressive entrance to Pardon hairpin — braking left very late, gearchange perfect. He manages a very creditable 40.62 but it's still not as good as Simon's 40.16 in the same car. Clearly I'm missing something.

Over lunch I seek out some of the younger drivers. Phil Cooke is my first target.

Now 35 and a dentist by profession, Phil watched motorsport with his father but that was as far as it went — there was no history of competition in the family. Much later he went to a hillclimb with a college friend and the friend's father, who was competing, and the bug

115

LIVING WITH SPEED

Unlike his co driver Ian Stringer, Tim Mason took the big Pilbeam into the Top 12 run off thanks to a time around 1 second better than Ian's.

bit. He bought a Caterham 'because I'd always wanted one' in the back end of 1989 and hillclimbed it as a standard road car in 1990. The Jedi followed in 1991. Whether or not he lifts the Leaders this year — and it is looking unlikely now — he has made a big impression on the 1100 class and is getting itchy feet.

'I've bought John Moulds' old 2 litre hillclimb engine and I'm just looking round for a suitable chassis.' He fancies a Pilbeam but is not sure the bank manager would approve. 'I'll have a quiet year next year and sort of build up to it' he thinks.

Despite the effectiveness of Phil's hybrid Jedi with its OMS-modified structure, Jedi creator John Corbyn does not seem inclined to change his long-standing devotion to spaceframe construction. He is here today, giving his new 130bhp Krauser engine another outing.

'The biggest problem with the 500 class at the moment is that there are no production two-strokes under 500,' John says. 'So what we've done is take an old Krauser which I've used in sidecar racing, of which there are quite a lot available now — the price is right — and we're going to develop it to work in a car. It's not very straightforward but it's starting to work.'

'I wouldn't even attempt to think about using a carbonfibre chassis because the only proper way of doing it is in an autoclave, which is a very very expensive bit of equipment. You've got to control it under proper temperature and pressure conditions. Unless you evacuate the resin it's heavy. I think a spaceframe, done properly, is still one of the best ways of going about it. And they're ever so easy to repair'. To support his argument, he points out that a MkIV Jedi spaceframe weighs 28kg, complete with suspension pick-up points and engine mounting brackets.

His Jedi, chassis 050 (he kept the number for himself for sentimental reasons), is particularly pretty, its red paint unspoiled by stickers, its ancillaries beautifully neat and making extensive use of carbonfibre. The black weave is evident in silencers, dash, vertical aerofoil surfaces, even the Burt strut.

None of this will be enough to tempt OMS enthusiast Paul Shipp into Jedi ownership. 'Jedis were always built as a 500 car, for an 1100 they're a little bit minimal.'

But the engineer at Ford's Dunton facility does share John's belief in bike engines. 'I think you're going to see more bike-engined cars in the 1600 class. Last year we were the only ones, this year there are three. The days of going out and spending twenty or thirty grand on a BDA may be coming to a close'.

'A new OMS, by the time you've paid for wheels and tyres and painted it, is ten grand, and the beauty of this sort of sport is that you can share it. Ten grand doesn't buy you a Westfield these days if you put a decent Vauxhall or BD in it and we go faster then they do.'

'I can't see people like myself and Mark Lawrence taking a step up from what we are doing now. The next class is the 2-litre class, serious engine money, serious chassis money, serious tyre budget, and at the end of the day you'll probably find that Mark has beaten all but three of the 2-litre cars anyway.'

Meanwhile, back at Steel King, the atmosphere is still relaxed. Roy is lying second after the first runs on 38.69, with Patrick Wood (who always goes well at Prescott) leading on 38.58 and Roger Moran third on 38.89. No one else is in the 38s and it looks as though the class winner will come from these three.

And so it proves. David Grace fails to get amongst the action, producing a best of 39.02, and after the second runs it's still Patrick who takes the afternoon's award — interestingly, after turning off the traction control as an experiment. The big question is, however, can he do it all again in the Top 12? Despite lots of class wins, Patrick has only ever taken one British Championship Top 12 run-off, albeit with a hill record, at Barbon in 1994. Will he double his tally today?

Before we find out, there are some congratulations due elsewhere, for Maggie Blankstone has just beaten her own Ladies Record by the very slimmest of margins, one hundredth of a second, driving the Pilbeam MP43C sports libre car shared with Jim Robinson. Driver after driver rushes up to shake her hand, hug her, kiss her. The First Lady of Hillclimbing is delighted — as much with the attention, I suspect, as the achievement.

In the second runs Roy turns up the heat, posting 38.30. Graham Priaulx improves to a threatening 38.91, Roger can manage no better than 38.87 and David is still slightly off the pace on 39.03. Can Patrick, who runs last, snatch it back?

He can't. The clock stops at 38.31 and the Target crew can't believe it. One hundredth adrift. Can it really be slipping away from them again?

Tension is high as the second runs approach. Roger Moran fits a brand new set of tyres, knowing that this is his last chance to stay in the championship race. He *must* to finish ahead of Roy to take the fight to the next round. Patrick doesn't do anything, except mentally chew his fingernails.

Bett Lane watches Roger fit the new tyres and thinks he is making a mistake. 'You need a couple of runs before they're at their best' she tells me.

Big surprise of the second runs is Richard Brown, who slices nearly a second and a half off his time to log 38.52. Graham Priaulx gets the message and also improves, to 38.60, while David Grace finally breaks 39 seconds by recording

116

CHAPTER 15

Bugatti Type 35T
Hugh Conway Jnr, Bugatti Handicap

If any one car is synonymous with Prescott hillclimb, it must be Hugh Conway Jnr's Bugatti 35T. Not only a fine example of one of the most sought-after vintage cars, it is all the more desirable because its history is so complete. And for 50 years of that history it has been making fairly regular excursions up this Gloucestershire hill.

By now it must be capable of finding its own way up, but just in case it can't, two of its former drivers are around today to help it: Prescott stalwart Rivers Fletcher and Medical Officer Richard Bergel.

Type 35s come in various guises, from 1.5 to 2.3 litres, supercharged and normally aspirated, but all are single overhead cam straight eights. This one was built as a 2 litre unsupercharged.

Originally sold to a Frenchman in 1925, it is normally listed as a '26 car because that was when it arrived in the UK. Before the War its string of competition-minded owners included Kay Petre, who raced it at Brooklands, and Sheila Darbyshire.

Around 1933 the original plain-bearing crank engine was replaced by a roller-bearing unit and the car renamed accordingly (35T instead of 35A) but apart from that the vehicle is remarkably original, still boasting factory bodywork — the stamp '40' can clearly be seen on the inside of the cockpit rear — and original chassis.

After the war ex-marine Ted Pool acquired the car and raced it despite having lost a leg in the hostilities. Hugh Conway Jnr tracked him down recently and was delighted to receive 1947 pictures of the car, showing it crashed right here at Prescott.

'It then passed through James Allington to Rivers Fletcher. Then it blew up again and was converted to a 2.3 litre car and bought in 1959 by an old friend of my father's, Hugh Bergel. He owned it for 19 years. His son Richard raced it frequently at vintage race meetings and he too crashed it twice, once at Rouen in France and then at Silverstone. After that Hugh sold it to father as a crashed car and the two of them rebuilt it more or less into its present state.

'Hugh and father both kept very meticulous records. The car did 10,000 miles on the road between 1959 and 1978, father took about two or three years to rebuild it and he did another 10,000. I've done about 3500, making 23,500 miles. Before that it was never registered for the road so that's the total — no miles at all for a 70 year-old car, extraordinary.

'It's had lots of rebuilds of course — I broke a halfshaft four weeks ago and had to rebuild the back axle — but what I like is its patina. It's still just a working car.'

Prescott, May meeting, as Hugh prepares to take a run after (bottom) investigating a fuel pressure problem.

Car on the Hill

117

LIVING WITH SPEED

Prescott, May meeting.

Maggie Blankstone

Woman on the Hill

Ask 100 competitors to name the best-known female hillclimber and a good 80 of them would say Maggie Blankstone. Her association with motorsport goes back nearly 40 years to when a car-mad 16 year-old girl first went marshalling. There was no history of motorsport in the family, her enthusiasm was entirely self-generated. It demonstrated an independence of thought and action which have served her well ever since.

It wasn't long until she obtained her driving licence, whereupon her father found his car 'borrowed' and entered into local rallies. 'I then met up with boyfriends who were in the car club, we teamed up together and

Maggie makes a habit of breaking the Prescott Ladies record. This shot is from 1995, when she did it with the 2 litre Pilbeam MP62.

that's how it started. It's gone on ever since — I've been competing about the same length of time as Roy Lane!'

Her motorsport experience is by no means confined to the hills. 'I did night rallying — the old "plot and bash" style of event — for a while and then I started autocrossing and sprinting. Later I went circuit racing and then I met up with Peter and we went hillclimbing together.'

Peter, whom she subsequently married, is just as much a hillclimbing institution as his wife, having started hillclimbing in the mid '60s. Unlike most husband and wife pairings, however, they frequently go their own way where machinery is concerned. Though they shared a Mallock for several years, 'when Peter was chasing the Hillclimb Championship in 1970-71, he had a single-seater and I had a Ginetta G12 which I campaigned for three or four years. So we towed two cars to the meetings. Then we were quite wealthy and we had a full-time mechanic, now we have to do it ourselves!'

The fact that the couple have owned a garage since 1971 — a Vauxhall dealership — helps their motorsport activities less than might be imagined. 'We keep our motorsport totally separate,' Maggie says. 'You can't afford to have somebody wanting his car serviced and then say "sorry, the boss's racing car is in".'

This year she and Peter are again doing their own thing automotively. Maggie, who has held the ladies record at Prescott since 1993, has teamed up with long-standing competitor Jim Robinson to drive a Pilbeam MP43C in the Sports Libre Over 2000 Class, a partnership she is 'enjoying thoroughly'. She does not expect to get down to Jim's times — 'he's normally two seconds quicker than me, I'm respecting the power of that car' — but will certainly get close enough to give him something to think about, and to provide constructive feedback about the car. For behind the smile there's an inner toughness about this white-haired lady which only the foolish ignore.

38.82. All three of them have thus leap-frogged Roger.

Roger's turn comes. The pressure is immense. He needs a sizeable improvement, at least half a second. One mistake could leave him sixth and end his title challenge. He powers off the line.

Bett was right. The tyres don't help. Roger's time is a lowly 40.31 and the man from Ludlow has to admit defeat. After a great first season with the big cars in which he has led the championship for most of the year, he has finally been hauled in by the old campaigner from Warwick. There are some moist eyes in the Moran camp, understandably. We learn later that he suffered an intermittent engine cutout on that run — what a time for it to happen!

So even before he takes the line Roy knows that he is the 1996 champion. Only Patrick can beat him now and second place is all Roy needs anyway.

In the circumstances Roy could be forgiven for taking it easy, but he doesn't, posting a small improvement to 38.28 and giving Patrick a little extra to do. Can he find 0.04 and break his jinx with the last run of the day?

The green comes up, and what happened next is best left to Patrick's own words.

'You're in a cocoon here. Focused on everything. Just check the instruments, everything's fine. Tighten the seatbelts one last graunchy bit. Put it into gear. You're so up there, you're like 150%.

'And I looked over, and as I looked over a photographer walked in front of the traffic lights and started clicking away. I was sat there, *and I couldn't see the stop-go lights!* So I started waving, then I started getting irritated — as you would, wouldn't you? — and then pointing at him and waving. It seemed to me like an eternity, like a minute, though it was probably 10 or 15 seconds.

'Dave Riley, Clerk of the Course, suddenly ran round and waved this guy aggressively out of the way. And then I left the line, and botched up the entry into Orchard, still thinking about the bloke. "What a pillock!" I was saying to myself.

'What I should have done, and what

118

CHAPTER 15

Winner and only entrant in the Prescott Wet T-shirt competition and (right) rolling out for the run that clinched the championship.

Roy would have done, is put my hand up, killed the engine, called the marshals over and explained the problem. I would have been rolled back off the line and given a fresh start. That's experience for you.'

The photographer's antics probably cost Patrick his second ever RAC win, for his time of 38.46 is no improvement and leaves him runner-up on the day.

In the emotion stakes, Patrick's disappointment is nothing compared with Roy's elation. Drivers, marshals, crew, practically everyone in the paddock wants to be the first to congratulate him, and the second he steps out of his car after his victory climb a throng of back-slappers, handshakers, kissers, jokers, photographers, and the just plain curious gathers around him. He's been here three times before but that doesn't stop

Patrick Wood: 'So up there'.

Championship Top Tens

RAC after 14 rounds			Leaders after 12 rounds		
1	Roy Lane	95	1	Justin Fletcher	79
2	Roger Moran	86	2	Martin Groves	76
3	Patrick Wood	78	3	Tom New	72
4	Tim Mason	63	4	Phil Cooke	70
5	David Grace	58	5	Mark Waldron	66
6	Bill Bristow	53	6	Mark Lawrence	64
7	Graham Priaulx	41	7	Tony Lambert	58
8	Simon Durling	34	8	Jim Robinson	57
9	George Ritchie	33	9	Pete Hannam	55
10	Richard Brown	31	10	Andrew Russell	48

him being overwhelmed. As the happy hubbub subsides, he's fighting back the tears.

The presentation starts with prizes for the kids' off-road cycle race — proper awards for various age classes, a genuine attempt to involve the younger hill-climbers in the day's sport. It continues with Maggie Blankstone being voted Man(!) of the Meeting, a title which does nothing to stem the air of jollity which is rapidly enveloping the entire proceedings. Roy gets a bucket of water thrown over him by John Chalmers as he walks up for his pot, though a less likely candidate for a wet T-shirt competition is hard to imagine. His shirt says 'I don't come here to play, I come here to win' but everyone here this afternoon knows that he really comes to do both. And if there's anyone in the paddock who be-

grudges the Steel King man his fourth title, they certainly aren't in evidence.

Justin Fletcher is cock-a-hoop at another new record and is now three points clear in the Leaders, and Martin Groves is not complaining either, as he too has set a new record today. From now on the Ricardo-sponsored title will be a fight between the two of them. One championship may be settled, the other is certainly not.

It has been a fascinating and exciting season so far, vastly more successful than Roy dared hope at the start. To wrap up the title with two rounds to go is to win decisively and conclusively. As I drive home I wonder if we will see the Ralt out for the final two rounds, for with the pressure off there is surely no better opportunity for a little experimentation. Time will tell.

119

LIVING WITH SPEED

Twelve titles, one photo: left to right Roy Lane (four times RAC champion), Tony Marsh (six times) and Sir Nicholas Williamson (twice).

No traction control here, not even a diff — the noisy end of Harry Foster's JP F3.

'One or two pheasants may be eaten later on today'

As far as Steel King is concerned, there's a very laid back air to the proceedings today. Roy is here to enjoy himself in what looks like very un-Wiscombe type weather — ie glorious sunshine. Yesterday, rather than enter Saturday's club meeting as a warm up for the Championship event on Sunday, he left the MP58 in the trailer and spent the day helping Tim Mason work on his MP50M. Of Roy's Ralt there is no sign, almost as if even the pressure of development is more than he fancies this weekend.

But Roy's attitude is certainly not typical of other sections of the paddock. While one championship may have been decided, the other most certainly has not. In the Leaders, Justin Fletcher and Martin Groves have everything to prove today.

Martin is still lying second in the Leaders to Justin and these two are the only ones who can now notch up a maximum score. 'If we both win our respective classes today that's where we'll stand,' says Martin. 'So then it's all down to Doune. And there's the same situation in the Midland Championship.'

I remark that Justin has something to prove at Doune, in view of his accident there in June, but Martin is not under any illusions. 'So do I, I've never been there before!'

He could be forgiven for giving less than 100% today, as his wife is heavily pregnant and he could become a father for a second time at any moment. However, he is banking on the new arrival on being a chip off the old block and timing his or her entrance to fit in with the Leaders. One must get one's priorities right, after all.

His first child, a girl of around two and a half, is already a common visitor to the paddock, having made her first

120

CHAPTER 16

Return to Wiscombe Park

meeting at the tender age of one week. Martin's wife Mandy does not compete, but it may only be a matter of time before her name appears on the entry list. 'I think she fancies a go; up to now she's had a worry that if she did anything to the car, it would upset my meeting. I'm sure she'll have a go at some stage.'

Thirty-one year-old Martin is unusual amongst top hillclimbers in that his connections with the motor trade and/or engineering are virtually nil, apart from around 6 months as a mechanic with the Reynard Formula 3 team in late 1990. Others can get trade-price parts and scrounge the use of the firm's facilities of an evening, but when you work in wholesale haberdashery and needlecraft there's no help to be had.

On the other side of the paddock is a bearded character who has no such problems, for he is a blacksmith, a man to whom fashioning metal is second nature. Mind you, he has no hope of winning either, for Harry Foster owns a venerable 1950s 500cc racer which today finds itself in the same class as the modern Jedis. However, he does have two '50s 500s to spar with, plus his own PB to aim at.

One of his sparring partners is Pete Wright, a civil engineer for Tarmac Construction. He's currently roadbuilding in Derby 'but this is what matters. This is our local track and we love it here. There can be nowhere better on a nice day.'

Under Harry's machine is what could flatteringly be called a catch tank, but is otherwise best described as an oil can hung underneath the chain with a lump cut out of it. 'In the best traditions of 500 ownership, we improvise' he laughs. The 'we' is Harry and Pete, who are old friends, Harry being in his 50s, Peter in his 'very, very late 40s'.

Looks like a toy, but appearances can be deceptive: the Cooper Mk8 of Pete Wright.

'You've got to slide it to make it work at all' — Mike Anthony nicely sideways at Sawbench.

Pete Wright leads Harry Foster to the line.

121

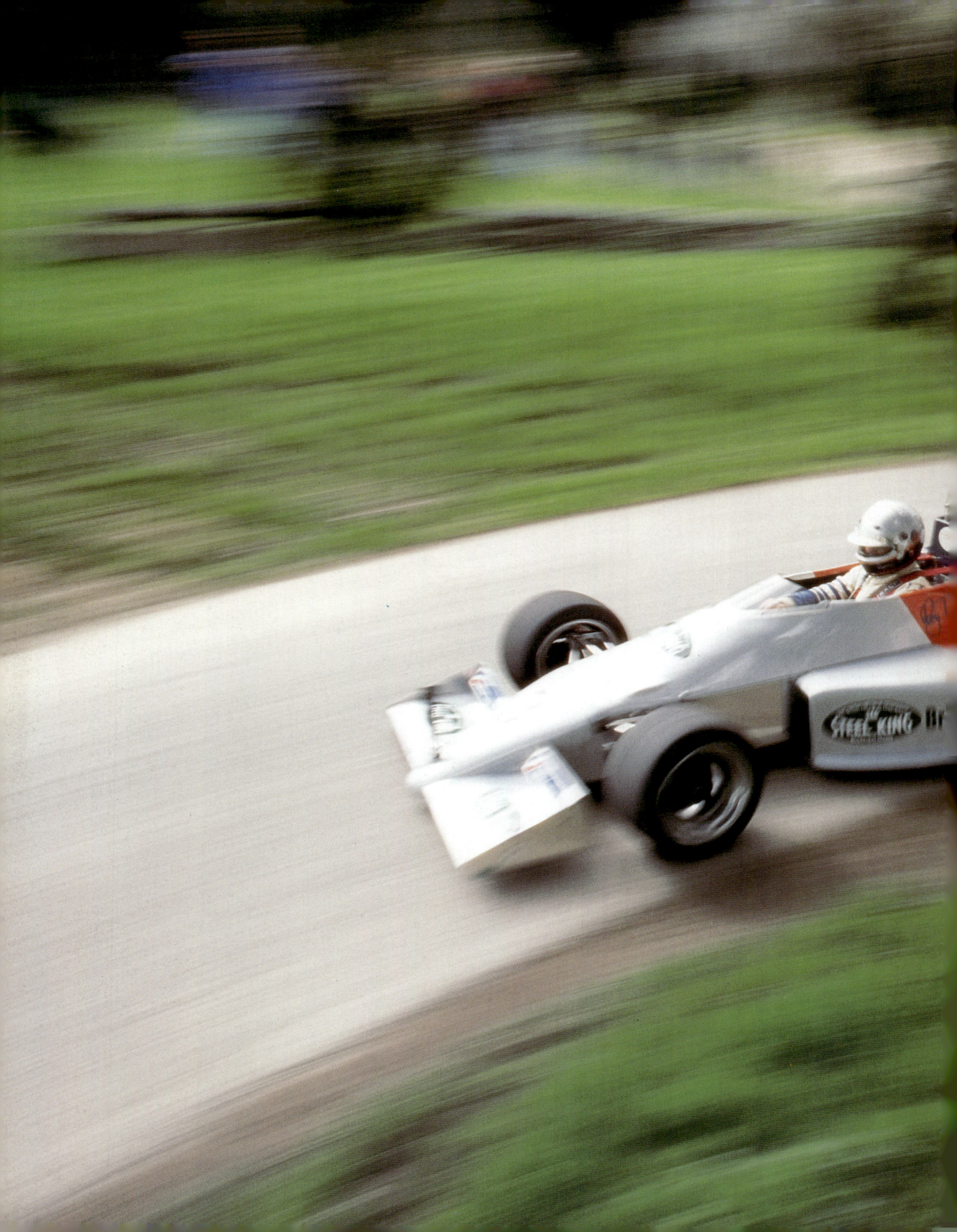
STEEL KING

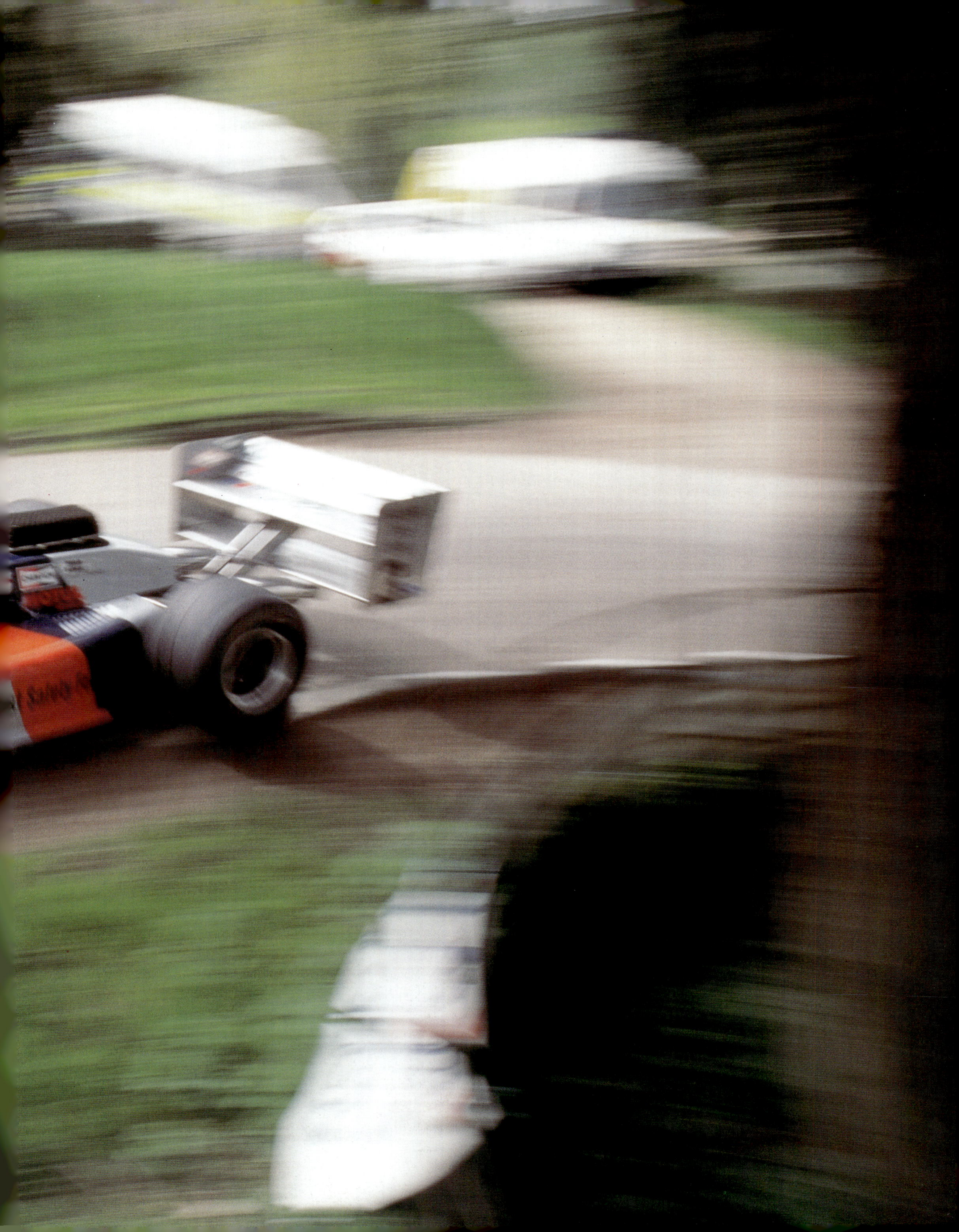

LIVING WITH SPEED

Car on the Hill

Mallock Mk20B
Martin Groves, Clubmans

Martin Groves and Mallock at the Doune September meeting (above left), and at the start of the Wiscombe Park event of the previous week (below). The top right shot shows the engine bay of this remarkably effective Mallock.

If road cars are too soft and too tame (and too expensive to repair), small racing cars too bike-oriented and large ones too costly, the Clubman's Class is for you. Front engines are obligatory, engine sizes and development are strictly controlled, and the result is that a serious and surprisingly quick racing machine can be created on relatively limited budget. Dozens of racing drivers cut their teeth on them before moving on. Hundreds of others are content not to move on, happy to stay in a class where competitive performance can be bought for a four-figure sum.

The Mallock practically created the Clubman's Class on the hills and remains the most popular make. As an indication of what can be achieved with one, consider Martin Groves' example.

There's nothing remarkable about the car's appearance. Indeed, its hard worked orange and yellow bodywork is best described as purposeful rather than pretty.

Martin concurs. 'I have got some new bodywork for it, but I don't see the point in putting it all on at the moment. We'll get it all done properly over the winter. It's worked very hard this car, double driven on a number of occasions this year. It's done 16-plus meetings already this season.'

An ex-circuit racing car, he bought it in late 1991 as a write-off without an engine, although it had been powered by a Formula Ford unit. 'All I collected was a bent chassis and a few boxes of bits.' 'We first had it out in the middle of '92. Since then it's generally got better and better. It's probably had its most notable results in the Channel Islands on the Val de Terres.'

Indeed it's the car's performance in the Channel Islands which most graphically illustrates how competitive a good Clubmans Car can be. He has had a personal battle with Roy Lane for the past five years on the Guernsey track, and currently the score is 3-2 to Martin, despite the enormous difference in horsepower. 'It's had a third place in the run off over there and a fourth and a fifth. It seems to suit that particular hill.

'The difference is, in a car like this you can drive the Esses section more or less flat out in third gear with both hands on the wheel and allow the car to drift through the left and right hand bends without really having to lift off. You just let the car flow, and I think that's where we make time.'

He first started competing in 1989 with a Special Saloon Anglia on the hills, using a 1760 crossflow Ford engine. But when the modified production car rules came in to supersede the Special Saloon cars, the Anglia by virtue of its engine found itself in the Sports Libre Class where it would have been uncompetitive.

A Clubmans car appealed because 'it is a controlled formula and everybody's running more or less the same equipment. Therefore it comes down to who's got the necessary skill and ability rather than who's got the largest pocket. It's certainly a very cost-effective class to run in, I don't spend any more money running this car than I did the Anglia.'

His actual costs have been inflated this year because of the need for a major rebuild to the 1700 motor, undertaken by John Beattie, but normally the biggest expenses are entry fees and a set of tyres. 'Most of us have just one set of tyres a year.' In total he spends some £3000-3500 per season.

'I do get some help from Brady Fabrications, they've rebuilt the chassis for me a couple of times after some major accidents, one of which was me driving, another one was another driver. Some places it's definitely an advantage to have someone else sharing, particularly at Prescott with its return road. If you're running second you've got the advantage of warm tyres. Most other places it's no great advantage and there's always the factor where someone else could ruin your day.'

'I'd love to have a go in a single-seater but with a young family I feel there's a limit to what I can put in financially. To go any faster than with this, I think you've got to look at the two litre racing car class. You're looking at potentially three times the initial expenditure at least and probably more than double the running costs. Therefore it's not on the agenda at the moment.'

124

CHAPTER 16

Both their cars look like Coopers, but only Pete's actually carries the famous name. Harry's machine is a 1951 JP F3, built by Glaswegian Joe Potts. Originally known for his racing motorcycles, Joe hillclimbed a Cooper MkIV and then laid down 34 of his own chassis along similar lines. Seven are known to have survived, but only a couple are still on the hills. Harry's is the only one still running with the original body.

Most had Norton engines in their day, but some were fitted with JAPs (as is Harry's) and two cars used a 1000 Vincent. 'When Joe Potts died in 1973, everything went in the skip, including the Manx Norton engines', Harry relates wistfully.

Pete's is a 1954 Cooper MkVIII, though there is also a MkV at home. The MkVIII is something of a fraud today, being fitted with a relatively modern grasstrack bike engine from a Jawa in the interests of power and of conserving the now-expensive JAP. 'Harry here made some plates for it so we could mount it in the car'. The two cars look quite different, the JP having a bluff nose and the Cooper looking much more sleek. The Scottish device's shape is dictated by the great big fuel tank positioned over the driver's knees, necessary in the JP's heyday as a typical fuel consumption on methanol was a mere 8mpg. The JP's handling varied considerably during the course of a race depending on fuel load, whereas the Cooper was less sensitive to load on account of its side tanks.

By rights, Harry and his Cooper should have the edge today on account of the Jawa's extra power, but the blacksmith is not beaten easily and at the end of the day there is only 0.12 between their best times and less than half a second between Pete and the slowest Jedi.

'They're not toys' Pete insists, 'though they look a bit like toys. Most people get quite a shock the first time they drive one. I've tried modern cars and although they're quicker — I ran in the Clubman's Class — they're definitely not as much fun as these'.

They certainly *look* fun, with their tail-happy antics at every hairpin. 'You've got to drive them like that,' Harry explains, 'because there's no diff, it's a solid rear axle. You've got to slide it to make it work at all, but it's controllable.'

Back with the '90s interpretation of bike-engined cars, Phil Cooke and Ian Chard can be expected to be fighting hammer and tongs for the 1100 class, and indeed after the first run Phil leads Ian by seven tenths, setting a new class record in the process of 37.81. And that's how it stays: Phil's next run is a poor (by his standards) 39.73, while Ian's is even poorer, the local driver coming to grief in the wooded section of the course.

Also fired up is Justin Fletcher. Martin Groves has already set a new Clubmans class record of 38.47 and Justin

Great to see a modern Ferrari being used in anger. This is Ed Stratton's F355GTS with which he won the Road Ferrari class.

knows he too must win to keep his edge in the Leaders. And win he does, with yet another new course record of 35.46, nearly a second and a half below his own record set as recently as May this year. What was that I said about things being laid back?

In the big racing car class, Sandra Tomlin has let someone share her car for the first time and has mixed feelings about the result. John Forsyth manages 39.88 in his first climb with the car, whereas Sandra is around 41. 'Rather startling isn't it!' she laughs. 'I never wanted to be shown up to be so slow!'

Lunchtime is a lazy affair and when the action restarts I am still too relaxed to fancy climbing right up to Martini, not straight away anyhow. I settle on the grass between Wis Corner and Bunny's Leap and observe techniques at the first turn.

Meanwhile the tannoy is asking for volunteers from the public to go pheasant marshalling. Quite whether the RAC regulations cover this activity is not clear, but all weekend drivers have been complaining that pheasants, which currently abound on the estate, are wandering all over the track. During practice for Saturday's club meeting, Basil Pitt had collected no less than three brace at a shot, to the detriment of his Ralt BDA's front wings (and the pheasants), as he bounded over Bunny's, perhaps inevitably earning himself the alliterative nickname 'Poacher Pitt'.

'If there are any people in the paddock who would be prepared to sign on as pheasant marshals for the rest of the afternoon we would be very pleased to see you and suggest what you can do' comes the plea.

The temptation for drivers seems to be to take Wis Corner too tight, which unsettles the car and ends up losing more time than it gains. Douglas Bennett in his Ford Escort is a good example: clearly fired up, he goes flat out over Bunny's Leap and lives to tell the tale.

In the bigger Road Saloon Class, Escort RS driver Stuart Browne takes the tight-line-round-Wis technique a stage further and tries autocrossing on the inside of the corner. His over enthusiasm costs him for the run is over a second down on his earlier attempt.

Andrew Short in yet another Escort makes a similar error but is determined to make it up over Bunny's Leap — the back goes light on the nearside and starts to slide, first to the right, then leftwards on to the grass. But somehow he invents a Fourth Law of Motion and reaches the Gate still pointing in the right direction. A few cars later Ian Williams in the Westfield S8 finds himself in exactly the same pickle and pays for it with a slower time. Successful hillclimbing is not only about pushing hard, it's also about judging when to stop pushing.

The most appealing sight among the road cars has got to be the Porsche 911 Carrera 3 of John Turpin. The brilliant blue projectile looks good, is driven with verve and has a wonderful rasp to its exhaust. I want one.

I climb up into the trees to watch Sawbench from the inside of the hairpin. Two black T-shirts emblazoned with

125

Tony Fletcher

Man on the Hill

'A chance would be a fine thing' is probably how RAC Championship Coordinator Tony Fletcher would react to the suggestion that he is the nearest thing you'll find to Bernie Ecclestone in hillclimbing. Where F1 pulls in millions, Tony is grateful to deal in thousands. But the parallel is true in that a good part of the sport's future lies in his hands.

He pays the RAC annually for the championship franchise and works full-time raising sponsorship money and organising the series. He does a similar job for the Midland Hillclimb Championship but has no involvement in other series other than as an occasional RAC steward.

Nevertheless he is often found scouting round lesser events. 'I quite enjoy going to club meetings, seeing who's coming up, because they're the future of the championship meetings. It's looking very bright at the moment because there are a lot of people at club level.'

Hillclimbing is in his blood. 'When I was about four my father was involved as a mechanic to Austen May, who drove a Cooper 500 in those days. I've been going hillclimbing ever since. I first became an RAC official in 1959 as a timekeeper', a role which he fulfilled for some 30 years.

Then in the mid '70s he became involved in the championship scene, an involvement which continues to this day. He complemented this by becoming clerk of the course at Loton Park. The regard in which he is held can be judged by the fact that in mid 1996 he accepted the presidency of the Hillclimb & Sprint Association.

Raising sponsorship money is 100% his responsibility 'and it is very critical. A year without sponsorship for the running of the championships costs me a lot of my own money — and we've now had two years without sponsorship for the British Hillclimb Championship.' By contrast the Midland Championship is supported by Bromsgrove-based Clark's Motor Group and by Avon Tyres through BMTR.

He knows full well that his job is impossible unless you take a positive attitude. For 1997 he is 'quite hopeful' that the gap in the British will be filled. 'We're talking to people all the time, if I wasn't then I wouldn't be doing this job. But it's never agreed until they sign on the dotted line. With next year being the 50th birthday of the British Championship, we obviously stand a better chance than we've stood for years.' (After this interview we learned that the 1997 championship would indeed by sponsored, by Liqui Moly UK.)

How has the sport changed? 'Immensely. The cars have changed, the venues have changed, everything has got better, everything is more professional although it is still an amateur sport. The standard of preparation of the cars, and the image which the sport portrays to the general public, is fantastic. All credit to the drivers for doing what they do.

'What we desperately need is television coverage. But we don't get television coverage until we can pay for it, you can't pay for television coverage until you get sponsorship, and sponsors won't come in until you've got television. It's a complete vicious circle.

'We'd love a higher profile, but I *don't* want the sport

A quiet moment on a busy afternoon: Tony Fletcher at the September Doune meeting.

to be seen to go professional. Once there's a lot of money in it — and we've seen this happen to other branches of motorsport — it kills the sport as we know it now. It's a very very fine balancing act, one we have to be extremely careful about.'

Which drivers would he count as the sport's all-time greats? 'Tony Marsh undoubtedly. Six times hillclimb champion with a 10-year gap in between, that's got to be fantastic. And Roy Lane, who's been with the sport almost as long as I have, a competitor for nearly 30 years.'

He values the family atmosphere and the continuity which it brings, saying 'we like to keep the people in the sport if we can.'

However, despite his best efforts some drivers he rates very highly have gone elsewhere. 'James Thomson, one year, a fantastic year, won the championship and then disappeared unfortunately. Martin Bolsover, three years on the trot and then went circuit racing. Andy Priaulx, did the sport for a couple of years, won the championship and then went circuit racing. It would be nice to keep these people; how do we do it?'

'One thing I'm very conscious of is encouraging young people.' For instance, one of the championships gives an award for the highest placed person under the age of 25. 'They don't get anything for it at the time but they get a number of free entries the following year.' This costs the championship quite a bit of money, because the championship funds then have to pay the club for those entries, but it hopefully encourages people to come into the sport and stay.

Among the current crop of young drivers in the smaller classes he particularly rates Martin Groves, Tom New, Justin Fletcher, and Tom Brown. 'They're the people who spring immediately to mind as potential future champions.'

Tony has no doubt that some if not all of these will hanker after a drive in unlimited capacity racing cars sooner or later. Indeed, Tom Brown has already had a taste of it courtesy of the Richard Brown/David Grace Ralt. 'It's a natural progression. The big class is almost the biggest one we've got; that's been the case for several years, and it's nice to see.'

'Team Filth' have decided to do the same thing, and I can't resist reading the shirt backs, which list all the hillclimbers' watering holes in the South West. Inside the shirts are Bill Chaplin and Livvy Klimpke, the duo whose shatteringly fast trike has been such a crowd-pleaser on the hills all season.

In full leathers Bill and Livvy look pretty formidable. If theirs was a road-going trike and the pair pulled up outside a cafe, the grannies inside would be reaching for their purses before Bill could hit the kill button. But it isn't, and in any case appearances are very deceptive. There's no aggression in their voices, just a West Country burr from Bill and a biker's irreverence from Livvy. Team Filth, I learn, has two full-time members and one honorary one, Simon Durling, who owes his position to a very convenient arrangement whereby the worn-out fronts from his Pilbeam find their way on to the back of the trike.

Back on the track, G15-mounted Andrew Russell is tackling the hairpin with real ability. He locks up slightly on the way in, takes full advantage of the tail-bias of the car to swing the back round, then straightens it all up and goes, very neatly done.

Shortly afterwards Roy Bray gives a demonstration of how hard you can drive an Escort Cosworth and still stay on the track. The 1994 South West Champion lifts the inside front on the way into

CHAPTER 16

*Simon Emmens'
Austin Cooper S was
easily a match for
Andrew Russell's
Ginetta G15 in
Modified Production
up to 1400.*

*Off the track, Team
Filth is not hard to
find.*

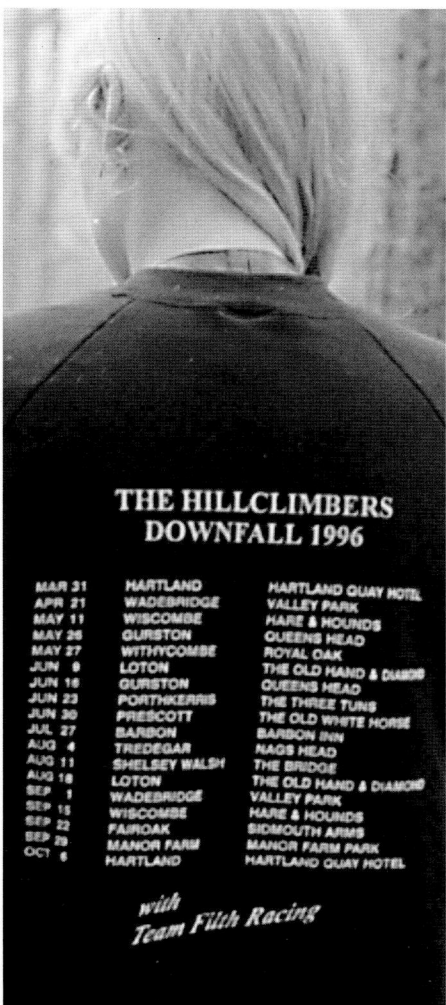

Sawbench and the inside rear all the way round, really hairy stuff. Even so it is not enough to displace similarly mounted Mark Spencer from second in Modified Production over 2000, top spot going to Mark Waldron in the TVR.

The Clubmans cars follow, and all eyes are on Martin Groves as he tries to keep his Leaders hopes alive. He's really trying, slides it on the curve into Sawbench, nearly loses it, just collects it in time. The result is another meteoric climb in an identical time to his first, record-breaking, attempt this morning. It may not be enough at the end of the season — everything depends on whether Justin Fletcher wins at Doune — but Martin is certainly keeping up the pressure. He can do no more than win — the rest is outside his control.

Equally spectacular is the Metro 6R4 of Andrew Fraser. He leaves his braking impossibly late, looks as though he can't possibly get round but does anyway. Mighty impressive. Co-driver Tim Painter doesn't look nearly as quick and this time impressions are not deceptive: he's a full second adrift. Splitting the two is Paul Parker in the big Royale, a result he's probably fairly content with since he is not too happy about the track conditions at Wiscombe.

He had voiced his concerns to me at Shelsley earlier in the season. 'I'm beginning to have my doubts about the safety of Castle Straight since they re-surfaced it, it has little or no grip at all now and in view of the inclement weather which is more customary at Wiscombe meetings it may be worth considering whether it's a championship venue any more. It's a good track, the layout of the track I have no question with, it's a good challenge. It doesn't suit this car because of the number of directional changes, particularly between Gate and Sawbench, but when things are right — certainly rarely at Wiscombe these days — we'll see off Tim and Andy.'

As we move into the racing car classes, grunt is replaced with revs and close-ratio gearboxes. Indeed, so close are some of the ratios on the 500s that you wonder momentarily if they've missed a gear and gone back into the same one. Among the small single seaters, the best attack at Sawbench is from Peter Smith in his Jedi Yamaha, who keeps the engine right on the cam all the way round.

Eventually it is time for the Top 12 and although the Championship no longer hangs on it, the tension still increases noticeably in the paddock. There is less chatter, more faces turned towards the timing board, more ears attuned to the commentary.

Tim Mason, who only just qualified for the run-off, gets off to a bad start with a stall on the line, repeating the problem which has dogged him for most of the season. In fact one reason for his lowly 12th in the running order is that earlier this afternoon he was given a failed run as a result of a stall in which the centre line of the rear wheels broke the light beam. This time he stops in time to be given a rerun.

The Brown family too is having a bad day, the Gould Ralt suffering from a lack of front grip to the point where the front tyres have actually been swapped for an older set in the hope of finding an improvement. Then Richard is delayed by an electrical glitch, eventually rushing to the start line under threat of the two-minute rule and only thanks to other competitors and mechanics who cluster round to help.

Out of his rhythm, he makes a poor

127

LIVING WITH SPEED

...Peter Sexton bends his Westfield SEi after overcooking the exit of the Gate...

Mishaps...

...while hard-charging Jedi driver Ian Chard charges a bit too hard and pays the price.

start and almost stalls. Despite knowing Wiscombe Park like the back of his hand — he is a director of Wiscombe Park Ltd — he finishes with a mediocre 37.16 which he improves to 36.67 second time up. Son Tom is slightly quicker in the same car at 36.59 but on his second run gets totally off line at Sawbench, only quick reactions saving the Gould Ralt from impact with the bank.

Two 2-litre drivers are among the elite, of which Justin Fletcher is predictably one. The other is Simon Frost who has made the long trip from Scotland worthwhile by qualifying eighth in an MP62 similar to Justin's. He eventually finishes last, but at least he made the grade.

Justin's MP62 meanwhile continues to put bigger cars to shame. 'This man will be absolute magic through the Esses' asserts commentator Jerry Sturman, and so it proves, Justin managing a fine 35.84 which leaves him third at the end of the first runs.

After coming third in the class event, Bill Bristow too has hopes of a good finish but blows his first run at Martini, where the nose clouts the bank and slows him to an uncompetitive 42.03.

Roger Moran is running last today, having won the class event, and so has the luxury of knowing what he has to do. Roy sets him a stiff but not unattainable target with a 35.32 first run.

'He looks absolutely committed as he comes up through to Sawbench,' enthuses Esses commentator Pat Jennings, 'round the hairpin and the tail hits the inside edge of the curve'. And he *just* shades out the old campaigner: 35.27 and the fastest Top 12 run so far.

This leaves Roger, Roy and Justin as the only three in the 35s at the end of the first runs, though Patrick Wood and Simon Durling are lurking just outside in the low 36s.

While Mark Waldron and Mark Spencer help Bill fit a new nosecone between runs, Jerry Sturman reads out some unofficial but reliable stopwatch times between the start and the Gate. These make very interesting listening, for the fastest to the Gate is not necessarily the fastest to the finish.

Quickest to this point is Roy on 12.99, testament to the massive torque of the 4 litre Judd, but second is Patrick Wood on 13.24, a sign that traction control really does pay dividends on the start line. And only a hundredth behind him is Bill Bristow, proving that Bill was not boasting when he claimed to enjoy particularly good traction from his home-developed rear suspension.

The same split time reveals how easily Tim Barrington's eventual ninth place could have been much higher. He bogs down his second-run start and by the Gate is a full three-quarters of a second adrift of his first run, but by the finish he is only 0.04 slower. Now if he had done a good start *and* a fast run... But hillclimbing is full of 'what ifs'.

Bill Bristow makes no mistake on his second attempt and comes away with 35.83, a fine result from a 2.5 litre car. This, and a big improvement from Patrick to 35.56, is enough to push Justin Fletcher down to fifth overall, leaving the top two spots to be fought over by the two men who have been sparring all season, Roger Moran and Roy Lane.

Again the split time is revealing, Roy dropping two tenths by the Gate compared to his first run. He finds a little extra elsewhere but it is not enough and he finishes with 35.30, a marginal improvement which is still slower than Roger's first attempt. Roger's second run is now a formality and he cruises up the hill to take the applause, an anticlimax for the crowd perhaps but a fitting reward for the man who has been in dominant form all weekend.

Jerry Sturman sums it up. 'It's been a great weekend for Roger, if he can't win the championship, the next best thing is to win here at Wiscombe. And he'll certainly be going for it next weekend at Doune.' He rounds the weekend off with the traditional thank you to all the marshals, whose normally purely nominal rewards have this weekend been augmented from an unlikely source: 'One or two pheasants may be eaten later on today perhaps', he adds knowingly before switching off the microphone.

Winning form.

ROGER MORAN

Championship Top Tens

RAC after 15 rounds			Leaders after 13 rounds		
1	Roy Lane	96	=1	Justin Fletcher	81
2	Roger Moran	89	=1	Martin Groves	81
3	Patrick Wood	81	=3	Tom New	75
4	Tim Mason	63	=3	Phil Cooke	75
5	Bill Bristow	59	5	Mark Waldron	72
6	David Grace	58	6	Mark Lawrence	64
7	Graham Priaulx	41	7	Pete Hannam	62
8	Simon Durling	39	8	Tony Lambert	58
9	George Ritchie	34	9	Jim Robinson	57
10	Richard Brown	33	10	Mark Coley	56

CHAPTER 17

'Eighteen till I die' (with acknowledgements to Brian Adams & R J Lange)

Return to Doune

Every year, Roy announces at the beginning of the season that he won't go to Doune in September. One visit per year, he asserts, is enough for such a far-flung venue. And every year he turns up at Doune in September.

This year of all years he could be forgiven for staying at home, for the Championship is already decided in his favour and following his second place at Wiscombe last weekend he has now come first or second in his ten best rounds of the championship, giving him 96 points out of a possible 100. The most he can achieve today is to raise it to 97, a distinctly academic reward for a 700 mile round trip.

But turn up he has, for the very simple reason that he wants to round off the season with a Saturday night party, which he is hosting jointly with several other competitors to celebrate a successful and highly enjoyable year.

'I think Roy's a bit lazy at the moment', Antony Lane observes on the Sunday morning, 'needs a win to do anything'. Is he referring to lack of motivation following his clinching of the championship, or is this a euphemism for 'Give dad some space, he's a bit hung over'? It seems prudent not to ask.

Certainly the season has taken its toll of men and machinery. David Grace's Ralt is suffering from transmission failure, an ignominious end to a highly promising first season. Tim Mason has also pulled out, after bending the car yesterday. Graham Priaulx's Pilbeam has a starting problem — the ring gear has gone. A similar problem afflicts Bill Bristow's car. Indeed, Bill is not a happy man: he's struggling here, unhappy about gear ratios, displeased with his times, looking stressed and agitated. There's an almost fatalistic note in his voice as he reels off the problems he and other competitors have suffered, as though he is sure they will not be the last.

He can't complain about the weather though. Today won't be as hot as the June meeting, but now that the sun has broken through the early morning mist the temperature is rising steadily. Not a breath of wind, scarcely a cloud in the sky, and a full entry list. What more do you need for a fine day's sport?

George Ritchie always goes well at Doune. Here he blasts past the old lady's bungalow on his way to fourth in the run-off.

Despite his alleged laziness, Roy was fastest in practice yesterday, the only driver under 40 seconds. Today will not be easy though, because although David Grace and Tim Mason are now off the scoreboard an even more formidable name is back on: Andy Priaulx. After storming to a hill record back in April the 1995 champion has been out of the Pilbeam's cockpit because of circuit racing commitments. Now he is back for an end-of-season fling, thanks to a new contract which is more tolerant of extra-circuit competition. Will he finish the season as impressively as he started?

He has a particular reason for wanting to compete today, because the Priaulxs are coming to the end of their three-year sponsorship deal with the Bank of Bermuda, assistance which has been worth £10,000 a season to them. The end of the deal, plus Andy's commitments elsewhere and Graham's desire to devote more time to supporting them, means that at the very least the distinctive metallic blue Pilbeam will be seen less next year. Probably the car will be sold, in which case this meeting will represent the end of a memorable era for the family.

It is an era from which Andy will move on with some sadness. Exciting

Helpers gather round David Grace's sick Ralt.

years may lay ahead, but the atmosphere of the hills is hard to forget. At Gurston Down we had discussed whether TV coverage might affect that atmosphere and Andy was not convinced that it would. 'The people here,' he said, looking round the paddock, 'are down home motorsport enthusiasts', implying that it would take more than a media man's wallet to channel their *joie de vivre* into something less wholesome. There was a wistful note in his voice, as though he were not entirely happy to be leaving the sport for more glamorous things.

Whether he can go out with a win today depends in no small measure on whether he can get happy in the car again after several months away. Graham's seat does not suit him, it puts him too close to the wheel; 'I feel like I'm fighting the car', he complains.

Patrick Wood is in philosophical

129

With this lot up front and virtually nothing at the back, weight distribution is not exactly ideal.

Car on the Hill

Maguire Mini
Dave & Sandy Robertson, Sports Libre Cars 1400-2000cc

Any resemblance between Sandy Robertson's Mini and the standard Longbridge item is merely incidental. For the car is a Maguire Mini, a pure space frame with a fibreglass Mini-shaped shell on top.

'It's a standard Mini gearbox casing', admits Sandy almost apologetically. The top and bottom front suspension arms are also 'original' but that's about as far as it goes.

Engine is 1594cc Ford crossflow unit with steel crank, steel rods, Cosworth pistons, full race heads, roller rocker assembly, titanium valve caps and special valve springs. Maximum revs are 10,500 but the unit is limited to nine.

It's grafted on to a Manx conversion gearbox; the standard casing with a special adaptor plate welded on, while on the clutch side of the engine there's a spacer plate to bring it back to the normal gearbox. The internals are a Jack Knight dog box with a sintered clutch and, for this year, a new Quaife diff.

Sandy explains: 'We used to have a Salisbury diff which was really twitchy. This one, first time I tried it here I went off, it was so easy to steer! That's making life a bit easier — you know, I'm getting older!'

Front hubs are F2 twin-pot callipers each side with Granada discs machined to suit, attached to steel driveshafts. The rear end is a fabricated twin swinging arm.

Two things strike you as you squeeze inside: the huge aluminium box to the left of the driver (the oil reservoir for the dry sump), and the large red light in front. This is a shift light, set to come on at the revs appropriate for maximum acceleration.

Sandy reckons its value is questionable, at least at Doune. 'On a hill like this you don't have time to look at the damn light.'

You look out over a dramatic power bulge which has less to do with the height of the Ford engine (it's a Lotus short-stroke block) than the fact that the whole body/

Sandy (left) and brother Dave.

chassis assembly sits about 5cm off the ground, making the power unit that much higher.

The car used to compete in the old Special Saloons category, but now finds itself in Sports Libre, where it is frankly outclassed against the Clubmans-and-then-some devices. By comparison it is nose heavy and hard work to drive; indeed the car is so light at the back that one person can pick it up; if you really tramp on the brakes the back tends to lift, which must be disconcerting to say the least.

As a result the brothers — Sandy co-drives it with his younger brother Dave — are considering replacing it with an ex Kenny Allen Ralt, one of the older aluminium-tub designs. It will be quite a wrench, as Sandy has been competing since 1979 and has always been faithful to Minis, starting with a Cooper S. He admits it will be a big leap, 'but everybody says the Mini is difficult to drive and these single seaters are easy.'

At the time of writing he has no idea what the Mini is worth. 'But I know what I've spent on the thing over the years!'

---

mood. 'This sport is not actually about driving skill, it's about commitment — especially somewhere like Doune as it happens. You can drive fairly quickly here without extending yourself or the car, but to go *very* quickly just requires huge commitment into a series of blind bends — and that, to put it crudely, is simply a question of balls. Sorting the car out actually doesn't become a problem because the performance of most of us is quite a long way below that of the car, the exceptions being the slow bits like East Brae and the safe bit like the Meadow.'

Steve Owen, meanwhile, has more practical things on his mind. Keen to see a good turnout of OMS cars for the end of the season, he has offered to help competitors with petrol money and has been rewarded with six cars on the entry list. Unusually, his sports libre car is not one of them, Steve opting instead to share with Paul Shipp. 'It's a long way to come with two cars and trailers', he explains. 'Paul's got to travel 550 miles to get here.'

Co-driving makes commercial and engineering sense too, because the open-wheeler has proved more popular than the sports car and it's logical to promote the more successful design. 'It's good for development, because that's the car we're trying to sell more of. If I'm in it as well we can get twice as much mileage on it, get on top of what happening with it.' Although OMS's main emphasis now is on the carbonfibre single-seater, like Mark Lawrence's, feedback from Paul Shipp's spaceframe design is by no means wasted because it uses the same geometry and shares many suspension parts.

Despite Steve's backup, Paul Shipp looks preoccupied and intense as he prepares for his first run. The 1370 Suzuki has recently been replaced by an 1100 unit so that the car can run in the next class down and in Steve's words the replacement power unit has taken 'a bit of sorting out. We've been struggling all weekend'

This morning they have changed the jetting and that seems to do the trick: Paul's first run of the day puts him

CHAPTER 17

firmly in the 44s, pretty much where they were in June with a bigger engine, and Steve later confirms the improvement with a 45. By the end of the day he too will be in the 44s, though neither of them will be in the top three, all of whom break the existing record of 43.41. Class leader Mark Lawrence breaks it with a vengeance, logging 42.96, the first ever sub-43 for the class.

Mark Lawrence's time would have been good enough for a middling position in the 2 Litre class, graphic evidence of the way the narrowness of Doune inhibits the big cars from getting their power down. And the 2-litres in turn seem nimble compared with the V8s, as Tom Brown points out.

Twenty-two year old Tom, who works on the family farm, has not had the best of luck at Doune this year, coming to grief in June with suspension failure on his 2-litre car and having his September meeting foreshortened by transmission problems on the Richard Brown/David Grace Ralt. But the fresh-faced young redhead has driven enough to notice the difference: 'With the 2-litre you can go through the bottom with plenty of road to play with, but the V8s are so big you can't do it, you run out of road. A 2-litre can get through the bottom part so much quicker than the big cars. I had ours on the barriers in the Esses yesterday, which you never would have done in a smaller car.'

Doune regular Martin Pieraccini concurs. 'This is not a power hill, it's a driver's hill.' And when I observe that the course looks frighteningly narrow he replies: 'You should try it from in here!'

Nevertheless he's a great Doune fan. 'It's a good place this. Nice holding paddock at the top as well. Up there you can unwind before you come down. I don't like places where you come straight back; you've done your run and you're parked again and the moment's gone, whereas up there it's all nice and peaceful.' He carried a walkie talkie once, to warn his helpers in the paddock if anything needed preparing, but these days he's content to let things take their course.

As is normal at Scottish events, sa-

Low-cost Libre: Donald McCaskill and his ever so slightly modified Mitsubishi Galant.

loons are well represented, but in addition to the modern machinery there are some interesting older tin-tops running in the Thoroughbred class, in particular Alistair Simpson's Sunbeam Rapier.

I seek the owner and find a quietly spoken man who runs a butcher's shop in the week and hails from Edzell, midway between Aberdeen and Dundee. Doune is not his favourite venue — 'it's a bit fearsome', Forrestburn suits both him and the car better. 'That's open, there's plenty of room to run off' he explains. He never competes in England but is not averse to the long drive to Rumster, up past Inverness. 'I enjoy the day out, it puts a bit of excitement in your life' — particularly as this is very much a road car, driven to and from events. Bend it and you're hitching a ride. 'But I'm sure the AA would get us home with it.'

In the early '60s when the Rapier was built, competition machinery was much less specialised than now, so it is appropriate that the Sunbeam still enjoys a varied diet. 'We've done a few historic rallies, like the Monte Carlo challenge, we've done that three times. We've also entered a few rallies in Ireland', he tells me. The car is also used regularly on the road, though he has a day-to-day car as well.

The four-cylinder Rootes block was eventually taken to quite a high state of tune in 1725cc Holbay form, but this one is relatively standard, still with its original 1600cc capacity but aided by SU carburettors, a different camshaft, and balancing.

'These things were more successful than Minis in their class' he reminds me.

'I've just gone to Yokohama tyres to give me a wee bit more grip, rather than the tall ones', but in other respects the car is very original, right down to the interior fittings. None of the panels have been replaced apart from the front wings, and the two-tone green paint is the original colour.

Despite being several decades ahead of the suspension design, the Japanese low-profile rubber seems to suit the car. 'It handles very well on the road', continues Alistair, 'and it's lowered the gearing, so that I can use overdrive second.' Normally the overdrive only works on third and top, but a simple wiring change is all that is needed to remove the electrical inhibition on the lower gears.

The Thoroughbred class runs a handicap, the principle being that you get points for beating your previous best by as big a percentage as you can. Isn't it open to being fiddled, I ask? Surely all you have to do is set a low standard with a poor first time?

'You can do that but you're soon noticed. That's called sandbagging isn't it? No, you've just got to improve your car and yourself.'

Rootes thoroughbred: the Simpson Rapier.

LIVING WITH SPEED

Liam Wood and friends unbend his Fiesta after a practice bump.

Today he has done just that, shaving a full five seconds off his previous best. 'It's mainly in the tyres,' he says, 'they help a lot.' With a run still to come he's second overall in the handicap, just behind Steven Donald's MGB Roadster, just ahead of Raymond Allerton's Jaguar XJ12L.

Alistair's clearly very fond of the car, which is just as well as his wife apparently won't let him sell it, so I feel very guilty about pointing out a fault, a fatigue crack in the offside rear wheel, propagating circumferentially in both directions from the brake adjuster access hole. But Alistair is unconcerned: 'I've got plenty of wheels' comes the reply.

Meanwhile a small crowd has been gathering around the paddock timing board as the Leaders chase reaches its climax. Martin Groves and Justin Fletcher are level on points but Justin will win in the event of a tie. So for Martin to take the crown, he must not only win his class but see Justin beaten in his.

Martin is now making his second run. He al-

Killing time in the queue: (top to bottom)
Graham Hickman, pensive,
Tim Thomson, intense
Roger Moran, thirsty.

ready leads his class comfortably on 42.23, the only man under 43 seconds, but is in no mood to rest on his laurels and takes the Mallock by the scruff of the neck to record 41.80, well under Graeme Wight Jnr's old 42.12 record. And this on his first ever visit to the course.

A spontaneous cheer breaks out as the time appears on scoreboard. 'That's fantastic, that's brilliant' says Roger Moran, and there are plenty who agree with him. Martin's Leaders season is through: he has done everything he could possibly do to lift the title and now all that remains is to wait for Justin's final run.

It's only a few minutes coming, but to Martin it must seem like hours. The omens do not look good because Justin is on fine form today and already leads the class with a record-beating 39.62. However Simon Frost, fresh from his Top 12 placing at Wiscombe, is also in record territory on 39.73; Martin's only hope is that he will pip Justin to the class win.

Conscious of the threat, Justin turns up the wick and goes even faster, recording a magnificent 39.38. It's enough to fend off the challenge from Simon, who can't quite match his first-run time, and enough to give the man from Shrewsbury the 1996 Leaders Championship. It has been a nail-biting climax to a splendid season.

Just as in June, class records are being smashed over and over again, none more so than in the 1600 class, where Graeme Wight Jnr slices over a second off to record 39.86, which makes it the first ever Doune sub-40 in a 1600cc car and the fourth fastest time of the day so far. Even allowing for the difficulties which the big cars face here, it's an astonishing feat for a 1600.

In all nine new records are set today, including one in the big racing car class where Andy Priaulx achieves 38.77, five hundredths better than his own record last year. Not quite an outright hill record, but there's still the Top 12 to come... Roger Moran and Roy Lane are in the 39s, none of the other V8s are under 40.

A glance at the Top 12 reveals two 1600s in the run-off (Graeme Wight Jnr and Kenny Allen), four 2-litres (Justin Fletcher, Simon Frost, Tim Thomson and Ken Snailham) and six cars over 2 litres. To be sure, there are more surprises to come.

George Ritchie gets the Top 12 off to a smoking start, literally, the tyres virtually lighting up on the MP72 as he makes the best getaway I have witnessed from any driver all season. He went well at Doune in June and seems intent on proving it was not a fluke. An eventual fourth place with a best of 39.34 is his reward.

By contrast Bill Bristow is still not quite in the groove, going off into very long grass at East Brae and damaging the nose. Patrick Wood too gets in a mess, misjudging Garden Gate and producing an unrepresentative time, but the day's highest flyers, Justin Fletcher and Graeme Wight Jnr, are simply unstoppable and go faster and faster, posting bests of 39.29 and 39.54 respectively, Graeme's time being achieved despite a brush with the barrier at Oak Tree.

The red flag goes up, there's a pheasant on the track. Several drivers cry in unison 'What only one, there's hundreds of 'em at Wiscombe mate!'. The pressure of competition is nearly over and you can sense relief in the hilarity.

Roy proceeds to post a respectable but hardly dramatic 39.63, perhaps intend-

David Grace

A chance meeting with Gurston Down landowner John Hitchins while holidaying in Greece got brewery executive David Grace interested in the sport in the early '80s. Another chance brought him face to face with an old college friend, Charles Wardle, at his first event. Through him he met his first racing partner, Jim Robinson, a pairing which was to span well over a decade.

They started in 'an old Mallock we found resting in a garage owned by a chap called Steve Madge. For about £500 we got that, plus a trailer load of bits, and during that winter we built it up as a Clubman's Mallock with a bit of an old nail of an engine. The following season we did all the Midland rounds, with reasonable success.'

One season on they had a Brian Hart pushrod unit and the car was much quicker. 'We made it much lighter, drilled holes in everything, cut an old VW Golf radiator in half, fitted a little tiny battery — every tweak we could think of. And it started to win.'

After two or three seasons in the Clubman's class the pair were winning regularly and set quite a few records, some of which stood for several years — indeed David's Gurston record stands to this day. The pair then graduated to a Mallock with a 2.2 Hart, 'a real beast — really overpowered for the chassis but very exciting to drive. You knew what oversteer was because you were sat on it'.

When they couldn't develop that Mallock any more without a lot of expense 'Jim decided he wanted a Pilbeam'.

So an MP43 sportscar was acquired from Mike Pilbeam and the pair worked frantically on it through the winter. 'The engine went out to 2.5 and at its first meeting, Prescott, we won the class first time out, having arrived about 2 o'clock in the afternoon. That was really good fun — gave me a feeling of how to control a rear-engined car and really rattled the top ten'.

Several successful seasons followed, with regular Top 12 run-off places. Eventually the MP43 sported the number 6. Along the way 'we upset a few of the prima donnas in the single seater unlimited class.' One of them was Max Harvey, who got so annoyed at being beaten that in the year he and Martyn Griffiths retired, he lent David his DFR-engined MP58.

'That was awe-inspiring to drive', recalls David. With Ian Dayson, son of competitor Bob Dayson, helping as mechanic, David finally had the power to challenge for the very top and by the end of the season he was strongly in contention, missing the championship on the last run of the year, at Doune, by a fraction of a second. That was 1992, and the beneficiary of David's near miss was Roy Lane.

Teamed up with Channel Islander Noel le Tissier, he made no mistake in '93 and '94, winning the championship on both occasions, but by 1995 Andy Priaulx had reached such a peak that no one could live with him; David was demoted to second.

By the end of the 1995 season both Noel and David were considering retirement. 'I'd done most things I could do and there's quite a lot of pressure on you at that end of the sport, because the car's quick and you're quick and you're expected to win everything. Sometimes it's nice not to have to. We decided to sell everything and take up crocheting or something.'

David decided to buy a Ducati 916 instead of a pair of large needles but there was a year's waiting list (for the Ducati that is). In the meantime Richard Brown suggested they put the DFR from the Pilbeam in the back of a Formula 3 Ralt chassis. Crocheting would have to wait.

The performance of the car speaks volumes for David Gould who developed it for them and David Grace now wonders if its success signals the beginning of the end for the Pilbeam MP58 monocoque. 'There are a few glum faces in the paddock again, something I loved to see when I had the sportscar. In fact, a couple of times in the wet I'd qualified the Mallock in a run-off and that *really* upset people.'

He finds it easier to drive an underpowered car flat out than a faster car at nine-tenths.

'There's something about having your foot nailed to the floor — you can concentrate on all the other things you've got to do.'

The partnership with Richard is clearly a happy one. 'We're like minded people, both reasonably quick so we give each other good feedback' and with Ian Dayson continuing to spanner, the Ralt is improving fast. The pressure to win could soon build again.

David has other ideas though. 'I'd love to see Tom Brown in the car because he's a quick driver and he's got youth on his side. That would be a new challenge, to develop a car and let someone else have a crack at the championship.'

David Grace (centre) gives Andy Priaulx a piggyback for the benefit of the camera, with a little help from Roy Lane. As Robin Boucher observes 'A lot of folk in the sport are fun-living people. In 30-odd years I could probably name on the fingers of one hand the objectionable people I have come across in the whole of hillclimbing and sprinting.'

Man on the Hill

Julie Chalmers

---

ing to find a little more for his last run of the day, but Andy Priaulx is not interested in tactics. He simply forces the big Pilbeam up the hill in the day's best time, 38.40.

Come the second runs, Bill Bristow's car looks somewhat the worse for wear, it's spare nose held on with a mixture of duct-tape and pop rivets and boasting end plates of different colours. But at least Bill has cheered up enough to smile at the situation, standing back to admire his handiwork and declaring 'That's better than the other one!' And even if the car is being wayward today, 'it's as good as gold,' he assures me, 'it does come back when it goes. I had it completely sideways at the Junction on my first class run.'

His effort is rewarded up to a point, literally, for he manages 41.01 on his second championship attempt which is enough for tenth place. Ahead of him come the 2-litre cars of Tim Thomson and Simon Frost.

As he sets off for his final run of the Championship, Roy knows that he must pull something out of the bag if he is to avoid finishing just one place up from the smaller cars, in seventh, which

LIVING WITH SPEED

Last run away... Bill Bristow's borrowed engine is up for sale on the Doune noticeboard.

ENGINE
FOR SALE AT END OF SEASON
2.5 BEATTIE-HART
(METHANOL-FUELLED)
333 bhp – very strong at mid-range

Consistent points scorer in British Championship Hill Climbs & Sprints
Possible in-car trial arranged

See Bill Bristow or phone John Beattie on 01952 727267

Final Championship Top Tens

	RAC after 16 rounds			Leaders after 14 rounds	
1	Roy Lane	96	1	Justin Fletcher	81
2	Roger Moran	90	2	Martin Groves	81
3	Patrick Wood	81	3	Tom New	78
4	Tim Mason	63	4	Phil Cooke	75
5	Bill Bristow	59	5	Mark Waldron	75
6	David Grace	58	6	Mark Lawrence	69
7	Graham Priaulx	41	7	Pete Hannam	62
8	George Ritchie	41	8	Tony Lambert	58
9	Simon Durling	39	9	Jim Robinson	57
10	Justin Fletcher	35	10	Mark Coley	56

would make him the slowest V8 in the run-off. He's renowned for delivering the goods when it really matters, but this time the old magic deserts him and he makes an uncharacteristic mistake. The car takes to the grass at East Brae and his day's sport is over. The side pods are full of grass but the car is undamaged, as is Roy's sense of humour. 'Fastest Flymo in town' he jests as he returns to the paddock. It will take more than a few green streaks on the paint to spoil his weekend.

This mistake leaves Graeme Wight Jnr sixth, Patrick Wood fifth, George Ritchie fourth and Justin Fletcher third.

Roy Lane finishes a splendid RAC season with a less than splendid run — 'Fastest Flymo in town', he quips.

Roger Moran, the only man apart from Roy who has looked likely to challenge Andy, can do nothing about the Guernseyman even after two runs, ending exactly half a second back on 38.90. No one else is under 39 at all.

Suddenly it's all over. Andy has no need to take his second run and the paddock waits to see if he will go for the record regardless, cruise up for the crowd, or not bother at all. Whatever he decides, he will end the season the way he started, with a win, making it two entries and two victories for the 1995 title holder.

While he is deciding, his father looks at the Pilbeam's left-hand skirt, for Andy has been cornering so hard through Meadow that he's worn it almost right through. A strip of it is hanging on by a few strands of glass.

Graham pulls it off. 'That's the end of that', he says, and the symbolism is not lost on those in earshot. The family attack on championship hillclimbing is over and it is impossible not to feel a little sad.

Andy takes a demonstration run, while the commentator sums up the mood of the meeting: 'Here's a man who can win the championship, go off and play on the circuits, come back here and take the place apart.'

Along with all the older drivers, Roy has been eclipsed by young talent today. The best drives have all come from the new generation, from Andy Priaulx, Justin Fletcher, Graeme Wight Jnr and Martin Groves, a foretaste perhaps of seasons to come.

The prizegiving at Doune is held indoors in what is still known as the Garden Centre on account of the building's original function. Perhaps because it is enclosed, it seems much more crowded than usual, with people standing on ta-

CHAPTER 17

*SEASON'S END:
◁ the Harratts pack up…
…the Lanes pack up…
▽
…and soon the Paddock is all but empty. ▷*

bles at the back and on the stairs leading to the balcony. Or maybe everyone wants to be there to bid the season goodbye (although for some it is not quite over as there are a few lesser events still to run).

Either way, the stars of the day are roundly applauded, particularly Graeme Wight Jnr whose 39.54 in a 1600 car must surely be the drive of the weekend. The stalwarts are not forgotten either, the Harratts, for instance, winning an award for the best prepared car on a Doune entry list.

Soon the laughter has died away and there are only an empty trophy table, a lot of entrants packing up to go home, and memories. I wander back to the car park and say my goodbyes along the way, to the Lanes and the Fletchers and to anyone else I come across en route. I walk slowly, reluctantly, savouring the moment.

The shadows are lengthening over the hills of Doune, and just like this morning the air is perfectly still and crystal clear. A soft golden light spreads over the land and the mountains look so close that you want to reach out and touch them. It is an evening in a thousand, the kind of evening which, if it were one in a hundred, would have the whole world wanting to live in Scotland. Truly we have seen Doune at its best this year.

As I climb into the BX and drive gently home it is the people rather than the cars which keep coming to mind, for they are what make hillclimbing special. Even allowing for the fact that this is a leisure activity and therefore shows participants at their best, and the fact that my association with Roy has lent me instant credibility, their warmth and friendliness has been exceptional.

Here is a sport where no one sets any store by your background or your wealth, only by your enthusiasm and your capacity for fun and sportsmanship. Hillclimbing is where the professionals like Willem Toet and Mike Pilbeam come to play at being amateurs, and where everyone else comes to play at being professional, and where nobody much tries to categorise you either way.

By next season a few will have retired or moved on to other things, but the rest will be back, including most of the ones who say they won't. For when you're tired of the hills you really are over the hill: the sport is a drug, it gets into your blood and the only fix is to tackle that strip of tarmac one more time.

As the golden light fades and the headlamps come on, I slip my favourite Brian Adams tape into the car stereo. The first track that plays is *18 till I die*.

Very appropriate really. A finer bunch of teenagers I have yet to meet.

135

At home with the Guv'nor

Initiation: the rebuilt Le Mans Sprite gave Roy his first taste of motorsport.

The Lotus 11 proved very successful but was also the cause of Roy's worst accident.

TAILPIECE 1

'If you're going to do something, do it properly'

A glance at the boy called Roy Lane in the years during and after the War would have given little clue as to the sporting future of this Leamington Spa lad. Unlike many drivers, who are born and brought up with cars and the motor trade and drift unquestioningly into motor sport simply because it seems a natural outlet, Roy's family had little to do with motor vehicles. In fact his father never drove one.

But he did drive, every day of his working life, for he was an engine driver, a fact which Roy recalls with great fondness.

'I used to take him his lunch because we lived only half a mile from the sheds. "Jump up on the footplate and let's go for a ride" he used to say, "shunt some wagons around." It was great! Other days he'd say "Come on, I'll turn you round on the turntable", so I used to jump up on the footplate with him and his fireman, swing round, come back out again and then it would be "Hang on, we'll go and hook some carriages on, just whip 'em up the road".

'Some days we'd wait for the signals. They'd sit there, have a smoke for a couple of hours, wait for a signal to go up, get out a pack of cards while they were waiting. The fireman and him always had a little piece of wood on the side, so they could play cards while they were waiting for signals. You couldn't visualise it now could you? It was the same in the sheds where they used to have their lunch, every table was covered in playing cards and cribbage boards.'

How many thousands of small boys the world over would have given up all their Christmas presents for lunchtimes like that?

That footplate has a lot to answer for, because undoubtedly the seeds of his interest in engineering were sown at this time. His brothers were also railwaymen, so there were other role models pointing him in the same direction. For a bright boy with a mechanical bent living in the manufacturing heartland of the Midlands, engineering was the obvious outlet.

He joined a local construction engineering company, Benfords, a few months after leaving school but he was not there long, because this was 1953, when every young man was required to spend two years in the forces doing National Service. Like millions of others, the teenage Lane signed up to do his patriotic duty.

The young Midlander, then just 18, found himself posted to Carlisle but his stay in the Border country lasted only a few weeks. Soon he was earmarked for the Royal Horse Guards and posted to Windsor, where for six months he performed royal guard duties.

At this point wheels were substituted for legs as Guardsman Lane found himself transferred to the armoured side of the regiment, where among other things he passed his driving test by 'driving armoured cars around the streets of London, Windsor and Maidenhead and terrorising all the locals'.

Another transfer followed, this time to the Inns of Court regiment which Roy describes as 'the territorial section of the Household Cavalry'. Within a year of 'terrorising the locals' as a trainee, Roy became an army driving instructor, so either the conscript learned fast or the forces were desperately short of instructors.

Tank testing followed, and somewhere in this busy programme he also participated in the Royal Tattoo in Edinburgh. A lot was packed into the two years: 'You never stopped anywhere', he recalls. 'I wasn't half pleased when I came out!' But the 20 year-old man who left in 1955 certainly knew a great deal more about engineering (and about life) than the 18 year-old youth who'd joined in 1953.

Despite this initiation into driving, and despite watching the Brandon Bees speedway team as a kid, motorsport did not really figure in Roy's life at that time. In the army his sports had been javelin throwing and cross-country running. Now his passion became cycle racing.

His approach, as with his motorsport later, was that there was no point in competing if you were not going to do your very best. He set about cycling with a discipline and dedication which earned him many trophies, including several Midland Time Trial Championships. Roy was one of the first cyclists to ride

Cycling in 1958. Roy did 50 miles in under 2 hours in this event.

Len Thorpe

137

LIVING WITH SPEED

A sprint meeting at Cirencester in 1967 with the Cooper, running on methanol.

25 miles in the hour, a feat he repeated some 26 times.

Stardom beckoned in 1957 when the British Olympic coach let it be known that Roy was being considered for the British team, but it was not to be. Instead of the successful season-long build up with which Roy had hoped to impress the selectors, he crashed badly and broke his collarbone.

Off work to recuperate (he'd rejoined Benfords on leaving the army), he used the time to train harder then ever and went on to record better times than before. But the moment had passed: by the time the next Olympiad came round, other riders' stars were in the ascendant and besides, Roy had other things on his mind.

One of them was Bett Cordwell. She too was an enthusiastic cyclist and it wasn't long before the two were inseparable. Bett and Roy were married in 1957, went cycling before and after their honeymoon (but for some inexplicable reason not during it) and have cycled regularly ever since. They bought a modest semidetached bungalow in Warwick, where they still live, added a dormer after the kids were born (Antony in 1960 and Julie in 1962) and earned a steady living working at Benfords, where Bett had also found employment. Sporting prowess apart, the Lanes were just like thousands of other families up and down the country.

By the early '60s, however, competitive cycling was losing its appeal for Roy. He'd never wanted to become 'an old snotty-nosed timeless cyclist' and even if he had, the doctor was advising against it. Like many top cyclists, Roy was developing back trouble, so on medical advice he started looking for an alternative sport.

He didn't have to look far, for at the back of Benfords' yard was a wall and on the other side of the wall was the Donald Healey Motor Company. 'I used to know one or two of the lads' Roy recounts, 'and occasionally went over there for a cup of tea at lunchtime. One particular day there was this blue Ecurie Ecosse Sprite sat there, damaged, and I learned that it had run about 22 hours at Le Mans before a Ferrari had gone in the back of it. I asked them what they were going to do with it.'

The company had planned to remove the engine and gearbox and scrap the rest, but Roy persuaded a rather surprised Geoff Healey, who until then had assumed Roy's loyalty to be strictly to two wheels, to sell the shell, gearbox and back axle to him instead. It was the start of Roy Lane, racing driver and car constructor.

When the crumpled shell was trailered back to the bungalow, friends and neighbours were less than impressed. Comments like 'Oh my God, have you gone into the scrap business?' abounded, but Roy was undaunted and inside the wood and asbestos garage in the back garden a revitalised 'Frogeye' slowly took shape. (I use quote marks because strictly speaking this wasn't a Frogeye at all: the distinctive nose had been redesigned and a hardtop added to improve aerodynamics for the 1961 Le Mans.)

Powered by a Formula Junior XSP racing engine, the Sprite took Roy through two seasons, circuit racing, hill-climbing and rallying, which in those days was perfectly practicable with just one car. Around the end of '64 it was sold less engine to John Moore and Roy went looking for something else to put the XSP into.

He found it in the shape of the ex-Mike Parkes' Lotus 11, which fortuitously was on offer without engine. Suitably lowered and with the diff re-engineered to keep the oil inside, the car proved very quick — too quick at Becketts one day, when Roy arrived at the Silverstone hairpin with no brakes at all. The short pipe connecting the two sides of the Girling calliper had fatigued through — a known problem for which the cure, Roy later discovered, was to bed the pipe in silicon. The result was a badly damaged car and a driver with a split lip, the worst accident he has suffered in his entire career. The wreckage was loaded aboard the trailer and a battered and a saddened Roy Lane towed it home behind the family's old A90 Westminster.

As a stopgap while he rebuilt the Lotus, Roy built up a Mini Cooper S around an engine he'd had laying around for some time and entered it in sprints during 1965 and '66. It was his first contact with sprinting and his last with front-wheel drive: he hated the car, with its cramped dimensions and nose-heavy handling.

Attention returned to the Lotus, which emerged from the garage shorn of its voluptuous bodywork and looking more like a Lotus 7 than an 11. It was

TAILPIECE 1

duly christened a Lotus 11/7 and in that form was very successful on the circuits.

At the end of the '66 season it was time for a garage clear out. The Mini went to Richard Martin-Hurst, the Lotus to ex-Rootes works rally driver Colin Malkin, in whose hands it proved highly successful. Roy found himself with a two tidy cheques and no cars. He had learned that if you build cars yourself, to a high standard, and then prove their abilities in competition, it is possible to generate enough profit to take the sting out of next year's costs. It is a philosophy which he has never deviated from and which leads those who don't know him to assume that he has far more cash then he actually has.

All season Roy had been eyeing single-seaters covetously, convincing himself that a no-compromise racing machine was the way to go. Now he had the resources to buy one.

A Type 56 Cooper to be precise. With a Lotus Twin-Cam inserted into the back, Roy tried a few sprints, but found himself a touch slower than the fast boys. 'I know what to do,' he thought, 'I'll stick a big supercharger on this.'

'So I stuck this bloody great Wade blower on, put a belt drive down the front of the engine, made all these bits and pieces at work during lunchbreaks and evenings and when everybody had disappeared, got the machine shop doing foreigners for me, built the thing up and entered it at Wiscombe Park in 1967, our first serious attempt at an RAC round. On methanol it went like an absolute dingbat.'

It was not the first hillclimb he'd entered — Roy had competed at Ragley Hall, Loton Park, Harewood and Prescott though to his chagrin Shelsley had rejected him as too inexperienced — but 14 May 1967 was certainly a turning point. For the first time he would be, if not a contender for FTD, at least one for the Top 12.

In fact he was to score his first ever RAC Championship point, qualifying tenth and finishing tenth 'after hitting the bank halfway up the top straight in the pouring rain. It was a dirty, wet, horrible meeting and by now we were in a

The supercharged Cooper contained a lot of undercover Bensons engineering and earned Roy his first ever RAC Championship point.

Guy Griffiths Motofoto

manky old Commer van that leaked water everywhere. We now had two children and there were no motorways in those days — it was 10 hours to get to Wiscombe Park with a trailer on the back.'

This could be interpreted as dedication to the sport to the detriment of all else, family included, but it would be an interpretation very wide of the mark. Then and now, it is rare indeed for Roy to attend a meeting without Bett, who is there not out of wifely duty but out of enjoyment. Even at this early stage of Roy's competitive career, the Lanes were so closely involved with the social side of the sport that to stay at home was to cut yourself off from friends, fun and fresh air.

Similarly, their children were brought up with the sport and regard it as an integral part of their lives. Unlike other drivers, Roy has never been emotionally torn between his sport and the need to spend time with his family. They are all there, by choice, willing him on, a factor which must surely explain at least some of his continuing success.

Indeed it was social side of the sport that played a large part in Roy's decision to quit circuit racing. For several years the Lanes attended both speed and circuit events, but despite meeting many 'super guys' on the circuits, Roy had felt less and less at ease with the circuit racing fraternity ever since an incident in the paddock at Silverstone several years before. A vintage car had been parked with the handbrake off and had rolled into Roy's Sprite, damaging it. When challenged, the owner — who Roy will not identify save that he was an upper-class establishment figure at the time — had merely said 'go away', only *much* less politely. There was pleasant classlessness to the speed scene which he found absent from circuit events.

Now with the children growing up, he found a more tangible factor in favour of the hills. 'What annoyed me with circuit racing was that you arrive at 6 o'clock in the morning, you're scrutineered at half past six and your race would be 5:30 in the evening. All these things are against it when you've got a family'. Hillclimbing may not offer long periods in the driving seat, but neither does it enforce long periods of idleness.

Although his involvement with the circuits ebbed and flowed, by the start of the '70s it had ebbed permanently and Roy's driving career had become solely concerned with sprints and hillclimbs, save for the occasional sporting trial in winter time, an activity he eventually abandoned in deference to his back.

Concentrating on speed events had practical benefits as well as social ones. Mechanical parts lasted longer, while accident damage was less common because you had only your own shortcomings to be wary of, not other people's. But most of all Roy relished the discipline of being able to concentrate utterly on one thing: getting from A to B as quickly as possible. 'I found it a tremendous challenge — still do.'

Roy recalls with a grin that the Wiscombe result had another effect: it forced Shelsley's Gerry Flewitt — 'the old sod' — to accept that 'this up and coming handsome young man was going to make the grade' and allow him to compete in top events there.

140

TAILPIECE 1

Brabham BT14 on the grid at Silverstone in 1968, Roy in cockpit, assistant Brian Simmonds crouching, Jim Knifton standing.

Facing page: The first Tech-Craft Buick at Prescott in 1969.

By now he had the single-seater bit between his teeth. At the end of the '67 season he sold the engine and supercharger to Malcolm Eaves, while the car went to Peter Bayliss, 'never ever to be seen again. I still have the chassis plate here, he's never come back for it.'

The competition potential of big stock-block American V8s was well demonstrated in the '60s and General Motors' all-alloy 3.5 litre V8 was particularly attractive to racing car builders on account of its strength and light weight. And the decision by Rover in 1968 to equip its big P5 saloon with a derivative of the engine served only to increase its profile and its accessibility. It was a trend not lost on the man from Warwick.

'I bought this Brabham BT14 less engine, with a gearbox. It was in a shocking state but I put a proper 3.5 litre Buick engine into it and off we went.'

Although he did not win any RAC rounds outright, Roy remembers 1968 as 'a super season'. Outright wins in sprints, at Silverstone and at non-RAC hillclimbs combined to make it undoubtedly his most successful year to date and even if the Brabham/Lane combination was not yet winning RAC rounds, it did start picking up points regularly, coming second to eventual champion Peter Lawson's 4WD BRM at Prescott for in-

Woodcote Corner with the second Tech-Craft Buick, 1969.

141

LIVING WITH SPEED

stance. Both of them beat the hill record, an achievement which in those days was worth a point in itself. At the end of the season Roy was in the top 10 of the RAC Championship and he has never been out of it since.

V8 power and R T Lane seemed to gel. By now he had developed a taste in racing cars, had begun to know what he liked and what he could perform well in. Give it ample torque for accelerating out of slow corners, gear it low so that you get a quick start and make the most of the rev band, and within the constraints of the above, keep it physically small to maximise manoeuvrability on the narrow hills. All his cars from this point on have exhibited these qualities to a greater or lesser extent, and the better the compromise between them, the better results he has achieved.

Every meeting Roy has ever entered is logged in a book, along with details of the car and the results achieved. For many years Julie has been in charge of timekeeping but back in 1968 she was still at junior school, so there are some gaps in Roy's handwritten entries.

He mulls through The Book, using it to spur memories of events long past. 'I went to Barbon!' he discovers, 'and

Technically the most interesting machine Roy ever drove, the 4WD Tech-Craft was also the least successful. The racing shot above was taken at Wiscombe in 1970, the others show it as it spent much of the season: in the paddock, being ministered to by its creator.

142

TAILPIECE 1

guess where I came? First in class and seventh in the Championship run-off!'

'It rained', adds Bett by way of explanation, as though it all happened just a week ago.

By 1969 Roy was getting ambitious. He'd spent countless hours improving other people's designs, now he wanted to build his own. So after a lot of agonising about the name between Roy and Brian Simmonds, who helped him with preparation and design for a number of years, the first Tech-Craft Buick took shape at the back of the bungalow in what was by this time a brick-built garage. Night after night the pair laboured, fortified by tea, raw enthusiasm and dreams of glory.

The effort paid dividends in a big way at Doune on 15 June 1969, when the new car scored its first outright win and broke the course record. It took 11 hours to get there, Bett remembers, but they came away with 11 points. A second win followed, at Great Auclum.

Emboldened, Roy and Brian decided that for 1970 they would build the car Roy had always fancied: a four-wheel drive single seater. It was too ambitious a venture to start from scratch, but Roy didn't need to; he'd learned that the damaged BRM Grand Prix 4WD car was for sale, with a spare transmission. Fitted with a 2.1-litre Tasman Formula version of the BRM P67 V8, it was the car that Peter Lawson had won the 1968 hill-climb championship with before John Cussins had crashed it at Prescott the following year.

It was worth buying for its transmission alone, which had been designed by Ferguson of tractor fame, a company heavily involved with 4WD development at the time and later to become part of the Ricardo group. Ferguson engineer Ossie Webb was persuaded to help, along with Jaguar suspension designer Stan Paskin, and so it was that the garage at the back of the bungalow spawned its second car.

(To be strictly correct it was the third, because the first Tech-Craft was sold, crashed, rebuilt around a new monocoque and then another identical car constructed around the repaired original shell).

The Tech-Craft BRM looked very neat, well thought out and a real threat to the existing machinery, but for once the engineering maxim that 'what looks right, is right' didn't hold good. The basic ingredients were a new monocoque fitted with the 2.1 litre version of the BRM V8 opened out to 2.2 litres and mated to the transmission of the damaged car, but the latter had been designed for only 1.5 litres. 'It was simply not up to the power and torque of the larger engine' Roy maintains. True, it had worked with the bigger engine in Peter Lawson's hands, but when confronted with a new chassis offering vastly better traction, the transmission cried 'enough', regularly.

The Tech-Craft BRM was plagued with mechanical failures all season and although the scoresheet for 1970 was not entirely bare, none of the first places related to RAC rounds.

At the end of a 'dreadful' season which nevertheless brought him seventh in the Championship, Roy had to face the fact that without investment on a scale which was simply out of reach, the concept could not be made competitive. The car was sold to John McCartney, in whose hands it proved reliable thanks

143

LIVING WITH SPEED

RTL tackles the Esses at Prescott in 1971 aboard his McLaren M10.

Facing page: McLaren M14D at Shelsley, 1973, surely the prettiest car Roy has ever driven.

When Cosworth abandoned any ambitions to be a Formula 1 constructor, Roy was offered the one and only all-Cosworth F1 car in the early '70s as a hillclimb project. Here he tests it at Silverstone before rejecting it as too fragile.

to the fitting of a 1.6 litre engine. It notched up a number of successes before finding a permanent home in the Coventry Museum. The damaged BRM, still complete apart from the loss of its engine, was sold Tom Wheatcroft for his museum at Donington Park, where it can still be seen.

There's a note of regret in Roy's voice as he relates these events, for during 1970 his dreams of Tech-Craft one day joining the ranks of the *grand constructeurs* like Ferrari and McLaren evaporated. He had entered the sport not just to win but to enjoy himself, but for Tech-Craft to succeed as a constructor at the very top of the motorsport pinnacle — and he could see no point in scratching around at the bottom — he would have to give up his job and take himself into a different arena altogether, an arena where he simply didn't feel at home: one of big numbers, big risks and ruthless business techniques.

The decision was made: there would be no more Tech-Craft cars.

As the 1970 season drew to a close, Roy faced the inescapable logic: if it were impractical to build his own car from scratch, he would have to drive somebody else's. But whose? 'I decided I would build myself a McLaren M10B.'

Having reached this conclusion, the pieces fell into place very well. Roy chuckles as he remembers.

'I bought a damaged monocoque that went in through the back door of McLaren's Formula 1 workshop one weekend and came out the following weekend rebuilt as a brand new tub'.

He then bought all the bits to finish it off himself and tried it out at Prescott towards the end of the 1970 season. The following year he took the car to fourth in the Championship, by way of two

144

TAILPIECE 1

wins at Prescott, one at Harewood and a number of placings.

Still that championship eluded him. Maybe a better car would help. He sold the M10B to Richard Shardlow and headed back to McLaren Cars. 'Entrance through the back door of course, I couldn't afford to go through the front door.'

Once inside he spied one of the previous year's F1 cars sitting in the corner, the ex-Andrea de Adamich Alfa Romeo engined M14D, sister car to the DFV-engined M14As of Denny Hulme and Peter Revson. The heavy, costly Alfa engine was of no interest, but the rest of the car certainly was and Roy came away with an engineless M14D for 'a very sensible figure'.

With a Chevrolet 5.7-litre V8 inserted, the M14D notched up two RAC wins, both at Prescott and both of them with a new record, enough to keep the number 4 on the nose for the 1973 season. (Today, incidentally, the M14D is mothballed back at McLaren, its Alfa engine reinstated.)

For the first time since his Sprite days, Roy kept a car for a second season, not least because he couldn't afford to do anything else. A better engine was substituted and a number of wins resulted in 1973, albeit none in the RAC series. Yet again the number 4 stayed on the nose.

Or rather it would have done if Roy had kept the car for a third year, but an offer from Terry Smith was accepted and the Lanes found themselves with a tidy bank account but no car for 1974.

The kitty was now large enough to afford a new car, a brand new McRae rolling chassis to be precise, which Roy built up around a special Bartz lightweight Chevrolet engine. The result was big, hairy and magnificent, the car which to this day remains Roy's favourite competition machine. It is also, incidentally, the only competition car Bett has ever driven. She tried it at Curborough, alternated between slow kangaroo-like jumps and sudden uncontrolled wheelies, and arrived back at the paddock announcing 'I'm not getting back in one of them!' She never has.

Part of his fondness for the car comes from the way it proved everybody wrong, a story he tells with evident self-satisfaction. 'Everybody who turned up at the first meeting in 1974 said "That car will never ever work." Mike McDowel said "Isn't it big. You'll never do any good with that". They all said "It's too big for the sport, it'll be clumbersome, no — that's no good" '.

In fact the McRae simply blew the opposition away, though not immediately — the rout would come in 1975. In 1974 it produced two RAC wins, at Great Auclum and Prescott, and took Roy to second in the Championship — ironically behind McDowel. Better still, Roy took a major championship for the first time, taking the BARC's FTD Trophy, backed in '74 by Castrol, outright.

This was solid success, more than enough to justify persevering with the car. Over the winter a different engine was fitted, with a special Alan Smith cross-over fuel injection system, and a vigorous weight-paring programme was pursued.

In this form the car was a devastatingly effective piece of machinery which was simply without peer in its day. With a now mature and very effective driver at the helm, the McRae won 23 out of the 28 meetings it contested in 1975, including 10 RAC rounds — enough to win the British Championship on a maximum 100 points, an achievement not to be equalled until Andy Priaulx's success 20 years later. Roy Lane, racing driver, had come of age.

By this stage the leaky Commer was gone and the family travelled in, if not style, at least relative comfort. In fact Roy describes their new transport quite glowingly as 'beautiful living quarters', but since the rest of the family roll around the floor at this description, it is reasonable to assume that it was palatial only by comparison with what had gone before. The vehicle actually consisted of a Ford Transit Luton van that had been converted on a local chicken farm. 'It had all the living accommodation, beds that dropped down — but we

145

LIVING WITH SPEED

Start line at Doune in 1974 with the McRae. Note the airbox, abandoned for 1975.

Hill-climbing's a hairy business. But when the driver's Roy Lane, the car's the Fenny Marine GM1, and the oil's Castrol, the toughest hills are flattened out.

Congratulations Roy, on being the outright winner of the R.A.C. Hill-Climb Championship, and the first driver ever to win without dropping a point.

Roy's 100-point RAC title prompted Castrol to commission this Brockbank cartoon in 1975.

used to put the car in as well. We used to load the car in on the carpets, take the car out, drop the beds down, live in there, put all the beds up, push the car in. We were always last to leave the meeting because we couldn't put the car in until we'd finished our meal and cleared everything up.'

Roy had always let it be known that once he'd won the Championship he'd pack up competing, but it was no particular surprise to find that nothing of the sort occurred. After 10 years on the hills, to stop now would have left a huge hole in the whole family's life. He kept the McRae for a third season, made a few

TAILPIECE 1

modifications to it and managed to retain the title in 1976, though it was a much harder task than before.

In fact the title chase looked like going right down to the wire at the last meeting of the season, Doune, but despite Alister Douglas Osborn taking the win with a new record in Scotland, once dropped scores had been accounted for Roy had clinched the RAC Championship — on equal points with runner-up ADO.

To retain the McRae for a fourth season would be inviting defeat, so the car was sold to Dave Harris, in whose hands it won the British Sprint Championship.

The Lanes at Gurston in 1975, the year dad won practically everything he entered.

Motor sport is dangerous! Roy broke his arm changing a wheel on the motorhome in 1974.

147

LIVING WITH SPEED

Above: The March 2-4-0 used in the early part of 1979 caused a sensation in the paddock but was too heavy to win on the faster hills. This shot was taken at Prescott.

The March 771 in four-wheeler guise in 1971, see here at Prescott.

Facing page: March 741 with 3 litre Cosworth DFV in 1977, at Shelsley start. Though Roy never took to the peaky engine, it did produce results.

Much later, Roy bought it back and stored it for many years before selling it to the US in 1995 for historic racing.

In the winter of 1976-77 the talk on the hills was of Cosworth powerplants and how an F1-derived engine offered a much better power to weight ratio than a production-block V8. It seemed the way to go.

'We bought a March 741 from Nick Williamson, complete with DFV engine — most likely the worst thing I ever bought. We came third overall in the championship and won a few meetings.

148

TAILPIECE 1

But being a 3 litre with no torque, the engine was pretty useless for hill-climbing. I used to break it quite often.'

Bearing in mind that in the '70s there were more competitors at the top level than there are today (though the number of entries in the top class is higher now), to come third represents a good season. But somehow the car did not suit.

Roy acknowledges that his dissatisfaction is based more on feeling than fact. 'Though I complain about it she did go well and she did produce some very good results for me. I won at Doune, for instance, something I didn't manage again until this year. One thing I always remember was that after Junction I could floor it. I used to hold my foot flat to the floor in that March Formula 1 car all the way to East Brae, the chassis worked that well. I can't do that today.'

Despite his reservations he persevered with the 741 for a second year, having lightened it, rebuilt the engine with torquier camshafts and made many other modifications during the closed season. He finished the 1978 season fifth after just one RAC Championship win, at Prescott, and then sold the car.

Roy had acquired a reputation for being something of a technical innovator. 'I'd won the championship a couple of times and I was now in the sport basically to enjoy myself. Engineering had always been one of my fortes and I had a lot of energy, I wanted to try new ideas, to do things differently from everybody else.' Innovative reputation or not, no one was prepared for what came next: the six wheeler.

'It was one of those Robin Herd/Roy Lane sessions, sat at the table one night, arguing which way we should go. Robin came up with this idea that four wheels at the back would be wonderful — which it was from a traction point of view, but the car was too bloody heavy!'

Robin had been influenced by Ken Tyrrell's six-wheeled P34, the idea of which was to use a narrow front track, to keep all the front rubber within the regulation nose width, and counter the consequent lack of front-end grip by adding an extra two front wheels.

March countered with the 761, a car with four rear wheels, and though the 761 was never successful on the circuits

LIVING WITH SPEED

3 litre F1 DFV-engined March 79S, at the Esses at Shelsley.

the idea had enough merit in Roy's eyes for him to buy the 1977 ex-Jody Scheckter March 771 from the factory and use it as the basis for a similar six-wheeler of his own, using the engine he'd retained from last year's 741. Robin provided a 761-style transmission on permanent loan and Roy built the 771 up as the March 2-4-0, using the traditional steam-engine nomenclature in recognition of the family's railway background.

'The six wheeler was very, very good. It steered well, it turned in, had good traction of course. Everybody said it wouldn't do this, it wouldn't do that, but it was superb. We got good results in the first four meetings, including a win at Wiscombe Park, but when we got to Shelsley in June it was just too heavy, 200 pounds too heavy.

'That's too much too make up when confronted with a steep hill like Shelsley Walsh, especially with a peaky engine like the DFV, where maximum power came at 11,000rpm. When you've got weight you need torque. It would be OK with a modern engine like the Judd, but then there would always be someone with the same engine without the weight...'

Immediately after Shelsley, Roy saw the writing on the wall and converted the car back to standard 771 specification. A conventional looking racing car appeared at Fintray the following weekend: the six-wheeler episode was over. What Roy didn't know at the time was that his run of wins in the RAC Championship was over too, for five long years. Although there would be many compensatory wins in sprints and in other hillclimbs, that victory by the six-wheeler at Wiscombe signalled for Roy the start of an RAC Championship drought which would not be broken until 1984.

At the end of the 1979 season the car was sold, less engine, to a circuit racer. Eventually exported to Italy, it still races in historic Formula 1 events. The special six-wheel gearbox casings went with it but not the internals, which are still on 'permanent loan', tucked away in a corner of Roy's workshop.

Something else significant happened in 1979, for in that year Roy became increasingly friendly with Richard Colton, whose Steel King shoe manufacturing company was to become his sponsor in later years. The arrangement has persisted to this day, one of the longest and happiest sponsor-driver pairings in motorsport, so long that many spectators cannot remember the day when Roy didn't drive a silver car.

With Roy always keen to keep the overall size of the car to a minimum (six-wheel episode notwithstanding!) he decided to try putting a Cosworth V8 into a Formula 2 chassis for the 1980 season, so the 2-4-0's engine was mated to a March 782 F2 chassis to create the March 79S. No RAC wins resulted, but a string of solid placings took him to third in the championship.

V8 engines were somewhat out of fashion on the hills by the early '80s. Lightweight four-cylinder power was the way to go, avowed Herd. Roy recalls that 'for 1981 Robin decided that I ought to try a Formula 2 car. He sold me, very cheaply, a brand new 801/812 cross which they prepared at the factory. I supplied the 2.5 Hart engine but the factory helped me a tremendous amount in preparing the car. It was a lovely car, ever so comfortable to drive, put its traction down, went round corners, did everything you wanted it to do, but did everything so bloody slowly it was unbelievable.' Fifth was the best he could manage in the championship. The 801/812

TAILPIECE 1

The four-cylinder era: Prescott start line in 1981, Roy driving a March 801/812 with Hart 2.5 engine. 'So bloody slow it was unbelievable'.

Tiring work this hillclimbing! (From nearest the camera) Roy Lane, Martyn Griffiths and Alister Douglas Osborn make themselves comfortable in the back of Roy's trailer.

went to the very bottom of Roy's list of favourite competition cars and has remained there ever since.

By the August Gurston Roy had replaced it with Roger Philpott's 2.3 Hart-powered 782. But this too was not one of his favourite cars and the two mounts between them could only take him to fifth in the championship.

In the winter of 1981-82 the thinking caps went back on in the brick garage. Pilbeams were beginning to make an impression and he seemed to be getting nowhere with Marchs. It was time for a clean break, a change of chassis.

Roy acquired the ex-Patrick Neve/Dave Harris Pilbeam MP42/46 from Martyn Griffiths and set about fitting it with Norrie Galbraith's 2.3 Euroracing BMW M12 engine for the start of 1982. The chassis itself came in for attention and was effectively turned into an MP50 by being shortened some 13cm and fitted with MP50 front suspension. According to present owner Dave Whitehead, the car has from then on always been an MP50 for practical purposes, even though some historians do not regard it so.

The 1982 season brought only sixth place, his worst position since the 4WD debacle of 1970, but there were sound practical reasons for sticking with the car for 1983 because during 1982 both Roy and Bett found themselves made redundant on the same day. Benfords had been hit hard by changes in its all-important export markets and overnight, without any warning, large numbers of staff were sacked. Suddenly the Lane family found itself without any income whatsoever.

So during 1982 a seminal decision was reached: they would strike out on their own, doing what they did best. And since the Tech-Craft name was already known by virtue of the three racers which bore it, what better title to give the new business? From now on Roy had a business as well as a sporting reason to succeed, because his cars had in effect became mobile advertisements for his expertise. Everyone wants to be associated with success.

Fifteen years on the business still trades along similar lines, though these days Roy's son Antony helps out increasingly in the modest industrial unit which has replaced the brick garage as the business premises. He will probably take over completely should Roy do the unthinkable and retire.

If the finances would not run to a new car, they could certainly manage a better engine, so for 1983 Euroracing enlarged the BMW to 2.6 and Roy improved his final finishing position to fourth. Perhaps the highlight of this season was his 20th win at Harewood, albeit at a BARC meeting. RAC wins still proved elusive — not since the six-wheeler at Wiscombe in 1979 had the man from Warwick received the winner's cup at an RAC round.

In spite of this frustration, fortunes were definitely on the upturn and in 1984, with the Pilbeam-BMW, Roy at last started showing some of his old form, finally ending his RAC drought with two top scores. The first was at Wiscombe Park's opening round, the second

151

Harewood paddock at the end of 1982, Antony prepares the March 782.

at Le Val des Terres, where despite winning the run-off he was beaten to FTD by local man Graham Priaulx's storming class run in the Tiga-BDX sportsracer. Roy also took the British Sprint Championship outright, even wheeling out the old McRae to take an outright win on the ultra-fast Isle of Man round before taking the Pilbeam to fifth in the hillclimb table.

At the end of the 1984 season the MP50 was sold less engine to Barrie Dutnall, who installed a 1600 BDA. It's now in the hands of Dave Whitehead, who has rebuilt it around a brand new 'replica' tub. Barrie passed the car on to Dave Abbott — who incidentally shared it with none other than hillclimbing scribe Jerry Sturman at Harewood on one occasion — and then it went to Dave Whitehead.

In what was by now time-honoured Lane fashion, Roy had sold his car less engine, for he had plans for a fourth-season with the BMW unit. He installed it in an ex-Martyn Griffiths Pilbeam MP53 and with his new chassis contested 26 meetings in 1985.

Still there was only one RAC win, this time at Shelsley Walsh, but at least he was stacking up the points, amassing enough to manage fourth place overall and to win the Birmingham Post Top Ten Challenge, the equivalent of the current Avon/BMTR series within the Midland Championship.

After a second successive fourth place finish at the end of the following year, 1986, there was more hard thinking done in the Lane household. The Pilbeam chassis was good and the BMW engine had served Roy well, far better than the Hart ever did, but still he was only picking up the occasional RAC hillclimb win. If he was to get back into serious contention he needed serious grunt, and that meant a V8. Tech-Craft was an established business now and the Lane finances had recovered somewhat after several rather lean years, so Roy took the plunge. He sold the MP53 to John Meredith and went to see Mike Pilbeam in Bourne.

'Antony, John Chalmers and myself went over to Pilbeam's and said "We want a car built like this" ', Roy recalls. With a 4-litre Cosworth DFL V8 in the back, the first MP58 was an immediate success and made 1987 Roy's best season since the Championship year of 1976, gaining him four wins and second overall. Martyn Griffiths dominated the results that year, but no matter, RTL and Steel King were back in the hunt!

Encouraged, the Steel King team stuck with the MP58 concept for a second year, and indeed for every year since, though three different MP58 chassis have passed through Roy's hands during this time. MP58/01 was retained for three years before being sold to Stonehaven's George Ritchie, to be replaced for 1991 by a slightly stiffer car with new coke-bottle style side pods, MP58/08. This too was powered by the

152

TAILPIECE 1

Spoilt for choice: Shelsley paddock in August 1986, Pilbeam MP53 and Tony Pond's loaned Metro 6R4 side by side.

trusty Cosworth DFL. At the end of 1994 this car was passed on to Simon Durling who together with co-driver Tim Barrington still runs it successfully — in fact the car was unbeaten at Gurston Down club events in 1996.

Roy then turned his attention to his current mount, MP58/09, which he acquired without engine from James Thompson. It had originally been earmarked for a new Al Melling-designed V8 but the project was abandoned following the death of his father Jim. The major difference between chassis number nine and its predecessors is its engine, for Roy had bought a V8 Judd from Leighton House, originally in 3.5 litre form. During the winter of 1994-5 it was enlarged to 4 litres by J&F Engines and the following winter it was comprehensively remapped, turning MP58/09 into the fastest car on the hills bar none.

The MP58 has been a great success story and has become the car to beat in top class British hillclimbing. Since 1987, when he got the fine MP58 chassis beneath him and V8 power once again behind him, Roy has never been out of the top three of the RAC Championship, reaching the very top once again in 1992, fully 16 years after his second title.

Now that 1996 has brought him a fourth title, what are his plans?

'Two or three people came up and said they were going to buy one of the cars, but nothing eventually came of it. So we're going to remap the 4 litre Judd again and we'll do what we want to do in 1997. I'm not going to seriously chase the Championship'. This last remark provokes knowing chortles from every family member in earshot, simultaneously.

'The Ralt we've got a little bit of suspension development to do on, so at some stage Antony, John and myself will all drive it, along with the Tiga — (Roy has for some years also owned a BMW-powered Tiga Sports Libre car). 'We'll do a social season, nothing too serious — we hope', he adds with a grin.

Talking of the Ralt brings us on to the subject of drivers, and which ones have impressed him most over the years. For it was the death of the driver he liked most of all, Mark Colton, which made the Ralt project possible. Mark, son of Roy's sponsor Richard Colton, was tragically killed in an MP72 at Craigantlet in 1995 in a freak accident which stunned the whole speed community.

Roy felt the loss particularly deeply. 'I brought him into the sport. I loaned him cars, I gave him drives — it was a terrible blow for all of us.'

Richard wanted the undamaged engine and rear suspension of the MP72 put to good use and it was this, plus funds from the sale of Roy's old McRae to America and the availability of a carbonfibre Ralt tub through David Gould, which prompted Roy to build the car.

'Some of the people I've got the greatest respect for are very young drivers,

LIVING WITH SPEED

James Thomson, for instance. He was a brilliant, natural driver, so relaxed, so likeable. He came, had a season when he could do no wrong, and left to go circuit racing in the early '80s — a bit like Andy Priaulx now.' Roy is the first to admit that had Andy Priaulx done a full hillclimbing season in 1996, he would probably have won the championship.

The most dedicated driver, the one Roy believes brought the most to the sport, is Martyn Griffiths. 'He was very fortunate in that he had a lot of financial support but he won the Championship five times and no one can take that away from him. Martyn's got to be the ultimate at the end of the day'.

The one champion driver Roy could

Two MP58s. Left is chassis 01 at Prescott, May 1988, where Roy set FTD and got 10 points for his trouble. Compare the squared-off side pods of this early car with the later 'coke bottle' shape of chassis 08 in the upper photo.

154

TAILPIECE 1

Mark Colton

Man on the Hill

To say that Mark Colton's death, in an accident during practice for Craigantlet's British Championship round, has stunned the hillclimb world would be an understatement. Only a small contingent of mainlanders had travelled to Northern Ireland for the event, but the sad news soon reached the wider speed event fraternity and was initially met with shocked disbelief.

During five short years in the sport at top level, the quietly spoken 34 year-old computer software engineer from Madingley, Cambridge, had become one of the leading British Hillclimb Championship contenders.

Mark's speed event career began in 1987 in a Porsche Carrera RS and, later, in a Lancia Delta Integrale. But he soon decided that single-seaters were the way to go. With father Richard a longtime motorsport enthusiast and already Roy Lane's major sponsor through his Steel King footwear concern, Roy was instrumental in giving Mark several outings in his F2 Ralt RT2 and Chevron B25.

The bug had really bitten by this time and 1990 saw Mark equipped with a new car, one of Mike Pilbeam's MP58 chassis (which, in various hands, was to win every subsequent hillclimb championship to date) powered by a 1600 Richardson BDA. Mark's first championship point wasn't long in coming at Bouley Bay, on his first visit to the Channel Islands. Following it up with a similar result at Prescott's Gold Cup meeting in September, he finished his maiden British Championship year with 25th overall in the smallest engined car to score points that year.

But with one of Brian Hart's stretched 2.8 four-cylinder units installed in the car the following year, his career began to gain momentum, though a setback to that 1991 season came at Barbon when he rolled the car at the Cumbrian course's notorious stone wall bordered top hairpin. Fortunately Mark was uninjured, which was more than could be said for his engine, as his foot had stuck on the throttle after the accident! He bounced back at Fintray a month later and still ended his championship season seventh overall.

The turning point came in 1992 with Ray Rowan's minimalist Roman chassis, the hybrid Toleman derivative that had taken the Midlander to the British title three years previously. Once again, equipped with 2.8 Hart power, the first British Championship win came in style at Doune, qualifying fastest and coming out on top in a three-way tussle with eventual champion Roy Lane and runner-up David Grace. Further wins at Wiscombe, and again at Doune, netted him third overall in the championship.

With the hillclimb reign of the Hart four-cylinder unit effectively ending with the '80s, V8 power was by now an essential part of the winning equation, as far as the British Championship was concerned. Cosworth V8s were already in wide use, but with the recent availability of the Judd CV, Colton installed one in the Roman chassis for 1993. It paid off with four wins and a part in one of the closest championship tussles of all time. Even with five runner-up placings, Mark again had to be content to shadow the Grace/Lane battle up front, albeit just three points behind the overall champion, who was Grace on this occasion.

Mark Colton after his 1994 record-breaking win at Lerghy Frissell.

Jerry Sturman

The death of Mark Colton stunned the hillclimbing fraternity and is still keenly felt, particularly by Roy Lane. This obituary by Jerry Sturman is reprinted with acknowledgement to *Motoring News*. It originally appeared in 1995.

The same combination in 1994 saw a repeat of the three-way battle up front.

Colton's Roman-Judd was supreme at Shelsley, with victories at both National meetings at the MAC's historic venue and the fastest speed ever recorded over the finish line — 144mph — assuring him of a place in the annals of the sport.

Wins at Prescott and over the inaugural Lerghy Frissel British Championship climb on the Isle of Man — together with runner-up placings at Loton, Wiscombe (twice), Barbon, Bouley, Craigantlet and Doune — saw him close the final year of his career just two points behind Grace in second.

This year Mark pioneered the development of Mike Pilbeam's state-of-the-art hillclimb machine, the MP72. The new car was a considerably revised derivative of the enormously successful Vauxhall-powered MP62 chassis and, despite initial teething problems expected with any new car, he was soon on the pace. Aided as always by longtime mechanic Mike Chittenden he was, apart from a brush with the barrier at Barbon's first corner, never out of the top four.

However, by the time he had scored the new car's first win, at Lerghy Frissel, it was clear that his main opposition was going to be Andy Priaulx's Pilbeam MP58-DFL. A superb battle with the young Guernseyman at Gurston Down saw both drivers inside the course record, Priaulx getting the last word with a record-breaking shot that would undoubtedly have been matched by Colton but for Mark's brilliantly recovered moment at Karousel.

Apart from the wet Shelsley round that followed, Andy won every subsequent round up to Craigantlet and was well on course for his first British Championship. But Mark never gave up the fight, scoring second places behind the young charger at Harewood and Val des Terres to give himself an outside chance of the title. And with Grace and Lane struggling a little this year, he was certainly capable of taking the runner-up slot for the second time in a row.

It was with this in mind that he travelled to Craigantlet last weekend.

Mark Colton was undoubtedly one of the major talents in the sport. Always a hard trier, there was no doubt that his determination and skill would have eventually brought him the ultimate hillclimb accolade. For his career to be brought to such an abrupt end is indeed a terrible blow, not only for the sport, but for all who know this quiet, undemonstrative competitor.

Motoring News offers its sincere condolences to Mark's family, to his constant companion Nicola, and to all his many friends and fellow competitors.

LIVING WITH SPEED

ROY T LANE: RAC British Hillclimb Championship Summary

Wins by date

No wins in 1967, unplaced in championship
1.6 Cooper-Ford (sc) Type 56

No wins in 1968, third in championship
3.5 Brabham-Buick BT14

2 wins for 1969, second in championship
3.5 Tech-Craft-Buick
| 15 June | Doune |
| 2 August | Great Auclum |

No wins in 1970, seventh in championship
Tech-Craft BRM p67 (also 5.0 McLarenChevrolet M10A/B, 5.0 McLaren-Chevrolet M10B, 3.5 Tech-Craft-Buick)

3 wins in 1971, fourth in championship
5.5 McLaren-Chevrolet M10B
2 May	Prescott
5 September	Prescott
12 September	Harewood

2 wins in 1972, fourth in championship
5.7 McLaren-Chevrolet M14D
| 4 June | Prescott |
| 3 September | Prescott |

No wins in 1973, fourth in championship
5.7 McLaren-Chevrolet M14D

2 wins in 1974, second in championship
5.0 McRae-Chevrolet GM1
| 10 August | Great Auclum |
| 1 September | Prescott |

11 wins in 1975, first in championship
5.0 McRae-Chevrolet GM1
4 May	Prescott
8 June	Shelsley Walsh
22 June	Doune
6 July	Harewood
13 July	Pontypool
24 July	Bouley Bay
26 July	Le Val des Terres
17 August	Shelsley Walsh
25 August	Gurston Down
7 September	Prescott
21 September	Doune

3 wins in 1976, first in championship
5.0 McRae-Chevrolet GM1
11 April	Wiscombe Park
2 May	Prescott
4 July	Harewood

3 wins in 1977, third in championship
3.0 March-Cosworth DFV 741
23 July	Le Val des Terres
4 September	Prescott
18 September	Doune

1 win in 1978, fifth in championship
3.0 March-Cosworth DFV 741
| 7 May | Prescott |

1 win in 1979, fourth in championship
3.0 March-Cosworth DFV 771 2-4-0
(also 3.0 March-Cosworth DFV 771)
| 1 April | Wiscombe Park |

No wins in 1980, third in championship
3.0 March-Cosworth DFV 782/79S

No wins in 1981, fifth in championship
2.5 March-Hart 802/812
(also 2.3 March-Hart 782)

No wins in 1982, sixth in championship
2.3 Pilbeam-BMW M12 MP50

No wins in 1983, fourth in championship
2.6 Pilbeam-BMW M12 MP50

2 wins in 1984, fifth in championship
2.6 Pilbeam-BMW M12 MP50
| 8 April | Wiscombe Park |
| 28 July | Le Val des Terres |

1 win in 1985, fourth in championship
2.6 Pilbeam-BMW M12 MP53
| 9 June | Shelsley Walsh |

1 win in 1986, fourth in championship
2.6 Pilbeam-BMW M12 MP53
| 31 March | Loton Park |

4 wins in 1987, second in championship
4.0 Pilbeam-Cosworth DFL MP58-1
24 May	Gurston Down
7 June	Shelsley Walsh
14 June	Fintray
8 August	Shelsley Walsh

2 wins in 1988, third in championship
4.0 Pilbeam-Cosworth DFL MP58-1
| 5 May | Prescott |
| 29 May | Gurston Down |

5 wins in 1989, second in championship
4.0 Pilbeam-Cosworth DFL MP58-1
20 May	Barbon
28 May	Gurston Down
25 June	Fintray
20 July	Bouley Bay
13 August	Shelsley Walsh

4 wins in 1990, second in championship
4.0 Pilbeam-Cosworth DFL MP58-1
16 April	Loton Park
29 April	Wiscombe Park
27 May	Gurston Down
19 July	Le Val des Terres

3 wins in 1991, third in championship
4.0 Pilbeam-Cosworth DFL MP58-8
19 May	Barbon
23 June	Fintray
1 September	Prescott

5 wins in 1992, first in championship
4.0 Pilbeam-Cosworth DFL MP58-8
3 May	Prescott
14 June	Harewood
28 June	Fintray
23 July	Bouley Bay
25 July	Le Val des Terres

6 wins in 1993, second in championship
4.0 Pilbeam-Cosworth DFL MP58-8
12 April	Loton Park
2 May	Prescott
30 May	Gurston Down
27 June	Fintray
22 July	Bouley Bay
12 September	Wiscombe Park

4 wins in 1994, third in championship
4.0 Pilbeam-Cosworth DFL MP58-8
(also 4.0 Pilbeam-Judd EV MP58-9)
29 May	Gurston Down
28 July	Bouley Bay
30 July	Le Val des Terres
4 September	Prescott

1 win in 1995, third in championship
4.0 Pilbeam-Judd EV MP58-9
| 17 April | Loton Park |

6 wins in 1996, first in championship
4.0 Pilbeam-Judd EV MP58-9
28 April	Wiscombe Park
5 May	Prescott
26 May	Gurston Down
2 June	Shelsley Walsh
23 June	Doune
1 September	Prescott

Total 72 wins

Wins by venue

Prescott	17
Gurston Down	8
Shelsley Walsh	7
Le Val des Terres	6
Wiscombe Park	6
Bouley Bay	5
Fintray	5
Doune	5
Harewood	4
Loton Park	4
Great Auclum	2
Barbon	2
Pontypool	1

Championship placings since 1967

First	4
Second	6
Third	7
Fourth	7
Fifth	3
Sixth	1
Seventh	1
Unplaced	1

TOTAL 30 SEASONS

---

never tune in to was Chris Cramer. 'He tried to be so serious, so professional, he was his own worst enemy. He had no social life, just one target, one focus, and that was to win. Once he'd done that he lost interest. When he was competing you could hardly have a conversation with him. But funnily enough, when he packed up racing he changed a lot.'

Roy himself has a unique place in the annals of the sport, a place which has brought perks from some unlikely quarters. One of them came in 1986 when his old friend Colin Malkin from Rover Group asked him to help publicise the Metro 6R4 rally car. The Group B hellraiser was coming to the end of its competition life, yet there were a number of homologation-prompted production models sitting waiting for a buyer. If Roy could run one on the hills it might help shift a few.

It sounded like too much fun to miss and Roy certainly made the most of the opportunity. He spent hours circulating Gaydon test track, breaking suspensions, breaking transmissions, generally getting to know what could be done with this very special 6R4 on which Cosworth had been let loose in the engine compartment. When he knew what it would do, he took it up Shelsley in anger in front of the Rover big brass. 'It was very good, though it was too heavy as it was a full rally car' he remembers. The same car, incidentally, won the Manx rally in the hands of Tony Pond shortly afterwards.

Another exciting interlude originated when the Bugatti factory was shifted to Italy to build the EB110. The company wanted to publicise the car — where better than at the Bugatti Owners Club's own hill, Prescott? And who better to use than one of the resident instructors at their Hillclimb Drivers School, Roy Lane?

He also has some interesting road cars

TAILPIECE 1

Roy and Bett trialing in 1988, at one of the last such events they entered.

Classic rallying with Antony in the Volvo during the 1995 Le Jog.

Roy's very original early Porsche 911 in the Rally of Wales.

of his own, including one of the original works Group B Audi Quattros. 'It's strictly for fun,' he explains. 'Big boys have to have big toys!' The Audi is currently tucked away, Roy preferring older rally cars which are eligible for historic rallying because the latter has replaced trialing as his winter motorsport. His current mounts are a Volvo Amazon-series saloon, which for some inexplicable reason insists on breaking its reverse gear, and a Porsche 911. Normal road car is a Land Rover Discovery, but under a dustsheet is a brilliant red Ferrari Testa Rossa which he bought damaged and has rebuilt to pristine condition.

Throughout his long and successful career Roy has never claimed any magic secret to success, ascribing it to nothing more dramatic then perseverance and attention to detail. 'If you're going to do something, do it properly. What's the point of spending money otherwise? That's why I get very annoyed with myself when I make mistakes, and sometimes I show it. Some people say I treat hillclimbing very professionally but I don't like to think that, because I like the sport so much. In fact I would hate to think that professionals are in our sport. But I do believe that if you're going to do something, you should do it properly.'

The standard of preparation of his cars is universally respected, but Roy admits that he is not the most aggressive driver on the hill. 'Aggression should only come out in the Top 12 run-off. You can't carry aggression all weekend, you just can't'. His success comes not from red mist but from self-discipline, intense concentration and careful preparation, which combine to allow him to drive extremely accurately and consistently.

'He very, very seldom makes a mistake', says Robin Boucher, who has watched him more times than he cares to remember. 'People like Roy are just amazing — still very competitive, though I won't say unbeatable.'

Tom Clapham, who started in the sport about the same year as Roy, concurs. 'I think he's a great guy, I've a lot of time for him. First time I ever saw Roy

LIVING WITH SPEED

The Lanes at the end of their fourth RAC title winning season. Left to right Antony, Bett, Liz, Christopher, Roy, Julie and John. The Ralt is on the left, the Pilbeam on the right.

was at Shelsley, one of the first times — maybe the first time — he ever went there. I've known him on and off ever since. Perhaps we get on well because we're both from the same era'.

Probably the best way to sum Roy up is to that he knows just how far to go, both in and out of the driving seat. Fast but never wild. Wily but never sneaky. Thrifty but never mean. A man who will approach the brink, but gets no kick from staring into the abyss.

There are some things about the sport he would like to change. He has fought long and hard for drivers to get more practice runs and therefore better value for their entry money, a plea which has been listened to at Gurston and Doune, to name but two, but which still falls on deaf ears in some quarters. He also feels strongly that double drivers should be obliged to each have their own tyres, at least at the top end of the sport where Championship points are at stake.

'I know from my own experience what a difference even a small amount of heat in a tyre can make to your times. There's no doubt that the second man up has a real — and in my view unfair — advantage.'

For the most part though, he believes that hillclimbing will continue to display the stability which has made it so attractive to legions of drivers fed up with constant rule changes in other branches of motorsport, as well as the social atmosphere which keeps people coming back long after they have sworn blind they will retire.

The man from Warwick knows that lure very well and plays down his own contribution to the atmosphere that creates it.

'Don't forget, when I'm gone the sport will still be there,' he says. 'Nobody is man over the sport.'

Maybe so. But it would not be the same without him.

158

TAILPIECE 2

'Pay attention to detail'

At work with the Guv'nor

After a season spent watching Roy Lane and other top competitors closely, you realise that there's no magic formula for developing a good hillclimb car. Finding those tenths is all about attention to detail, methodical development, and avoidance of false economy — not exciting qualities but fundamental ones nevertheless. Oh, and buying a suitable car in the first place.

'Suitable' of course means all things to all men. It can mean acquiring a tired ex-F3 circuit car for an attractive price and rebuilding it to hillclimb specification. It can mean saving most of that effort and buying a Pilbeam, still the only big series-built single-seater designed specifically for speed events. Or it could simply mean acquiring a road car with the right balance of speed and handling to worry the rest of the class.

I asked Roy how he would set about developing each of these types of vehicles, starting with the one demanding the most work — the F3 car.

Bearing in mind how stiffly sprung circuit cars have become, and how many bumps and camber changes there are on the hills, there are no prizes for predicting his first priority — sorting the suspension.

'The first thing you'll do is go down about 20% on the spring rates. Also readjust the dampers, take some of the stiffness out of them on both bump and rebound. You would also work on anti-roll bars, making them softer. Perhaps try a bit more downforce front and rear, also it might be a good idea to give yourself a bit more adjustment on the front and rear wings.

'You'll probably need it, because however you set the car up you'll end up juggling with it on the day — hills vary so much. I went to Loton Park a couple of weeks back thinking I had a very good set up developed from the last few years, but in practice we had to fiddle around with the front anti-roll bar, then the rear bar, then we lifted the car a little bit at the back and by the end of all this we'd made it very good, steering-wise. Loton Park is *so* important on steering, getting the car to turn in efficiently while keeping your downforce on. Our juggling round brought us — for that weekend, those weather conditions and the track as it was last weekend — an ideal set up. But we might go there in June and find it different all over again!'

I asked what he would expect to have to change if the weather got hot.

'In most cases the hotter a track gets, the more you need to inflate the tyres. When it gets really hot, like last summer when we had some beautiful days at Loton Park, we were going up 2-3 lb/in^2 on pressure to help deal with the heat in the track. Provided you make the most of the hot track in that way, you could expect to see your times come down in good weather because warm tyres work so much better.

'Tyres demand a total rethink if you're starting with a circuit car. That will be on radials whereas you need the quick heat build-up of a crossply. In the distance most circuit racers take to warm their tyres up, you'll have gone up *and* down the hill!

'In recent years Avon have had a virtual monopoly on crossply racing tyres, but interestingly enough now that we're

A Pilbeam chassis like this MP58 is simple, light and effective, but there's no denying that it costs much more than developing a F3 car of your own.

Author's note: this final chapter was written several months after the rest of the book, as the 1997 season was getting under way.

John Chalmers

LIVING WITH SPEED

getting into the 1997 season I've seen someone running on Hoosier tyres. They're an American make, also crossply. I used them years and years ago, they were one of our suppliers, and they were very, very good.

'Suspension work is much more important than the state of tune of the engine — most Formula 3 engines are very driveable these days.

'You would regear it though. On the circuits, that car was going a heck of a lot faster than it ever will in hillclimbing. With a 2 litre engine of say 160bhp, the fastest you'll ever go even in sprinting is only around 120mph.

'Hewland gearboxes lend themselves to easy ratio changes, but that's not enough on its own. You'd most likely have to lower the crown wheel and pinion too, because most of them run a 10:31 crown wheel and pinion, whereas you'll find yourself needing an 8:31. You *can* rely on changing gear ratios alone and at some venues you'll get away with it, but when you get to a place like Wiscombe, with its tight hairpins at Sawbench and Martini, you'll get caught out. They're both very low-gear corners.'

Would you need a heavy duty first gear, I wondered, remembering that all the big single seaters use double-width first gears to cope with the punishment of repeated fast starts?

'Not for a formula 3 car. With a formula 2 car you might though. Over the years lots of people have used Formula 2 cars. The March 782 was perhaps the best of all the circuit cars you could adapt to hillclimbing, it was superb. It was basically a soft car, with soft bars, and had a fair amount of downforce, so there was nothing really trick needed to make a 782 really good on hills. But most of the cars that followed it, like the March 792 and 802, were very stiff, rigid, heavy cars, constructed a lot more heavily than a Pilbeam, for instance, which we'll go on to later.

'The next stage is to look at the fuel system. You don't need big tanks on a hillclimb car, and it's not good enough

Suspension settings represent the biggest single difference between a circuit car and a hillclimb car like an MP58. Springs, dampers and rollbars all need to be changed.

Right: no need for a big fuel tank on a hillclimb car. This is Roy's MP58.

TAILPIECE 2

to leave all the capacity there and just have a little bit of fuel sloshing around in the bottom. With the rapid change of attitude experienced by hillclimb cars, you could easily find the fuel system sucking fresh air at a vital moment.

'Most racing cars have bag tanks, so it's quite easy to take the original tank out and put a smaller one in. My Tiga sports car, for instance, was made to take about 40 gallons of fuel. So we pulled the bag tank out and fitted a 3 gallon aluminium tank instead.

'Admittedly there are other ways of doing it. Russ Ward's car for instance, has still got its original rubber bag tanks inside but with one side of the car blanked off. But he drained all the fuel out recently and found he'd been carrying nine gallons! That's a total waste of time, 70 lb of unnecessary weight.

'Our Ralt has got a rubber tank behind the seat and it just holds 3 gallons. It's nice and tall so with pick-up right in the bottom there's always plenty of head.'

What about braking systems?

'With an ex-circuit car, the one thing you must always do is change the brake pads. Circuit cars either run carbon-metallic or some other very hard pad, in lots of cases they even drive round with a foot on the brake to put some temperature into the pads. That's no good on a hillclimb, you ain't got time to do that.

'So what most people do is deglaze the disc — regrind it to remove the glaze that builds up as a result of using a hardened pad — and put a soft pad in. Mintex make a fabulous range of very soft pads which we all use in hillclimbs. They give you ultra grip from the word go. At Prescott for instance, you can dive into Ettore's at 100mph and slam on the brakes and you know they're going to work. Try that with a circuit set-up and you'll go straight on.'

But presumably such soft pads only have a short life, I queried?

'Not really, because your mileage is so low. If you're only doing, say 20 meetings a year, those pads will be no problem at all. I make a point of starting off each season with everything new, but most competitors will tell you they've had the same pads for three or four years! Hillclimbers are the worst people in the world for *buying* anything, they're so tight!'

We haven't talked about fuels, I reminded him.

'These days with hillclimb cars you're stuck with petrol or methanol, both of them have got to be virtually straight. I run both my cars on BP Super Unleaded petrol, because that's got a better octane rating than four-star now. The Judd engines are lean-burn engines and don't need the lead. The CV likes a little bit of fuel, if you take a plug out it's always a dark brown, but the plugs in the EV are always white.

'Petrol is very kind to engines and makes them very sharp if they're tuned properly. Methanol is a fast-burning fuel which gives you a lot of torque. A lot of what people say about methanol being hard on engines is untrue: it's kind to engines once they're running, because the high water content means that they run cool. But if methanol is left in a standing engine, it can affect it very badly, so much so that the fuel system is best left drained because the methanol eats away at the pump.

'When people first started using methanol they used to drop the fuel out at the end of the day and put the petrol back in, altering the jets to suit. (You've got to change the jets because you need twice to three times as much fuel throughput as with petrol — after all, the water doesn't burn!)

'For the same reason you can't just put methanol into any old tank: you need a proper aluminium construction, perhaps even treated inside to stop corrosion.

'But if you've got a high enough compression to burn it properly (at least 12:1), an engine running on methanol will give you more horsepower and more torque.'

This took us on to the subject of engines, and how they have developed.

'Engines have changed so much over the past few years. They've gone off the points and the plugs and the coils and they're now very easily manageable if you've got a computer and the facilities to get inside the thing. Then you can

LIVING WITH SPEED

This is how an MP58 looks when stripped down. Careful maintenance between meetings can make the difference between a successful weekend and a frustrating one.

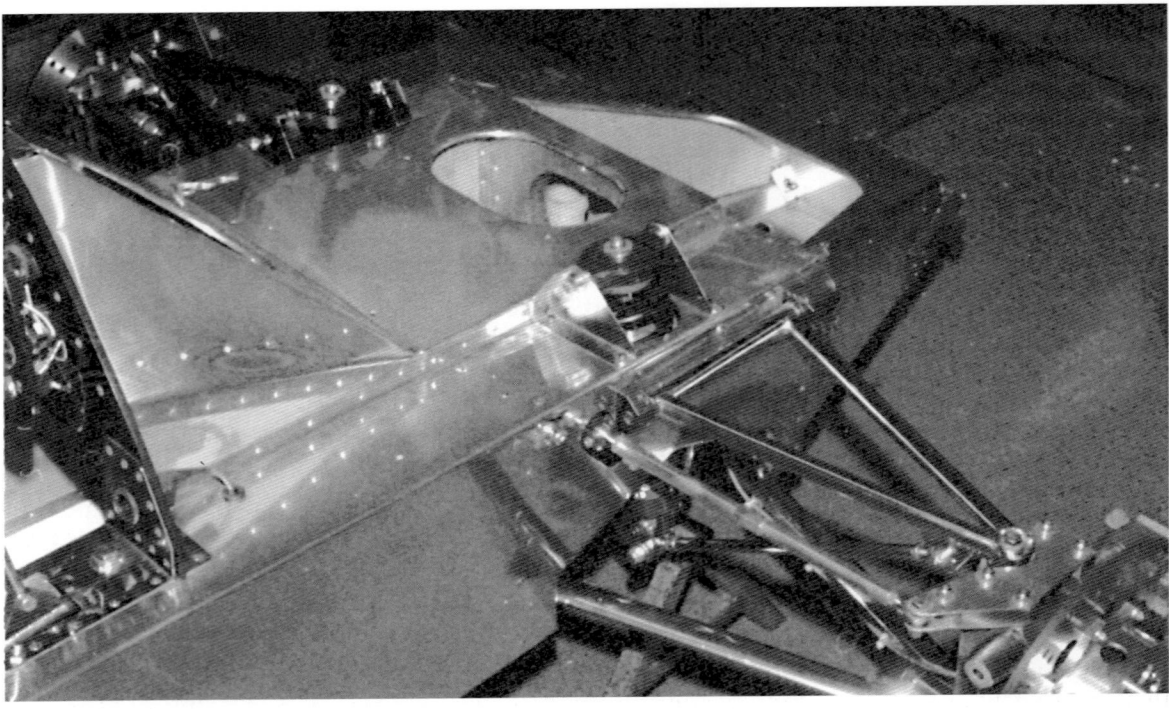

John Chalmers

scale the characteristics right down to exactly what you want.

'The approach I would take with our mythical F3 car is exactly the same as we've done with our Judd F1 engines. We've brought the torque range down the scale simply by modifying the engine management.

'Years ago you'd have been changing all sorts of mechanical parts to achieve this, but in the first year we ran the Judd it was a straight 3.5 litre F1 engine apart from the management. Even since we've enlarged it to 4 litres we've stuck to most of the same innards, including the cams. Only the management side and the advance and retard arrangements — which are in any case part of the computer management — have been altered.'

What management system does he recommend?

'I think Zytech has got to be the best. There are some other very good ones though, like the Weber Alpha. We fitted that to a 2 litre Hart engine a few years ago and I was amazed how it transformed it. Motec is fitted on our Judd CV and that too is very good.'

Roy sees his strengths as being in the chassis and transmission department rather than the engine and makes no claim to be a wizard engine builder.

'I tend to leave engines to specialists, who've got their own dynos and can do the job properly. I don't believe in using Joe Bloggs with a shed down the bottom of his garden. That's why I use J&F Engines or Engine Developments at Rugby, I like to know I'm dealing with a company whose reputation matters to them.

'For the same reason I don't have any particularly profound views about lubricants — I simply make sure I use good quality oils and that I listen very carefully to the engine builder's recommendations. We're running 100% full synthetics this year, both in engines and gearboxes, simply because the engine builders and oil companies recommend it.

'Cheap oils are false economy — you may think you're saving a few bob but it's nothing compared to the cost of a crankshaft regrind or a new cam. We have used Shell and Mobil in the past, but right now I'm using the Motel 300 range of racing oils and they're absolutely superb. My engine was stripped last winter after two years of use and the engine builders would have been quite happy to put the same bearings back in. We didn't, but they would have if I'd asked. You've got to remember that during those seasons my engine was run on a total of three test beds, which together add up to over 20h, and two full seasons of sprinting and hillclimbing, some 45-50 meetings. For a racing engine, that's a lot of use.

'I've had customers come to me with a sick engine and I take one look and say "Oh my God, you've run this on some cheap and nasty oil which perhaps I shouldn't mention". And they say "Yeah, I got it from the goody shop down the road." Enough said. You should always use the best oils in competition cars.'

He went on to point out that although hillclimbing is kind to engines in that blow-ups are rare, because the engines are only stressed in short bursts, it is relatively hard in terms of wear.

'Where our damage is done is in starting up from cold so often. We don't just start them once or twice a weekend, we start them lots and lots of times, from cold, and that's when the wear occurs. That's why we always pre-heat our en-

162

TAILPIECE 2

gines — an engine heater is a good investment.

'Having said all that, with a hillclimb car the most critical lubrication item is the transmission rather than the engine. In all honesty, the gearboxes on my sort of car really aren't up to the strength needed for our type of engines. Last weekend at Wiscombe, for instance, Richard Brown, myself and Tim Mason all suffered transmission failures. Admittedly three at once was exceptional, even for a warm day when the increased grip puts that much more stress on the transmissions, but it does illustrate how marginal they are.

'When you've got an engine that's giving out in excess of 600hp it's hard to find a transmission that can take it. With our standing starts, we give gearboxes and driveshafts a lot more hammer than most people in motorsport.'

'Clutches take a lot of stick too. With a racing engine you can choose from three types: sintered, cerametallic, or carbon. For years I've run carbon clutches because they're nice to drive with, they last a long time, and they've got a lovely feel to them. But they're F1 technology, very expensive.

'Next down is the cerametallic, and a lot of people use them because they last quite well and are nice and driveable. Sintered clutches are the cheapest form of competition clutch and therefore by far the most popular. At Tech-Craft I keep far larger stocks of these than any other type. But they do tend to snatch a bit, they're either in or out. All are available with one to four plates, depending on the amount of power you're trying to transmit.

'Our imaginary F3 car would be using a twin-plate carbon clutch. But 10 years ago you'd have had just a single-plate sintered clutch.'

Would any alterations be required to the steering?

'On purpose-built competition cars, steering ratios are rarely altered. But if you're trying to make something of a roadgoing Escort, for example, one of the first things to do is put a quick rack in it. The difference between three turns and one and a half is quite marked.'

Still with our hypothetical F3 car, I asked what changes he would make to bodywork. I'd noticed lots of aerodynamic tweaks in the paddock, some people adding bits on, others stripping bits off. What would be his approach?

'Why carry excess weight?', he answered, and then added with a chuckle that the driver himself was a bit overweight this year.

'I seem to work for hours and hours trimming down the weight of the car. We've got my Pilbeam down to a very nice light weight now, for what it is, the power to weight ratio is tremendous — but I'm afraid the driver has put on weight at the same time.

'It's ironic really. You run a little tiny thin disk to keep weight down, you trim weight off here, trim weight off there. You have new bits made in lighter materials — instead of glass you have it made in Kevlar, instead of 16 gauge aluminium you use 18 gauge, and this year we've replaced the aluminium skid blocks with titanium ones which are half the weight. We've bored big diameter holes in the wing mountings to lighten them by 3-4kg. We even skimmed down the outer bodies of the constant velocity joints. Doing this to all four joints can save you a couple of kilos. All in all last winter we removed about 8-10kg in weight. The only trouble is, I've gone and put it all back on again!'

This time last year, I reminded him, he'd lost about half a stone in preparation for the start of the season.

'Actually I have trimmed down a bit. I've cycled about 400 miles since Christmas, maybe more, although the exercise is not necessarily to lose weight, it's to keep myself very fit and keep my reactions quick. I think that's very important in motorsport; if you're fit and healthy your reactions will look after you.'

This led us on to the subject of ergonomics.

'This is *so* important, being comfortable in the car. Lots of people think they should sit over the top of the steering wheel with their arms stretched right out "like a racing driver". You should never be like that.

'I don't like my arms fully extended but I do like to be far enough forward that I can get on to the gearstick quickly. You've got to remember that when you're sprinting or hillclimbing everything's happening so much quicker than on a circuit. If you're doing a fast run up Loton Park everything's happening so fast that you've got to be able to know exactly, within a split second, where everything is. It's all *instant*, to keep the momentum, to keep the power on. With circuit cars people don't bother so much.

'It's worth spending hours to get yourself comfortable in a seat that fits you properly. You mustn't be floating around, you want a good belt that's going to anchor you in place, because it's ever so important, especially in a single seater, to feel the car through your body.

'It's so easy to mould your own seat — you get a two-pack kit and a plastic bag and you make your own seats. We've done it in both my cars. This is why at the moment I'm driving the Pilbeam rather than the Ralt. I'm ever so comfortable in the Pilbeam because I've been driving it for three or four years and I've got really used to it. I climb into the Ralt and I feel very uncomfortable. It's a nice position, but it's still not quite right and I'm having great difficulty working out what the difference is.

'Think about pedal positions too — they're adjustable on most cars these days. Every time we ready my car for the next weekend's meeting I sit in it and ask myself "can I improve it, can I heel and toe, can I get my right foot on to the accelerator at the same time as I'm braking?". I need it when I'm going into Pardon at 95mph, I need to be able to brake and flip the accelerator as the same time to get a nice clean change down. The same going into the Esses, I like to be able to drag a brake, turn my foot sideways and blip it while I change back into first. It needs to flow, the rhythm is so important.'

Now that we've reworked our imaginary F3 car, we've gone as far as we can in the workshop and it's ready to roll, as far as we can tell. So I asked him what testing procedure he would adopt.

'You should always go and have a test day, get yourself comfortable in the car,

163

make sure you're happy with your braking, make sure you're happy with your tyres. Somewhere like Curborough, or Three Sisters, or that big airfield down at Swindon. Don't rely on race days to sort the car out. It's the same argument I use about never putting an engine into a car without running it on a dyno first. It's false economy not to set it up properly, because a simple problem which could have been easily cured on a test bed can prevent you getting the car started all weekend. I don't want aggravation, I want the car to go. If you're serious about competing, if you've set out to win the British Hillclimb Championship, or the British Sprint Championship, you've got to do the job properly.'

'On the test track, you start off by bedding brakes in and checking that your gear ratios are right. Then start to explore the handling — is she steering well, not oversteering too much, not understeering too much? Have you got enough downforce? In a single seater or sports car you've got plenty of adjustment, so it's always worth the investment of a day on a test track to explore these things.'

I asked him how he would tune out understeer.

'Colin Chapman's rule of thumb is that you combat understeer by softening the front and stiffening the rear. You can do that with spring rates, roll bar settings, or both. But lots of people forget that there is also another option, which you can use if adjusting spring rates doesn't completely cure the problem — you can lift the back. This puts a bit more weight on to the front end which can be especially useful if the understeer is making itself felt mainly under braking. A bit of extra weight transfer will help you steer.

'Wing adjustment is all very well, but it will only help you on fast corners. If you have a problem at Sawbench, you won't be adjusting wings, you'll be adjusting anti-roll bars and springs.'

By now we'd rebuilt our F3 car and it was time to look at our other specimen types of hillclimb car, namely Pilbeams and road cars. Bearing in mind the interest in carbon tubs and the fact that

Two 5.5 inch grand prix clutches, the left one sintered, the other carbon.

Pilbeams are all aluminium, I asked Roy for his thoughts on the pros and cons of the two materials.

'All the Pilbeams so far have been aluminium and aluminium honeycomb monocoques, because they're easy to repair. For instance, I had a bad accident in Ireland one year, we took it over to Mike at Bourne, he repaired it and we won Shelsley with it the following weekend. You couldn't have done that with a carbon tub.'

'Sure, there are people who can repair carbon monocoques but they seem to take a long time. Carbon monocoques are very nice, and pound for pound stronger than aluminium, but the nature of the material means that you can't use it thin, so there's a weight penalty with them — up to a third heavier than my Pilbeam. Nevertheless they probably are the future because if you tried to create something as strong from ally it would be even heavier.

'With the Ralt they tried to minimise the weight problem by using a honeycomb structure and then covering it with carbon. That's why it's so thick. It was something of a halfway house — F1 monocoques now tend to be pure carbon, without honeycomb. They're even stronger.

'The Ralts weren't particularly successful in F3, because they were so heavy. I spoke to a chap at the Racing Car show who actually worked on my Ralt when it was an F3 car and he said the biggest problem with them on the circuits was that they were about 25kg overweight. You just can't carry that penalty. But ironically, it's that very characteristic which gives them great potential for hillclimbing, as they're strong enough to take a V8 without too much modification.

'Remember that Mike has studied hillclimbs for a long time now, ever since he came into the sport with Alister Douglas Osborn back in the '70s, and the Pilbeam is as a result a purpose-built car. It's light, has decent suspension movement and good brakes. It's built for the job. Most Pilbeams don't need a lot of development, they basically set up right to start with. You might adjust your springs a little bit, or your dampers or your wings, but the car is near enough there. Pilbeams come with ready-made tanks that carry a gallon or a gallon and half maximum, that's all.'

'A few years ago Roger Moran asked me what I wanted for a F2 Ralt I had. I said "Look Roger, you're a serious sort of chap, I know you want to carry on in this sport, why are you talking to me about messing around with my Ralt? It's a beautiful car, but it's not a patch on a Pilbeam MP62."

'Later Roger told me it was the best advice I'd ever given to anybody. If a man is serious about hillclimbing, he will go and buy a Pilbeam.'

'At the moment', he adds significantly.

So Mike Pilbeam was the first to make a serious effort to design a 'production' big racing car for the hills?

'Exactly. You think of the cars I've had. Formula 1 cars like the six-wheeler or the March 741. Formula 5000 cars like the McRae. You can make them work — as we did with the McRae very successfully — but they were hard work to adapt. For years I never wanted to

164

TAILPIECE 2

Ergonomics are vitally important. Forget about how you think racing drivers should sit, just find a position that is comfortable for you, that locates you well and where everything falls quickly to hand.

change to a Pilbeam because everybody else was going that way, but in the end I did and it was worth it. I had a very lean period for years because I was a stubborn devil and wanted to stick to what I was doing. But a car like the March 802, lovely though it was, could never be as light and nimble as a Pilbeam.

However, he is still not convinced that the MP72 is a real advance over the MP58.

'Strange car the MP72, I think it's a car you have to get used to — and I think Roger is now getting used to it. I've driven his one twice, only down hills mind you, and it feels very nervous, very twitchy at the front. It's got a superb back end, but it feels to me as though it wants a front end like an MP58! For me the MP58 is still one of the best chassis in the world for hillclimbing.'

We move on to road cars, and what he does to prepare them for the hills.

'Suppose you bring your standard road car to my driving school, or you want to compete in it. Now tyre technicians have played around and done a lot of work to decide on the best tyre pressures for it, but for road use these are a compromise between handling and comfort. So I often say at the school that it's worth putting another 4-6 lb/in^2 in the tyres. The handbook figures are the minimum you'll ever want in competition — for a wet day at Shelsley, they could be ideal. But when it's dry and warm, anything up to 8 lb/in^2 extra front and rear might transform the car.'

I ask him whether he's looking for grip or for feel.

'You're looking for feel, and for not bending tyres over going round corners. Think of yourself going round Ettore's on standard tyre pressures, with the tyres buckling right over, you're trying to keep the tyre upright to help it work. It'll give a shaky, vibratory ride home if you leave it that way, but on the track you'll feel the benefit.

'With modern road cars the number of things you can do in the paddock to set the car up are very limited. Take the latest TVRs, for instance, tyre pressures are probably one of the only adjustments the man in the street can make. That and dampers, which on most good sports cars are adjustable; a bit more bump and rebound could be worth a tenth or two. Roll bars for instance, can't be adjusted as easily as on a circuit car, maybe not at all, what with all the bodywork covering them over.

'In days gone by, people changed needles and jets and adjusted timing in the paddock. Nowadays, engine management systems and the availability of chips have made it very easy to tune an engine on the day. It's nice to be able to pull a chip out and put another one in — if you know what you're doing.

'Other than that most of the things you'll be doing concern scrutineering, but they don't help you go faster — apart from catch tanks.

'They can actually increase power. Whether your car has a sealed breathing system or not, divert it into a catch tank. Not only do the scrutineers like it, but you'll notice an increase in power, provided you also remember to seal up the breather entrance into the inlet side of the engine. When you start driving that car hard, it's going to produce heavy oil mist. The more space you give it to breathe, the better it will perform. You'll also need a Burt strut — an indicator on the front of the car to break the beam.

'In the road classes there's no requirement for roll bars or cages, but scrutineers are very fussy about the negative side of the battery being marked with yellow tape.

'They also like to see batteries in boxes, or at least with their terminals covered. It's a good idea to mark switches clearly on a competition car of any sort, especially the ignition switch, though you don't need a master switch on the outside of the car in a road class.

'For car drivers racing overalls and helmets are compulsory now, but many bikers still use leathers because they offer better protection if your backside ends up slithering along the tarmac.

'Gloves and shoes are not compulsory but are recommended. Gloves are a fire precaution, but I admit I feel very uncomfortable with gloves on and still prefer to drive without them. I only wear them on a cold wet day to help me grip the wheel. One reason I don't wear them is because I use a suede steering wheel, which doesn't slide inside the glove very easily.'

(Another feature of his steering wheels, I noticed, is the four-leaf clover on the boss. However, Roy insists he is not superstitious.)

'Make sure there's nothing rolling around inside the car', he continued. 'Nothing rolling around inside the boot. Leave the spare wheel in the paddock. Make sure you come armed with tools, a decent quick-lift jack, wheel spanners, a good battery and a foot pump with a gauge that works. Pay attention to detail. Write down things that you've tried, what worked and what didn't, because although at the time you think you'll remember it, two weeks later you'll have practically forgotten what you've done, and a month later you've have totally forgotten.'

There it is again, that not-so-secret magic formula from the man who has done it all and is still doing it. Pay attention to detail.

The message is: don't meddle around on the fringes, get stuck in and enjoy it.

APPENDIX A

The Hillclimb & Sprint Association

It was back in 1979 that the Hillclimb & Sprint Association was formed with the aim of promoting the interests of speed event competitors. Leading lights in what was, at the time, something of a radical organisation were friends and former Leaders champions John Meredith (noted for his exploits in Mini-based machines), and the three-wheeling exponent of a spectacular supercharged Austin Healey Sprite, Russ Ward.

Together with an increasing number of competitors, both had long felt that what seemed to be an entirely separate faction was making the rules. They believed that a united voice was needed to put forward the views of competitors — the very group of people for whom, after all, this somewhat insular sport existed in the first place.

Inevitably, there were those who baulked at the idea of what they thought would become a 'drivers trade union'. But in fact the Association was never intended to be anything of the kind and now, almost 20 years on, has become a respected voice within the sport. The HSA liaises closely with motor sport's governing body, the RACMSA, on all matters concerning hillclimbing and sprinting, particularly regarding safety, and is recognised by competitors and organisers alike as the club that really does have competitors' best interests at heart.

Current HSA President Tony Fletcher, the man behind the country's leading hillclimb championships and himself a member of that original 1979 committee, sees the HSA's role increasingly as an advisory one. Indeed with top-level competitor Patrick Wood chairing a committee made up largely of active hillclimbers and sprinters, the Association is ideally placed to be involved at the sharp end of what is becoming an ever more active and complex branch of motorsport.

Unlike many motor clubs, the Association does not exist to promote events *per se*, although the HSA's annual Curborough Test Day, together with two competitive meetings at the Lichfield sprint course, have proved highly popular for many years now. Despite its 800 strong membership encompassing many of the top names in the sport, including reigning Hillclimb and Sprint Champions Roy Lane and Chris Hill (the latter a serving HSA committee member), the 'grass roots' club competitor is seen as vital to the future of the sport.

To this end the Association has run, and continues to run, championships to encourage newcomers to hillclimbing and sprinting — one of its most notable achievements in that sphere being a championship that pioneered a breakthrough for disabled drivers. In fact this ground-breaking series opened doors to motorsport participation which, for this enthusiastic minority, had hitherto remained firmly shut.

Flagship of the HSA is its bi-monthly magazine *Speedscene*. Originated by Richard Culverhouse, developed by Robin Boucher and with *Autosport* and *Motoring News* freelance journalist Jerry Sturman occupying the editorial chair for the last eight years, it is the only publication exclusively devoted to hillclimbing and sprinting nationwide. With the invaluable assistance of a wide range of contributors from across the British Isles, all major meetings and a good cross-section of club events are covered in words and pictures.

Not only that, the magazine's contents range from technical articles, through driver profiles, to tips on how to tackle the country's speed venues — neither are the sport's historical roots forgotten. Free to HSA members and available by subscription to nonmembers, one of *Speedscene's* key functions is to offer a medium for readers to express their own views on hillclimb- and sprint-related topics — its pages are open to all.

For membership details of the Hillclimb & Sprint Association, contact Shirley Tewson, 11 Offchurch Village, Leamington Spa, Warks CV33 9AP. Tel 01926 424609.

The HSA is run by drivers for drivers. If you want to join you talk to Shirley Tewson, if you want to advertise in its magazine, you talk to her husband Tony. And here they are in their preferred environment, the cockpit of their PDQ Pilbeam, at the August Shelsley meeting.

APPENDIX B

Championship Winners of the RAC & Leaders Championships

RAC British Hillclimb Championship 1947-96

Year	Driver	Car	Championship Sponsor
1947	Raymond Mays	2.0s ERA R4D	
1948	Raymond Mays	2.0s ERA R4D	
1949	Sydney Allard	3.7 Allard-Steyr	
1950	Dennis Poore	3.8s Alfa Romeo 8C-35	
1951	Ken Wharton	1.1 Cooper-JAP Mk4	
1952	Ken Wharton	1.0s Cooper-JAP Mk4	
1953	Ken Wharton	1.0s Cooper-JAP Mk4 / 2.0s ERA R11B	
1954	Ken Wharton	1.1s Cooper-JAP MK4 / 2.0s ERA R4D	
1955	Tony Marsh	1.1 Cooper-JAP Mk8	
1956	Tony Marsh	1.1 Cooper-JAP Mk8	
1957	Tony Marsh	1.1 Cooper-JAP Mk8	
1958	David Boshier-Jones	1.1 Cooper-JAP	
1959	David Boshier-Jones	1.1 Cooper-JAP	
1960	David Boshier-Jones	1.1 Cooper-JAP	
1961	David Good	1.1 Cooper-JAP	
1962	Arthur Owen	2.5 Cooper-Climax FPF T53	
1963	Peter Westbury	2.6s Felday-Daimler	
1964	Peter Westbury	2.5 Ferguson-Climax FPF P99	
1965	Tony Marsh	4.3 Marsh-GM	
1966	Tony Marsh	4.3 Marsh-GM	
1967	Tony Marsh	4.3 Marsh-GM / 4.3 Marsh-GM 4WD	
1968	Peter Lawson	2.1 BRM P67 4WD	
1969	David Hepworth	4.5 Hepworth-GM 4WD	Shell
1970	Sir Nicholas Williamson	5.0 McLaren-Chevrolet M10A	Shell
1971	David Hepworth	5.0 Hepworth GM 4WD	Shell
1972	Sir Nicholas Williamson	2.0 March-BDA/Hart 712S	Shell
1973	Mike McDowel	5.0 Brabham-Repco BT36X	
1974	Mike McDowel	5.0 Brabham-Repco BT36X	
1975	Roy Lane	5.0 McRae-Chevrolet GM1	
1976	Roy Lane	5.0 McRae-Chevrolet GM1	
1977	Alister Douglas Osborn	3.0 Pilbeam-DFV R22	
1978	David Franklin	2.0 March-BMW M12 742	
1979	Martyn Griffiths	2.2 Pilbeam-Hart MP40/01	
1980	Chris Cramer	2.2 March-Hart 782/79B	
1981	James Thomson	2.5 Pilbeam-Hart MP40/02	
1982	Martin Bolsover	2.5 Pilbeam-Hart MP50/02	Pace Petroleum
1983	Martin Bolsover	2.8 Pilbeam-Hart MP50/02	Pace Petroleum
1984	Martin Bolsover	2.8 Pilbeam-Hart MP50/02 / 2.8 Pilbeam-Hart MP43/02	Pace Petroleum
1985	Chris Cramer	2.5 Gould-Hart 84	
1986	Martyn Griffiths	2.8 Pilbeam-Hart MP53H/04	Guyson USA
1987	Martyn Griffiths	2.8 Pilbeam-Hart MP53H/04	Guyson USA
1988	Charles Wardle	5.0 Pilbeam-Repco MP47/RB	Guyson USA
1989	Ray Rowan	2.8 Roman-Hart IVH	Guyson Beadblast
1990	Martyn Griffiths	3.5 Pilbeam-DFR MP58/05	Guyson Beadblast
1991	Martyn Griffiths	3.5 Pilbeam-DFR MP58/05	Guyson Beadblast
1992	Roy Lane	4.0 Pilbeam-DFL MP58/08	Proteus Petroleum*
1993	David Grace	3.5 Pilbeam-DFR MP58/05	Gulf Oil*
1994	David Grace	3.5 Pilbeam-DFR MP58/05	Gulf Oil*
1995	Andy Priaulx	4.0 Pilbeam-DFL MP58/03	
1996	Roy Lane	4.0 Pilbeam-Judd EV MP58/09	

Championships marked* sponsored in association with Autosport magazine

RAC British Leaders Hillclimb Championship 1970-96

Note: Because of the RACMSA's rationalisation of motorsport disciplines, from 1992 onwards 'RAC British' was dropped and the title became RACMSA Leaders Hillclimb Championship

Year	Driver	Car	Championship Sponsor
1970	Chris Cramer	1.3 Mini Cooper S	Shell
1971	'SM Smith' (Tony Bancroft)	4.7 TVR Tuscan	Shell
1972	Chris Cramer	1.3 Mallock-BL Mk11	Shell
1973	Alex Brown	1.1 Ginetta-Imp G17	Woking Motors
1974	Martyn Griffiths	1.6 Mallock-Ford TC Mk8B	Woking Motors
1975	Alan Richards	1.0s Gryphon-Ford AR3	Woking Motors
1976	Russ Ward	1.3s Austin Healey Sprite	
1977	John Meredith	1.4 Mini Cooper S	
1978	Charles Barter	1.1 Davrian-Imp Mk7	Haynes Publishing
1979	John Meredith	1.0 Mini-Imp	Haynes Publishing
1980	Charles Barter	1.2 Davrian/Imp	Haynes Publishing
1981	Barrogill Angus	2.0 Stiletto-BMW	Haynes Publishing
1982	Charles Wardle	1.6 Mallock-BDA Mk21	Haynes Publishing
1983	Brian Walker	2.5 Skoda-Hart S110R	Aston Martin
1984	Ken Snailham	1.6 Lotus Ford TC 7	Aston Martin
1985	Russ Ward	1.1 Saracen-BDJ M85	Aston Martin
1986	Dave Whitehead	1.3 Stiletto-BDH	AWS Group
1987	Mike Kerr	3.9 Skoda-Rover S110R	Bratt
1988	Simon Frost	1.6 Lotus-Ford TC 7	Edwards Catering Co
1989	John Whyte	1.3 Stiletto-BDH	Audi
1990	Graham Hickman	6.3 Skoda-Chevrolet	
1991	Mike Lee	1.3 Mallock-BDH Mk16	
1992	Bill Bristow	1.8 Caterham-Ford Super 7	
1993	Tony Lambert	3.0t Ferrari 308GT4	Bridgestone
1994	Roger Moran	1.6 Pilbeam-Vauxhall MP62/04	Bridgestone
1995	Roger Moran	2.0 Pilbeam-Vauxhall MP62/04	
1996	Justin Fletcher	2.0 Pilbeam-Vauxhall MP62/09	Ricardo

APPENDIX C

Speed championships in the UK

RAC BRITISH HILLCLIMB CHAMPIONSHIP
Sponsor: 1997 — Liqui Moly UK, 1996 — None.
Scope: Nationwide series.
Eligible cars: Modified Production, Clubmans, Sports Libre, Racing.
Scoring: Top 12 run-off basis, with qualifying open to Hillclimb Super Sports (originally Clubmans) and onwards.
Contact: Tony Fletcher, 5 Barrie Avenue, Offmore Farm, Kidderminster, Worcs DY10 3QN. Tel 01562 754243.

RACMSA HILLCLIMB LEADERS CHAMPIONSHIP
Sponsor: 1996 — Ricardo, 1997 — none.
Scope: Nationwide series.
Eligible cars: As above.
Scoring: Class based, points on class position.
Contact: Tony Fletcher (as above).

RAC BRITISH SPRINT CHAMPIONSHIP
Sponsor: Farndon Engineering.
Scope: Nationwide series.
Eligible cars: Similar to RAC Hillclimb, plus additional classes for Road Saloons, Sports and Kitcars.
Scoring: As RAC Hillclimb but qualifying is open to full range of classes.
Contact: Robin Boucher, 3 Swift Park Grove, Spennells, Kidderminster, Worcs DY10 3QN. Tel 01562 751163.

RACMSA SPRINT LEADERS CHAMPIONSHIP
Sponsor: Farndon Engineering.
Scope: Nationwide National B series.
Eligible cars: As above.
Scoring: Class based, similar to Hillclimb Leaders, though points not scored solely on class position, but on a 'time relative to class winner' basis.
Contact: Robin Boucher (as above).

MIDLAND HILLCLIMB CHAMPIONSHIP
Sponsor: Clarks Motor Group.
Scope: Series based at Loton Park, Prescott and Shelsley Walsh.
Eligible cars: Similar to British series, but with roadgoing sub-divisions in 2-litre and unlimited capacity Modified Production classes.
Scoring: Class based, similar to Hillclimb Leaders.
Contact: Tony Fletcher, 5 Barrie Avenue, Offmore Farm, Kidderminster, Worcs DY10 3QN. Tel 01562 754243.

AVON/BMTR TOP TEN CHALLENGE
Sponsor: BMTR.
Scope: Run concurrent with Midland Hillclimb Championship.
Eligible cars: Similar to British series.
Scoring: Top 12 run-off basis similar to, and sometimes concurrent with, British series events.
Contact: Tony Fletcher (as above).

PAUL MATTY SPORTS CARS CLASSIC CHALLENGE
Sponsor: Paul Matty Sportscars.
Scope: Run concurrent with Midland Hillclimb Championship.
Eligible cars: Classic Cars built up to and including 1970 in Saloon, Sports, and Sportsracing/Racing categories.
Scoring: Class-based handicap.
Contact: Tony Fletcher (as above).

ANICC HILLCLIMB CHAMPIONSHIP
Sponsor: Anno Lead.
Scope: Northern Ireland-based series.
Eligible cars: Full range of categories to local Ulster regulations.
Scoring: On an outright and class-position basis, with separate Leaders championship for the latter.
Contact: Michael Beattie, 11 Windermere Drive, Belfast BT8 4XD. Tel 01232 703505.

ANICC SPRINT CHAMPIONSHIP
Sponsor: Kittle Brothers.
Other details as for ANICC Hillclimb Championship.

SCOTTISH HILLCLIMB CHAMPIONSHIP
Sponsor: Grampian TV/Guyson.
Scope and Eligible cars: Full range of classes from roadgoing to racing, all under Scottish regulations.
Scoring: On an outright and class position basis.
Contact: Robert Smith, 29 Sorn Street, Catrine, Ayrshire KA5 6LR. Tel 01290 551464.

SCOTTISH SPRINT CHAMPIONSHIP
Sponsor: Guyson.
Other details as for Scottish Hillclimb Championship.

CCC/BARC/HSA SPEED CHAMPIONSHIP
Sponsor: Cars & Car Conversions magazine.
Scope: British-based National B series.
Eligible cars: Standard Production, Roadgoing, Kit and Formula Ford cars plus British Championship classes.
Scoring: Class-based system which disregards non-registered contenders.
Contact: Ian Bax, 34 Norfolk Farm Road, Pyrford, Surrey GU22 8LF. Tel 01483 284594.

MIDLAND SPEED CHAMPIONSHIP
Sponsor: Rover Mower.
Scope: Nationwide National B series.
Eligible cars: Full range of classes, from standard production to racing.
Scoring: Outright and class based system similar to Sprint Leaders.
Contact: Robin Boucher (as above).

GURSTON DOWN HILLCLIMB CHAMPIONSHIP/
GURSTON DOWN TOP TEN CHALLENGE
Sponsor: Wrynams of Salisbury.
Scope: Single venue series for BARC (SW Centre) members.
Eligible cars: To BARC (SW) classes, similar to British series but with Modified Production categories split into Saloon, Marque Sports, and kit-derived cars.
Scoring: Both series run concurrently — bogey time basis for Hillclimb Championship and outright fastest time basis for Top Ten Challenge.
Contact: Jane Harratt, Lower Minchington Farmhouse, Blandford, Dorset DT11 8DH. Tel 01725 552832.

HAREWOOD HILLCLIMB CHAMPIONSHIP /
HAREWOOD FTD CHAMPIONSHIP
Scope: Single venue series for BARC (Yorkshire Centre) members.
Eligible cars: To BARC (Yorks) classes, similar to British series but with additional classes for Touring, Marque Sports and Formula Ford cars.
Scoring: Similar to Gurston Down series.
Contact: Chris Seaman, Seaman Photographers Ltd, 193 London Road, Sheffield S2 4LJ. Tel 0114 258 5695.

ASWMC HILLCLIMB CHAMPIONSHIP
Sponsor: TSR Performance.
Eligible cars: Full range to Association of Southwest Motor Club regulations.
Scoring: Class-based on bogey times.
Contact: Nick Crocker, 114 Clifton Road, Paignton, Devon TQ3 3LD. Tel 01803 553836.

ASWMC SPRINT CHAMPIONSHIP
Details as for ASWMC Hillclimb series.

LONGTON & DMC SPEED CHAMPIONSHIP
Contact: Jerry Hylton, Town End Cottage, Smithy Lane, Stalmine, nr Blackpool FY6 0LE. Tel 01253 700697.

ASEMC SPEED CHAMPIONSHIP
Contact: Ray Heal, Beards Farm, Hurstmonceux, Hailsham, E Sussex BN27 4QN.

NOTTINGHAM SCC SPEED CHAMPIONSHIP
Contact: Stephen Miles, Tel 0115 9227974.

MID CHESHIRE MRC HILLCLIMB & SPRINT CHAMPIONSHIP
Sponsor: Hammonds Bedrooms.
Contact: Graham Keen, 3 Riddings Road, Timperley, Altrincham, Cheshire WA15 6BW. Tel 0161 976 3004.

SOUTH OF ENGLAND SPEED CHAMPIONSHIP
Sponsor: Polkacrest.
Contact: Steve Medhurst, 9 Maxton Close, Bearstead, Kent, ME14 4QD. Tel 01622 730899.

ONE-MAKE SERIES

PAUL MATTY SPORTS CARS LOTUS CHAMPIONSHIP
Contact: Paul Matty, Meneatt Farmhouse, Shelsley Kings, Worcestershire WR6 6SA.

CASTROL FERRARI CHALLENGE
Contact: Richard Allen, Thoby Lodge, Thoby Lane, Mountnessing, Brentwood, Essex CM15 0TB. Tel 01708 702090.

CLUB ALPINE RENAULT CHAMPIONSHIP
Contact: P Gibson, 85 Stonehill Road, Leigh-on-Sea, Essex SS9 4AX.

930 SPORT PORSCHE CHAMPIONSHIP
Contact: S Wilson, 14 Longdin Street, Latchford, Warrington WA14 1PW.

REVINGTON SPARES TR REGISTER SPRINT & HILLCLIMB CHAMPIONSHIP
Contact: Malcolm Tidball, 10 Vicarage Street, Tintinhull, Yeovil, Somerset.

RYOBI 1DC MORGAN HILLCLIMB & SPRINT CHAMPIONSHIP
Contact: Mrs S Jones, Kyrewood House, Tenbury Wells, Worcestershire WR15 8SG.

MORGAN NORTHERN SPEED CHAMPIONSHIP
Contact: D Mason, 94 Bradley Road, Bradley, Huddersfield HD2 1QY.

MG MOSS NORWESTER NATIONAL SPEED CHAMPIONSHIP
Contact: Jim Garvey, Beechcourt, 394 New Street, Biddulph Moor, Stoke-on-Trent, Staffs ST8 7LR.

CATERHAM SPORTS SCHOLARSHIP
Contact: Entreprix Ltd, 20 Lovies Lane, Diss, Norfolk IP22 2LR.

RELIANT SABRE & SCIMITAR OC SPRINT & HILLCLIMB CHAMPIONSHIP
Contact: Shaun Byrne, 59 North Drive, Harwell, Didcot, Oxfordshire, OX11 0PD.

Notes:
1. *In most championships scoring is based on class results, even in one-make series.*
2. *Most of the information is based on the 1996 series.*